THEOLOGY AND SLAVERY

Theology and Slavery

CHARLES HODGE AND

HORACE BUSHNELL

David Torbett

MERCER UNIVERSITY PRESS

MACON, GEORGIA

ISBN 978-088146-032-2
MUP/H724

First Edition.

Books published by Mercer University Press are printed on acid
free paper that meets the requirements of American National
Standard for Information Sciences—Permanence of Paper for
Printed Library Materials.

Library of Congress Cataloging-in-Publication Data

Torbett, David.
Theology and slavery : Charles Hodge and Horace Bushnell / David Torbett.
-- 1st ed.
p. cm.
Includes bibliographical references and index.
ISBN-13: 978-0-88146-032-2 (hardcover : alk. paper)
ISBN-10: 0-88146-032-X (hardcover : alk. paper)
1. Slavery and the church—United States—History—19th century.
2. Slavery—Moral and ethical aspects—United States—History—19th
century. 3. Hodge, Charles, 1797-1878—Political and social views.
4. Bushnell, Horace, 1802-1876—Political and social views. 5. United
States—Race relations—History—19th century. 6. Racism—United
States—History—19th century. 7. Racism—Religious
aspects—Christianity—History—19th century. 8. Protestantism—United
States—History—19th century. 9. Theology—United States—History—19th
century. 10. United States—Church history—19th century. I. Title.
E449.T68 2006
241'.675092273--dc22
2006022094

To Jill

For her faith

Contents

Abbreviations

BRPR	*Biblical Repertory and Princeton Review*
PCH-FLPU	Papers of Charles Hodge, Firestone Library, Princeton University

Preface

The story of racial slavery in America is a fundamental chapter in the history of American Christianity. Most of the major players in the slavery controversy—from radical abolitionists to proslavery fire-eaters and all positions in between—were Christian and drew on Christian traditions and principles to support their stances. All, in the words of Lincoln, "read the same Bible and pray to the same God." Slavery was the burning moral issue of the nineteenth century that preoccupied American Christians, brought them to a point of crisis, and divided them against each other, splitting the major American Protestant denominations. The repercussions of this crisis continued to affect American Christians as they faced subsequent controversies over race—from Reconstruction to the Civil Rights Era and up to the present time.

Not only was the nineteenth century an era of crisis over slavery, it also marked the emergence of two distinct and enduring voices in American Protestantism: a "conservative" view, which stood firmly behind an inerrantist interpretation of the Bible, and a "liberal" view, which upheld an open-ended, imaginative interpretation of Scripture and found divine revelation not only in the Bible but in the totality of human experience.

Against this backdrop, the views of two Northern nineteenth-century theologians, Charles Hodge and Horace Bushnell, stand out. Hodge was the archconservative Presbyterian professor at Princeton Theological Seminary whose writings continue to serve as an authority for evangelical Protestants. Bushnell, a Congregationalist minister in Hartford, Connecticut, was dubbed the "father of American religious liberalism." Together they represent two poles of thought that continually assert themselves when American Protestants speak out on social issues. Even if many American

Christians no longer recognize these theologians' names, they feel their influence. Hodge and Bushnell both addressed the problem of racial slavery. Together, their stances on the most important moral issue of their day provide a case study for the moral implications of each of these enduring polarities.

This is a case study with surprising results. Many Americans might imagine an easy coalition between conservative Protestantism, slavery, and racism. It is easy to recall the ways in which defenders of racial slavery (and other forms of racial discrimination) have wrapped their arguments in a mantle of religious orthodoxy, both before and after the Civil War. In fact, upon hearing the terms "conservative Protestantism" and "slavery" and "race" mentioned in the same sentence, some Americans would immediately imagine a burning cross. By contrast, many Americans would associate liberal Protestantism with Yankee abolitionists and later Northern civil rights workers.

Hodge and Bushnell upset these conventional understandings of the relationships of conservative and liberal Protestantism to slavery and race. Few would be surprised to learn that of these two theologians, Hodge, the conservative, was the weaker opponent of slavery. What is surprising is that the liberal Bushnell, despite his stronger opposition to slavery, embraced peculiar theories of African inferiority that Hodge did not. Bushnell, unlike Hodge, repeatedly predicted that the end of slavery would be a precursor of the extinction of the African people on the American continent. This important and ironic difference between Hodge and Bushnell is rooted in their broader theological differences. It is precisely because of their religious beliefs that they took the stances they did.

Because Hodge believed in an inerrant Bible, which he understood to permit slavery, he could not condemn slaveholding as a "sin per se." But while Hodge's biblicism prevented him from being an abolitionist, it also prevented him from being a fire-breathing *defender* of Southern slavery. Hodge, even though he held some racial prejudices, still believed in the biblical doctrine of the essential unity and equality of all people of all races. Therefore he could not defend American *racial* slavery as an essentially good or permanent institution.

Bushnell, on the other hand, was not bound to an inerrantist interpretation of the Bible. He was free to denounce slavery as an essentially evil institution. However, it was precisely this open-ended understanding of religious truth that led to Bushnell's racist assumptions and his racial extinction theory. For Bushnell, being "open-minded" meant being open to views of human nature and of race that were new in the nineteenth-century: views that emanated from the Romantic movement in philosophy and literature and the new science of ethnology. Bushnell, unlike Hodge, embraced an organic model for human society that dovetailed with Anglo-Saxon racism. Bushnell, unlike Hodge, sympathetically engaged the "polygenetic theory of human origins": a contemporary pseudoscientific theory that posited the permanent and innate inferiority of nonwhites. Charles Hodge, the conservative, though he was not immune to old-fashioned racial *prejudices*, clearly rejected this new-fangled, unbiblical racial *theory*.

This case study will prove the following thesis: *1) Charles Hodge's particular constellation of theological method, normative principles, anthropological assumptions, predominant loyalties, and circumstantial considerations enabled and inspired his defense of involuntary servitude per se. This same constellation also enabled and inspired his moderate opposition to slavery as it was practiced in the United States. 2) Horace Bushnell's particular constellation of theological method, normative principles, anthropological assumptions, predominant loyalties, and circumstantial considerations enabled and inspired his opposition to slavery and his post-Civil War support of African-American suffrage. This same constellation also enabled and inspired him to embrace theories of Anglo-Saxon superiority and African inferiority.*

Chapter one will introduce the reader to Hodge and Bushnell by describing the events surrounding the publication of their first major statements on slavery. It will also restate and define the terms of our thesis. The second chapter will discuss important aspects of Hodge's and Bushnell's historical context, including the particular characteristics of American slavery, nineteenth-century understandings of race, some important intellectual trends of Hodge's and Bushnell's day, and three typical contemporary moral attitudes toward slavery. Chapter three will focus on Charles Hodge, his life, his thought, and especially his statements on slavery and race, which he made over a thirty-year period. Chapter four will analyze Bushnell's statements on slavery and race, placing them in the context of his biography and his general theological commitments, and comparing his views to Hodge's. Chapter five will describe how both men's dissonant attitudes toward slavery and race affected their enduring intellectual legacies. Finally, we will draw some conclusions about what twenty-first-century Christian theologians might learn from this case study of theology and slavery.

Many able scholars have examined Hodge and Bushnell, and they have not ignored their views on slavery. However, I know of no other book-length comparison of just these two figures especially devoted to this topic. This project originated as a doctoral dissertation, which was completed in the beginning of 2002. While I was finishing the dissertation and in the process of rewriting it as a book, a number of excellent studies were published that shed light on Hodge, Bushnell, slavery, and nineteenth-century American theology in general. I was able to engage a number of them in the following pages. However, there are three comprehensive studies that, though I refer to them in footnotes, I wish I had time to engage further: Gary Dorrien's *The Making of American Liberal Theology: 1805–1900* (Westminster John Knox, 2001), Mark Noll's *America's God: From Jonathan Edwards to Abraham Lincoln* (Oxford, 2002), and E. Brooks Holifield's *Theology in America: Christian Thought from the Puritans to the Civil War* (Yale, 2003). In some of the quotes from primary sources below I have taken the liberty of modernizing the spelling and punctuation.

I am indebted to more people than I can name for helping me with this project. I would like to express my special thanks to Mark Valeri, my dissertation advisor, who continued to help me in numerous ways even after my dissertation was finished. I would also like to thank a number of teachers, colleagues, family members, and friends who read and offered comments on either part or all of the manuscript, either as a dissertation or in its revised form. These include the other members of my dissertation committee, John Stewart and Douglas Ottati, as well as James Smylie, Robert Tucker, Dawn DeVries, Stanley Skreslet, Ivory Lyons, Samuel Roberts, Walter David Jesse Torbett, and Jill Torbett. I am grateful to Marc Jolley and the editorial team at Mercer University Press for reading the manuscript, suggesting revisions, and, of course, publishing it.

I am grateful to many other teachers, including Gabriel Fackre and Max Stackhouse, for their wisdom and encouragement. I am thankful for the institutions that have provided resources and helped to support me as I finished this project: Union Theological Seminary and Presbyterian School of Christian Education (with its great library), Mount Union College (its faculty, staff, and library), and Ashland University. I am grateful to the archivists at the libraries of Yale and Princeton Universities. I would also like to thank Louise Stevenson for allowing me to make use of her primary research and cite her email.

I would like to thank my parents (David and Alice Torbett), my children (Thomas and Nora), and especially my wife Jill for supporting me in many different ways throughout the whole project. I pray that God will use these scholarly efforts to strengthen the church.

Introduction

The decade of the 1830s was the end of the era of compromise and the beginning of the era of crisis in the American conflict over slavery. The fierce rhetoric of the rising generation of abolitionists and proslavery advocates foreshadowed the bloody war that would ultimately divide the United States. It was during this decade that two influential American Protestant theologians, Charles Hodge and Horace Bushnell, made their first major statements on slavery. Each delivered a singularly ambivalent message, containing discordant themes that each would repeat over the next thirty years. Both of their views on racial slavery were grounded in and, to an extent, resulted from their particular theological orientations. This chapter will describe the events surrounding the publication of their first major statements on slavery, as well as state and define the thesis their case study proves.

From Compromise to Crisis

Since the time of the American Revolution, slavery in the United States had been a source of tension. Samuel Hopkins, a New England Congregationalist minister, pricked the conscience of the Continental Congress in 1776 by calling attention to the inconsistency "of promoting the slavery of the Africans, at the same time we are asserting our own civil liberty." Even slaveholders of the revolutionary generation, like Thomas Jefferson, were troubled by the irony. Nevertheless, slaveholders preserved the institution, even working an implicit affirmation of it into the US Constitution.[1]

Yet for decades, this tension did not erupt into divisive conflict. A critical mass of white Americans, Northern and Southern, managed to diffuse it by reaching a kind of consensus, one that acknowledged slavery as a moral problem but permitted its temporary existence. They agreed that slavery was an evil and that it ought gradually to be abolished. They assumed that even slaveholders did not like the institution and would cooperate in its gradual elimination by voluntarily freeing or "manumitting" their slaves. But they also agreed that slavery was, at least for the time being, a necessary evil that should not be abolished too quickly. They assumed that most black slaves were not ready for immediate freedom. They doubted that the black and white races could ever coexist freely as equals in the United States. They supported a form of segregation: the American Colonization Society's plan of sending freed slaves to settle in the new colony of Liberia as the humanitarian solution to America's racial problem. This compromise consensus found its way into a number of public and private documents in the early nineteenth century.[2]

But this consensus dissolved in the 1830s, and an era of crisis began. A number of factors, not the least of which was simply the passing of a generation, made this a decade "of remarkable change, almost a revolution, in the nation's attitude toward slavery in its midst." A younger, fiercer generation of advocates arose, taking stands on both sides of the issue. Whether they attacked slavery or defended it, they rejected the old compromise of gradual abolition, voluntary manumission, and colonization. In the North, abolitionists

---

[1] Samuel Hopkins, quoted in Joseph A. Conforti, *Samuel Hopkins and the New Divinity Movement: Calvinism, the Congregational Ministry, and Reform in New England between the Great Awakenings* (Grand Rapids: Christian University Press, 1981) 128. Paul Finkleman, *Slavery and the Founders: Race and Liberty in the Age of Jefferson* (Armonk NY: M. E. Sharpe, 1996) 62.

[2] A good example is the Resolution of the Presbyterian General Assembly of 1818, which we will discuss presently.

like William Lloyd Garrison decried slavery, not as a necessary evil but as a heinous sin. They demanded immediate abolition and rejected colonization as a cruel scheme to deport free blacks. In the South, proslavery advocates like Thomas Roderick Dew defended slavery, not as a necessary evil but as a benefit to civilization and to both races. They saw no need for abolition, immediate or gradual, and rejected colonization as unnecessary.[3]

This increasingly bitter war of words foreshadowed the bitter and bloody Civil War that was to come. Indeed, the bloodshed over slavery was already beginning. The nightmare of a massive servile rebellion had long haunted the collective consciousness (and perhaps also the collective conscience) of white Americans. In Virginia in August 1831, Nat Turner confirmed those anxieties by leading a rebellion that left fifty-seven white people dead. Garrison, a pacifist, regretted such violence but saw it as a necessary consequence of the sin of slavery and predicted more bloodshed in the future. Many white Americans, Northern and Southern, believed Garrison's and other abolitionists' words fanned the flames of rebellion and sought to muzzle them with force. In every region of the country, angry mobs attacked abolitionists periodically throughout the decade, sometimes with deadly results.[4]

Two Theologians, Two Anxious Audiences, Two Dissonant Statements

It was during this decade that Charles Hodge (1797–1878) and Horace Bushnell (1802–1876), "arguably the greatest theological voices in mid-century America,"[5] made their first significant statements on slavery. Hodge's article "Slavery" appeared in the

---

[3] Sydney Ahlstrom, *A Religious History of the American People* (New Haven: Yale University Press, 1972) 651–54.

[4] Louis Filler, *The Crusade against Slavery, 1830–1860* (New York: Harper and Row, Publishers, 1960) 52, 64, 71, 77–81.

[5] Robert Bruce Mullin, *The Puritan as Yankee: A Life of Horace Bushnell*, with a foreword by Allen C. Guelzo (Grand Rapids: Eerdmans Publishing Company, 2002) 157.

journal he edited, the *Biblical Repertory and Princeton Review*, in 1836. Bushnell touched on slavery in his first published sermon in 1835,[6] but he first addressed the topic at length in his 1839 *Discourse on the Slavery Question*. Hodge and Bushnell, who represented two distinct theological points of view, addressed two anxious and divided audiences with two singularly dissonant messages on slavery.

A Book Review. Charles Hodge was a professor at the Presbyterian Princeton Theological Seminary. The large readership of his journal, the *Princeton Review*, was a testament to the respect he garnered among Presbyterians and other American Protestants. Hodge was unashamedly conservative in an era when Presbyterian churchmen were expected to be conservative. He was later to boast (with a straight face) before a large admiring audience, "a new idea never originated at Princeton Seminary."[7] The foundation of Hodge's conservatism was an infallible Bible, which he called a compendium of "facts" to be studied with the inductive method.[8]

Hodge published his article "Slavery" on the eve of the Presbyterian Church's national General Assembly of 1836, where a crisis was anticipated to erupt. The previous year, the Chillicothe Presbytery had introduced a memorial that condemned "buying, selling, or holding slaves" as "a heinous sin and scandal." It advocated immediate emancipation and rejected the colonization scheme as "unjust and cruel."[9] Using the fiery rhetoric of a new generation of abolitionists, this memorial of 1835 struck at the heart of a compromise that had placated Presbyterians for years, ever since Northern and Southern Presbyterians at the General Assembly of

---

[6] Horace Bushnell, *Crisis of the Church* (Hartford: Daniel Burgess and Company, 1835) 18–20.

[7] Archibald Alexander Hodge, *The Life of Charles Hodge, by His Son* (London: T. Nelson, 1880) 521.

[8] Charles Hodge, *Systematic Theology*, 3 vols. (New York: Charles Scribner, 1871; reprint, Grand Rapids: Eerdmans Publishing Company, 1997) 1:10–11 (page numbers correspond to the reprint edition).

[9] Memorial of the Chillicothe Presbytery, quoted in Charles Hodge, "The General Assembly of 1835," *Biblical Repertory and Princeton Review* (hereafter *BRPR*) 7/3 (July 1835): 450–51.

1818 had agreed to affirm the moderate antislavery policy of gradual abolition, voluntary manumission, and colonization.[10] The General Assembly of 1835 referred the volatile memorial of the Chillicothe presbytery to a committee, which deferred general discussion until the next year. The General Assembly of 1836 could no longer dodge the question: would Presbyterians as a whole continue to support the old compromise of 1818 or would they embrace the new spirit of immediate abolition? Both sides of the argument had strong advocates. The issue had the potential to split the church.[11] Undoubtedly, many Presbyterians stood poised to see where Hodge, the "Princeton theologian," would weigh in on the 1836 debate on slavery.

Hodge's "Slavery" seemed at first to be a proslavery tract. Hodge attacked the new crop of "abolitionists" who called slavery a "heinous crime" and demanded immediate emancipation. Hodge blamed them for the social unrest that currently wracked the country. He argued on the basis of a number of biblical texts that slavery *per se* ("slaveholding in itself considered") was not a sin and should not in itself be the subject of church discipline.[12] Such an argument might have been expected from Hodge, who had previously owned more than one slave.[13] The article, which was ostensibly a review of William Ellery Channing's *Slavery*, was in fact a thinly-veiled attack on the memorial of the Chillicothe Presbytery, and apparently it worked. The 1836 General Assembly did not approve the memorial.

---

[10] The Resolution on Slavery of the General Assembly of the Presbyterian Church (U.S.A.) of 1818 denounced "the voluntary enslaving of one's fellow man" as contrary to "the Golden Rule," Yet it also sympathized with the concerns of slaveholders and welcomed them into communion, warned against immediate emancipation, and urged the support of the American Colonization Society. See Andrew E. Murray, *Presbyterians and the Negro—a History* (Philadelphia: Presbyterian Historical Society, 1966) 26.

[11] Disagreement over slavery was indeed a factor in the split of the Presbyterian denomination into the Old School and New School in 1838.

[12] Charles Hodge, "Slavery," *BRPR* 8/2 (April 1836): 269, 278–89, 299–302.

[13] The known details of Hodge's slaveholding, along with the particular aspects of the practice of slavery in New Jersey, will be discussed in a later chapter.

For another year, at least, the Presbyterian Church remained out of the abolitionist camp.

Even so, Hodge's article was not intended as a defense of Southern slavery. First of all, while Hodge was not willing to side with the new generation of abolitionists who condemned slavery as a sin in all cases, neither was he willing to side with the new generation of proslavery writers who considered slavery a "positive good." Like the Presbyterian General Assembly of 1818, Hodge affirmed the moderate position that the existence of slavery within the borders of the United States was an unfortunate situation that ought gradually to be changed. Furthermore, when Hodge defended slavery *per se* as not necessarily sinful, he was not defending African slavery in the Southern United States specifically. He was defending involuntary servitude in its most abstract sense, "an obligation to labor for the benefit of the master, without the contract or consent of the servant."[14] Hodge made a distinction between slavery *per se* and unjust "Southern slave laws," which "forbid the instruction of slaves; which interfere with their marital or parental rights;" and "which subject them to the insults and oppression of the whites."[15] Hodge argued that these laws ought to be done away with and that such a humanitarian reform of Southern slavery would be a prelude to the end of slavery in the United States.

In a manner strangely reminiscent of Garrison, Hodge said that if Southerners did not reform the inhumane aspects of slavery, then a bloody servile rebellion lurked ominously in their future. Hodge, of course, did not advocate such a rebellion, but he warned that it might be unstoppable. "The South," he wrote, "must choose between emancipation by the silent and holy influence of the gospel...or abide the issue of a long continued conflict with the laws of God."[16]

---

[14] Hodge, "Slavery," 279n. Hodge was quoting William Paley, *Moral and Political Philosophy*, 8th ed. (Boston: West and Richardson, 1815) 155.

[15] Hodge, "Slavery," 278.

[16] Ibid., 310.

Then in a convoluted passage Hodge addressed the issue of race. He considered the possibility that slaves, if freed, might ultimately become United States citizens. Hodge argued that the fear of this future possibility was not an excuse for hindering gradual emancipation. While he did not unequivocally affirm racial equality, he reminded his readers that African slaves were human beings and that "their color does not place them beyond the operation of the gospel."[17]

One historian called Hodge's article "manna from heaven to proslavery Southerners."[18] Yet its qualifications made it an ambivalent gift. It appears that if Southern slaveholders—like the ancient Israelites—found "manna from heaven" in Hodge's 1836 article, they also found—like the ancient Israelites—that gifts that fall from heaven are not always as free as they seem. Furthermore, Southerners were careful—unlike the ancient Israelites—not to gather up too much of this "manna," lest it spoil. When in 1860 Ebenezer N. Eliot included "Slavery" and Hodge's later article "Civil Government" (1851) in his *Cotton Is King, and Proslavery Arguments*, he excised some of the passages that fit awkwardly into proslavery propaganda.[19]

A Thursday Evening Lecture. Horace Bushnell, a popular Congregationalist minister at North Church in Hartford, Connecticut, would never be one to boast (as Charles Hodge did) that "a new idea never once originated" in the context of his ministry. On the contrary, he strived to be broad-minded and creative. He saw religious truth as too great and too subtle to be contained in rigid logical formulas, even if those formulas claimed to be based on biblical propositions. Bushnell spoke of truth as a complex of emotions and attitudes, which are communicated through the

---

[17] Ibid.

[18] H. Shelton Smith, *In His Image, but...Racism in Southern Religion, 1790–1810* (Durham NC: Duke University Press, 1972) 80.

[19] E. N. Elliot, ed., *Cotton Is King and Proslavery Arguments*, 3d ed. (Augusta GA: Pritchard, Abbot and Loomis, 1860; reprint, New York: Johnson Reprint Corp. 1968) 811–77 (page numbers correspond to the reprint edition).

mysterious bonds of organic human communities. These views would later embroil him in conflicts with his colleagues in the ministry who doubted his orthodoxy, and they would ultimately distinguish him as the "Father of American religious liberalism."[20]

Bushnell delivered his *Discourse on the Slavery Question* as a public lecture at North Church on Thursday evening, 10 January 1839. As did Charles Hodge in 1836, Bushnell made his first major statement on slavery to a hotly divided audience. Not all New Englanders were abolitionists, despite what some Southerners thought. Garrison was a Bostonian, but so was the mob that tarred and feathered him in 1835. Connecticut, with its disproportionate number of antiabolitionist riots, was probably "the most anti-abolitionist, anti-African-American state in New England."[21] Bushnell's own congregation was divided over slavery,[22] as were the crowd of visitors, "men and women, Whigs, 'Locos,' colonizationists, and 'abolitionists of every degree and temperature, from 55% to 210%'"[23] who waited to hear what the famous preacher had to say.

Bushnell, for his part, said two surprising things. First, he stated that slavery was wrong and should be done away with as soon as possible. He criticized the tactics of Garrison and the abolitionists but basically agreed with them in principle, saying that slavery deprives people of their humanity, of their families, of their souls—that it effectively turns a human being into a "muscular tool." He called for the end of slavery, saying, "there can be no

---

[20] Sydney Ahlstrom, "Theology in America: A Historical Survey," in *The Shaping of American Religion,* vol. 1 of *Religion in American Life*, ed. James Ward Smith and A. Leland Jamison (Princeton: Princeton University Press, 1961) 279–85.

[21] Robert L. Edwards, *Of Singular Genius, of Singular Grace: A Biography of Horace Bushnell* (Cleveland: Pilgrim Press, 1992) 51.

[22] Bushnell acknowledged his divided congregation when he dedicated the printed edition of this discourse to them, wishing that "it were possible to make it more agreeable to their views." Horace Bushnell, *Discourse on the Slavery Question: Delivered in the North Church, Hartford, Thursday Evening, Jan. 10, 1839* (Hartford: Case, Tiffany, and Company, 1839) inscription.

[23] Edwards, *Singular Genius,* 51. Edwards is quoting Russell G. Talcott to John Seymour, 15 January 1839.

consequences" of the abolition of slavery that are "worse than the thing itself." He opposed remunerating slaveholders for emancipated slaves. He criticized well-intended advocates of colonization, who erred in upholding it as "a complete remedy for slavery." He even criticized New England merchants who profited from slavery. In fact, his denunciation of slavery, in his time and for his audience, was rather bold.[24]

But then, in the middle of his antislavery argument, Bushnell made an alarming statement on race. He asked, "what will be the result to the slaves, if emancipated," and answered his own question by responding, "I am obliged to say that I do not anticipate any...bright destiny opening on the African race in this country." He expected "that the African race, in this country, would soon begin to dwindle towards extinction" in the same manner as the American Indians and other "barbarous" peoples in America. He did not doubt that a number of individual former slaves might survive and even thrive after emancipation: "The difficulty is to elevate the race, *as a race*, among us." He opined, "They need five hundred or a thousand years of cultivation to give them a fair chance. They cannot maintain the competition, they will be preyed upon and overreached, they will not respect themselves, they will grow discouraged, they will, many of them, betake themselves to idleness, vice, and crime; by all these conjoint influences they will be kept down and gradually diminished in numbers."[25]

Such theories on race were not entirely original. But they were unusual in the middle of an antislavery argument. In fact, Bushnell harped on this racial extinction theory to the point of endangering his humanitarian argument for abolishing slavery. If his dire predictions for freed slaves were true, would not abolition be a disservice to them? Bushnell's vague "answer" to this question was, "Though [emancipation] opens no very bright and hopeful prospect to the

---

[24] Bushnell, *Discourse on the Slavery Question*, 6–7, 9, 24.
[25] Ibid., 11–12.

African race, it will at least bring them to an acknowledgment of their manhood."[26]

What Did They Say, and Why Did They Say It? With varying emphases, Hodge and Bushnell continued to play these distinctly dissonant chords for decades. Up until, during, and after the Civil War, Hodge continued to defend slavery *per se* as not necessarily sinful. But he also continued to criticize the actual practice of slavery in the United States, hoping for its ultimate demise and expressing cautious optimism about the future of the African-American people following emancipation. Bushnell, meanwhile, continued to combine rigorous opposition to African-American slavery with predictions of the extinction of the black race on the American continent.

Their apparent ambivalence has made these theologians a puzzle, both to their contemporaries and to later historians. Scholars differ regarding the issues of what Hodge and Bushnell actually meant when they spoke out on slavery and race, whether their positions changed over time, and upon what their statements were based. According to some, Hodge and Bushnell simply reflected the prejudices and presuppositions of their social peers. Others find their statements on slavery and race to be more deeply rooted in particular sets of religious commitments.[27]

Statement of Purpose

Hodge and Bushnell, despite their apparent ambivalence, did indeed maintain consistent and coherent positions on slavery and race, though both of their positions contained a degree of flexibility that allowed them to adjust to changing circumstances. Furthermore, neither of their views on slavery and race were simply reflections of the prejudices and presuppositions of their societies. Rather, their positions were deeply grounded in particular religious commitments.

Theological commitments were not the only factors influencing Hodge and Bushnell's statements on slavery and race, but they were

---

[26] Ibid., *Discourse on the Slavery Question*, 14.
[27] I will cite examples in later chapters.

essential factors. These commitments had their own integrity. They cannot be reduced to epiphenomena—that is, to aspects of other, supposedly more important factors. They shaped the ways in which Hodge and Bushnell negotiated the options their culture presented for understanding and responding to the problems of slavery and race. It was because of, not in spite of, Charles Hodge's theological "conservatism" that he was an opponent (albeit at times a weak one) of slavery. It was because of, not in spite of, Bushnell's theological "liberalism" that he was an opponent of slavery *and* that he held to a theory of African-American extinction.

Together Hodge and Bushnell provide a case study that proves the following thesis: *1) Charles Hodge's particular constellation of theological method, normative principles, anthropological assumptions, predominant loyalties, and circumstantial considerations enabled and inspired his defense of involuntary servitude per se. This same constellation also enabled and inspired his moderate opposition to slavery as it was practiced in the United States. 2) Horace Bushnell's particular constellation of theological method, normative principles, anthropological assumptions, predominant loyalties, and circumstantial considerations enabled and inspired his opposition to slavery and his post-Civil-War support of African-American suffrage. This same constellation also enabled and inspired him to embrace theories of Anglo-Saxon superiority and African inferiority.*

"Practical Reasoning" and "the Truth." This thesis statement includes certain technical terms, which belong to the academic discipline of ethics, that require further definition.[28]

"Normative principles," "Anthropological assumptions," "predominant loyalties," and "circumstantial considerations" are "elements of practical reasoning."[29] They describe a universal process of

---

[28] Of course, using these terms is not the only way to make ethical analysis. I make no attempt to defend this particular approach in opposition to others. I hope my argument as a whole will demonstrate that this approach is valid.

[29] Douglas F. Ottati, "Assessing Moral Arguments: A Study Paper" (1987), typed manuscript (photocopy) 1, Union Theological Seminary-Presbyterian School of Christian Education, Richmond, VA. Ottati uses slightly different terminology for

moral deliberation. Whenever anyone—a Christian theologian, an atheist philosopher, or an ordinary person of indeterminate beliefs—articulates a moral "policy," a systematic attempt at moral guidance, he or she touches on something like these four base points, either implicitly or explicitly.[30]

These are "formal" elements of practical reason. They do not imply any specific theological or philosophical content, but they "attract" a certain content.[31] The policy-maker "fills" these formal containers with specific ideas drawn from his or her experience or from any number of traditions. For theologians like Hodge and Bushnell, these elements would attract a specifically theological content.

These elements are systemically interrelated. Each factor influences all the others: "If one brings about a significant change in one sector, the entire pattern will be modified."[32] However, these elements are also relatively independent. No single element or combination of elements dominates or controls the others in a predictable way.[33]

"Normative principles" are rules. Rules govern the means by which a person might pursue a given end. People operate under different rules. They also have different understandings of the extent to which rules allow for exceptions or might be applied differently under different circumstances. One says a great deal about the rigidity of one's rules by what one calls them. While Charles Hodge

---

two elements. "Circumstantial considerations" is my paraphrase of Ottati's "an interpretation of circumstances." Where I use the term "normative principles," Ottati uses the term "moral values" and lists "norms, guidelines, and principles" as synonyms. Other ethicists, whom I will cite presently, also use slightly different vocabulary with essentially the same meaning.

[30] Ralph B. Potter, *War and Moral Discourse* (Richmond VA: John Knox Press, 1970) 23.

[31] Charles M. Swezey, "What Is Theological Ethics?: A Study of the Thought of James M. Gustafson" (Ph.D. diss., Vanderbilt University, 1978) 4, 15.

[32] Potter, *War*, 28.

[33] Arthur J. Dyck, *On Human Care: An Introduction to Ethics* (Nashville: Abingdon Press, 1977) 20.

preferred to speak of strict and rigid divine "laws," Bushnell favored the more flexible term "principle of virtue."

"Anthropological assumptions" are beliefs about human nature—assumptions about what makes a human being a moral agent: what capacities people have, what limitations they labor under, what environmental or inherent factors influence them, and the extent to which human beings differ, either as individuals or as groups. Under this rubric, a religious theist might ask, what is the human being's relationship to God and to his or her fellow creatures? One's anthropological assumptions also include one's understanding of race and racial differences.

"Predominant loyalties" are the good or goods that the moral agent pursues: the cause or causes that motivate the agent, the goal or goals that the agent keeps in sight.[34] As we shall see, Both Hodge and Bushnell were loyal to their own versions of an ideal Christian society, and these visions drove their policies on slavery.

The fourth element listed is "circumstantial considerations." Any human action takes place in a particular context; every circumstance includes a number of variable factors that require consideration. Every moral policy requires "an empirical definition of the situation" in which a decision is being made, though ethicists differ in how they interpret historical circumstances and the extent to which they allow the contingencies of a particular situation to determine the final policy.[35]

This leaves one more technical term to be defined, "theological method." While this term may be used in different ways, here it will have a limited meaning. It is *the method a theologian uses to know the truth*, particularly *true knowledge of God*. A theologian's method deals with questions like, which sources (Scripture, tradition, reason, and/or experience) are the reliable sources of divine truth?;[36] how do

---

[34] Potter, *War*, 23–24.

[35] Ibid., 23.

[36] These four terms are from the "Methodist quadrilateral," a helpful tool for analyzing a theologian's method. See Max Stackhouse, *Public Theology and Political*

these different sources relate to each other?; how are such sources inspired or authorized by God?; and how are they to be interpreted and applied?

There are a number of reasons why "theological method" is in a separate category from the four "elements of practical reasoning." Unlike the four formal elements of practical reasoning, which do not necessarily imply a theological content, theological method is by definition "theological." The question of truth belongs to a more theoretical level of discourse than do the elements of practical reasoning.[37] When we discuss the validity of our basic sources of truth, even if we use secular language, we inevitably ask questions about human limitations and ultimate authority. These are religious questions, whether or not the person asking them is "religious" in the conventional sense. One's estimate of reliable sources of knowledge is a "factor of religious belief" that "conditions" his or her moral choices.[38]

It was this religious issue that most clearly separated Hodge and Bushnell. Though Bushnell and Hodge would have agreed on little else, they would have at least agreed that they had profoundly different understandings of the source of religious truth. Hodge, who reviewed three of Bushnell's books for the *Princeton Review*, was scandalized by Bushnell's skepticism about theological language and attacked Bushnell's poetic, metaphorical interpretation of the Bible,

---

Economy: Christian Stewardship in Modern Society (Lanham MD: University Press of America, 1991) 1–15.

[37] Swezey, "What Is Theological Ethics," 1–2. See also James M. Gustafson, *Christian Ethics and the Community* (Philadelphia: United Church Press, a Pilgrim Press Book, 1971) 84–85, 87.

[38] Swezey lists five: an overarching "task of theology," which is to articulate a "vision of God," and four subordinate "issues that occur perennially" in the course of this task: "the relation of good and evil, the nature of religious participation, estimates of reliable sources of knowledge, and the character of moral guidance." See "The Role of Religious Participation and Religious Belief in Biomedical Decision Making," in *Society's Choices: Social and Ethical Decision Making in Biomedicine*, ed. Ruth Ellen Bulger, Elizabeth Meyer Bobby, and Harvey V. Fineberg (Washington D C: National Academy Press, 1995) 361.

saying, "The Bible is not a cunningly devised fable."[39] Bushnell (who rarely responded to critics) did not argue with Hodge directly on this or any other matter, but he dismissed the biblical inerrantism Hodge and others affirmed. Those who make "the divine authority of the Scriptures...depend on the question of their most rigid, strictest, most punctual infallibility" force the Scriptures "to stand or fall by mere minima, and not by anything principal in them, or their inspiration," he wrote.[40]

Furthermore, the "truth" question most clearly distinguishes the two groups Hodge and Bushnell represent, conservative and liberal American Protestants. In subsequent decades, whenever a public argument has erupted between these two groups—whether over teaching Darwinian evolution in public schools, or abortion, or gay marriage, or gay ordination, or some other issue—invariably one group has argued that its view is the biblical truth and the other group has argued that the Bible needs to be interpreted in the light of other sources of knowledge.[41]

Surely methodological differences are not the *only* important factors in any of these conflicts. Nevertheless methodological differences are important. They were important for Hodge and Bushnell. They affected the moral stances they took, particularly on slavery and race, in surprising ways. Our focus is limited to understanding Hodge and Bushnell in their own historical contexts, but if we understand what moral consequences two sets of theological ideas have had in the past, we should have a clue as to what consequences similar sets of ideas would have in the present and in the future. The examples of Hodge and Bushnell provide warning and encouragement to many twenty-first-century theologians who, in

---

[39] Charles Hodge, "Bushnell's Discourses," *BRPR* 21/2 (April 1849): 291.

[40] Horace Bushnell, *Nature and the Supernatural: as Together Constituting the One System of God* (New York: Charles Scribner's Sons, 1903) 21.

[41] See for example the conversation between Paul E. Capetz and Fred W. Beuttler concerning ordination of homosexuals in the *Journal of Presbyterian History* 79/1 (Spring 2001): 1–45.

various ways and to varying degrees, continue to espouse their doctrines.

But in order to understand the ethical consequences of Hodge's and Bushnell's beliefs, one must understand the historical situation in which they lived, made judgments, and expressed their ideas, which is the purpose of the next chapter.

1

Slavery and Race in the United States

When Hodge and Bushnell's contemporaries spoke out on American slavery, they addressed a specific historical institution, using the language of specific cultural and intellectual environment. Though diverse, their arguments tended to cluster around typical stances. This chapter will first identify three specific qualities of American slavery. It will then discuss three intellectual traditions that generally influenced antebellum moral arguments on any subject. Finally it will describe three typical positions that dominated the American public debate on slavery.

Features of American Slavery

Slavery in the United States had a combination of at least three qualities that made it a "peculiar institution," a unique form of bonded labor. It was chattel slavery; it was Southern slavery; and, most importantly, it was racial slavery.

Chattel Slavery. The African-American slave was not like the indentured servant, whose period of servitude was temporary, or the English villein, whose "servitude was peculiarly confined to the territorial domain of his lord."[1] The African slave in North America was legally "chattel": a species of movable property, like a piece of

---

[1] David Brion Davis, *The Problem of Slavery in Western Culture* (Ithaca NY: Cornell University Press, 1966) 39.

furniture. The master could buy the slave, sell the slave, give the slave away, and generally use the slave as the master saw fit. A slave was a slave for life unless freed by the master. Even the slave's children belonged to the master. The master's power over the slave was virtually absolute. It must be so, wrote one Southern judge, in order to "render submission of the slave perfect."[2] Chattel slavery was not unique to the antebellum United States, but it did distinguish slavery in the US from some other forms of bonded labor.

It is important to note, however, that the term "chattel" was a legal convention, not a philosophical definition of the American slave.[3] Though chattel in the eyes of the law, the slave was still a human being in the eyes of God. As contradictory as this might seem to us today, this was what American slaveholders affirmed. However inhumanely masters treated slaves, they did not as a rule understand them to be literally things or animals.[4] Even Southern slave laws did not generally push the logic of chattel slavery to the extreme. Negatively, the law recognized the slave as a moral agent who could legitimately be punished for crimes. Positively, some laws existed to protect the lives and safety of slaves.[5] However, slaves had little or no power to assert these legal "rights." The black slave usually could not testify against a white person in court or legally protect himself with force. Protection of the slave's humanity was ordinarily left up to the conscience of master.[6] Furthermore, having had the misfortune of being labeled chattel, the American slave had little opportunity of becoming anything else. That there were laws against manumission of slaves, particularly in the Southern states in the nineteenth

---

[2] Thomas Ruffin, *The Papers of Thomas Ruffin*, vol. 4 of 4, ed. J. G. deRoulhac Hamilton (Raleigh NC: n.p., 1918–1920), quoted in Eugene Genovese, *Roll Jordan Roll: The World the Slaves Made* (New York: Vintage, 1976) 35.

[3] William Summer Jenkins, *Pro-Slavery Thought in the Old South* (Chapel Hill: University of North Carolina Press, 1935) 228–30.

[4] Winthrop Jordan, *White over Black: American Attitudes toward the Negro, 1550–1812* (Chapel Hill: University of North Carolina Press) 232.

[5] Genovese, *Roll Jordan Roll*, 25–31.

[6] Ibid., 30.

century, was one of the peculiar attributes of African-American slavery.[7]

Southern Slavery. Another significant particularity of African slavery in the United States was that it dominated one section of the country. It was primarily a Southern agrarian institution. Slave labor was employed to some degree in all the original thirteen colonies, but the states north of Maryland and Delaware took steps to emancipate slaves shortly after the American Revolution (though some states used gradualist methods, with the result that complete abolition did not occur in the North until well into the nineteenth century). In the South, however, after the invention of the cotton gin in 1793, slavery became intrenched. By Hodge and Bushnell's day, African slavery had become the staple source of labor for Southern agriculture (a major export industry consisting primarily of cotton but also tobacco, rice, and other crops) and a bone of contention in a growing sectional conflict that was to disrupt both the churches and the nation.[8]

Racial Slavery. The most significant distinguishing mark of slavery in the United States was that it was thoroughly racial. Other forms of slavery throughout history involved the captivity of some "other" person, an outsider to the slaveholder's ethnic group. However, African-American slavery was unique in the extent to which it distinguished the ethnicities of the slaves and masters. It is fair to say that in the history of western civilization, at least until the twentieth century, there has never been as thorough a distinction made between peoples as there has been between "white" and "black," or to use Winthrop Jordan's wording, "white over black," in the United States. Slavery in the US both depended on and broadened this distinction. Clarity requires that we first discuss the idea of race in general, then the particular dichotomy of "white over black."

---

[7] Davis, *Problem of Slavery*, 29, 54, 57.

[8] Ralph Flanders, "Slavery," in *Dictionary of American History*, 6 vols., ed. James Thruslow and R.V. Gleman (New York: Charles Scribner's Sons, 1940) 5:95–96.

In recent years, historians have argued that "the so-called races of mankind" are simply social constructs: "the fortuitous and arbitrary inventions of European and American history, the by-products of Europe's religious, economic, and imperial expansion across the seas of the earth."[9] But the age-old notion that races are essential and obvious categories persists.

The term "race" has historically referred to an ethnic group whose members have a cultural and blood relation, a people who share a common historical heritage and a common gene pool. Racial thinkers assume that each "race" has particular organically interconnected physical, psychological, and spiritual qualities. Consistent racial thinkers understand the marks of race to be permanent and indelible: one cannot change one's racial identity or be initiated into another race by culture. Racial thinkers often express a distaste for intermarriage between members of different races. They usually understand their own race to be the superior one.[10] In the nineteenth-century United States, many of Hodge and Bushnell's "white" peers showed (to varying degrees) all these aspects of racial thinking, including the belief that the light-skinned European type was the normative or superior race.

Yet there was only a vague consensus as to what the physical and spiritual qualities of races were, as to the precise dividing lines between races, and even as to what to call them. Nineteenth-century Americans often spoke of "three great races of man," the African, the Oriental, and the Occidental. Many saw these three groups as descendants of three sons of Noah—Ham, Shem, and Japheth, respectively. Others spoke of four or five great races, placing the

---

[9] David Brion Davis, "Constructing Race: A Reflection," *William and Mary Quarterly*, 3d ser., 14/1 (January 1997): 7.

[10] Au'Ra Muhammad Abdullah Ilahi, "Racism," in *Historical Encyclopedia of World Slavery*, 2 vols., ed. Junius Rodriguez (Santa Barbara CA: ABC-CLIO, Inc., 1997) offers this similar working definition of "racism": "Racist doctrine evolved in early colonial America to place humanity into compartmentalized groups based on distinctive physical, social, and mental traits, which presumably established a ranking founded upon the 'unilinear evolutionist' thinking of the time" (2:537).

American Indian in a separate category or distinguishing the Asian from the Near Eastern "Semite." Some referred to races with geographic terms: Ethiopian, Mongolian, Caucasian, American, and Malay. Most often people divided races by colors—red, yellow, black, and white.[11] Some divided the "white" European race into Anglo-Saxon (or Teutonic or Germanic), Iberian, Celtic, and other "races." Nevertheless, "the concept of race, polysemic though it remained, was so widely used that it achieved normative status."[12]

Though the idea of race has a long history in the west, it has always carried with it an inherent ambiguity. Many of the same traditions that developed, preserved, and encouraged racial thinking also had elements that challenged it. In Western civilization, the idea of race has always existed in tension with another enduring idea, one that was affirmed by the Judeo-Christian tradition and, with different emphases, by the predominant Western philosophical traditions since the time of Plato—the idea of human unity.

Human unity means that human beings are in every sense of the word a family. That is to say, they are all literally related, descended from the same primordial grandparents, Adam and Eve (a tradition that was taken literally not only by theologians but also by scientists, well into the nineteenth century). They are alike in kind, created in the image of God (to use biblical language), distinguished from other creatures by being blessed with a rational and moral nature. Finally, human beings are a family in the sense that they are joined together. They are social creatures, interdependent and therefore morally obligated to each other. Because all people are essentially similar,

---

[11] Thomas F. Gossett, *Race: The History of an Idea in America* (Dallas: Southern Methodist University Press, 1963) 35–37. The word "Caucasian," which is still used to describe the white race, was coined by the eighteenth-century anthropologist Johann Friedrich Blumenbach, whose collection of skulls included one from the Caucasian mountain region of Russia, which Blumenbach thought to resemble the German cranium.

[12] Maurice Olender, *The Languages of Paradise: Race, Religion and Philology in the Nineteenth Century*, trans. Arthur Goldhammer (Cambridge: Harvard University Press, 1992) 57. Olender is writing about nineteenth-century Europe, but his statement accurately describes the situation in the United States.

each person is to use his or her own experience as a gauge for how to treat others. Western theologians and philosophers over the centuries united in affirming some version of the "golden rule": "Do unto others as you would have them do unto you."[13] The idea of human unity wove together a web of religious, intellectual, and moral suppositions. If one attacked one aspect of the idea by making hard distinctions between races, one threatened to unravel the whole fabric.

Nevertheless, throughout the history of Western civilization (including the history of antebellum America), people did make such distinctions. The idea of human unity did not absolutely preclude the notion of racial differences. Whether or not people share a common human nature, it remains a fact that people (and peoples) differ. The trick for any thinker who wished to be consistent was to reconcile such perceived (or assumed) differences with the orthodox tenet of the unity of humankind, a tenuous task. It involved drawing a line between peoples that was bold enough to see but not so bold as to deny a group of people the dignity of a human nature. Often, especially during and after the Enlightenment, the debated question was whether the differences between races were innate and permanent or the temporary results of environmental factors. Few thinkers came down solidly on either side of the nature/nurture debate, however. Most theorists mixed nature and nurture together, with various degrees of logical consistency.[14] Despite all the difficulties and ambiguities that were inherent in the idea of race, white Americans in the nineteenth century appeared to be determined to make rigid racial distinctions, the most rigid being between "black" and "white."

Slavery in the United States was not just racial slavery. It was African slavery. To be a slave one needed to be of African heritage. By the beginning of the eighteenth century, most of the Anglo-American colonies had taken steps to distinguish the African people

---

[13] Gossett, *Race*, 7–9.

[14] See the example of Samuel Stanhope Smith, below pp. 36–37.

as an enslavable race.[15] To be "black" and to be a slave had become, legally and even linguistically, virtually identical. Conversely, to be "white" had come to be virtually synonymous with being free, or at least potentially free.[16]

Anti-black prejudice was deeply seated in the white American's mind. Most nineteenth-century white Americans regarded the African as the dullest, most savage, most oversexed, and ugliest specimen of humanity. When in 1787 Thomas Jefferson opined that blacks were "in reason much inferior," that they were "more ardent after their female," and that they were obviously less attractive than whites, he was articulating views that had prevailed and would continue to prevail in white American society for many decades.[17]

In Hodge and Bushnell's day, discrimination against African Americans extended beyond slavery. The "freedom" of a free black in the South or the North was not equal to that of a white citizen in the eyes of the law. One activity that was singled out for disapproval in the North and the South, both by law and by custom, was sexual union between blacks and whites, though of course such unions occurred.[18] Those who disapproved of "amalgamation" were not simply horrified at the idea of intertwining black and white bodies, though expressions of this kind of distaste were plentiful. They wanted to maintain a distinction between black and white peoples in

---

[15] An example of this racial definition is a Carolina law of 1696, which defined slaves as "All Negroes, Mollatoes and Indians which at any time heretofore have been Bought and Sold or now are to be taken to be or hereafter Shall be Bought and Sold...and their children." Quoted in Mariam E. Sirmans, *Colonial South Carolina: A Political History* (Chapel Hill: University of North Carolina Press) 65.

[16] Gossett, *Race*, 29–31. See also Edmund S. Morgan, *American Slavery, American Freedom: The Ordeal of Colonial Virginia* (New York: W. W. Norton, 1975) 381.

[17] Thomas Jefferson, *Notes on the State of Virginia*, ed. William Peden (Chapel Hill: University of North Carolina Press, 1955) 137–43.

[18] For example, Massachusetts law forbade marriage between whites, Africans, and Indians from 1705 to 1843. See Louis Ruchames, ed., *Racial Thought in America Volume 1: From the Puritans to Abraham Lincoln* (Amherst: University of Massachusetts Press, 1969) 307.

order to preserve the United States as a white country. They feared the creation of a "mongrel race" of future Americans. They presumed, along with one Virginia politician, "that no white man will look forward with any complacency to that condition of society, in which the two races will be blended together."[19]

A second argument for the incompatibility of the black and white races in America presented itself, sometimes accompanying assumptions of African inferiority, sometimes standing alone— namely that, right or wrong, white prejudice against blacks was so powerful and so permanent that it prevented the two races from ever living together happily and on equal terms in the United States. This argument was usually accompanied by a claim that blacks were similarly hostile to whites: white Americans could never be sure when slaves or former slaves would decide to execute vengeance on the race that oppressed them.[20]

These assumptions of racial incompatibility pressed a question on any white person who tried to envision the end of slavery in the United States: what would the future of former slaves be? How would the nation negotiate the differences, not to mention the hostility, between the two races once the restraints of slavery had been removed? How would one avoid the nightmare scenario described by Thomas Jefferson, one of divisions and "convulsions, which will probably never end but in the extermination of one or the other race"?[21]

No historian, and very few Americans, would deny that the sharp dichotomy of white over black pervaded American culture in the nineteenth century (and not only in the nineteenth century). Historians differ as to the dichotomy's origin, especially as to its relationship with slavery. Was slavery, as Jordan says, simply an aspect of a color-based prejudice that dwelled deep within the

---

[19] Alexander Smyth, quoted in Jordan, *White over Black*, 581.

[20] George M. Fredrickson, *The Black Image in the White Mind: The Debate on Afro-American Character and Destiny, 1817–1914* (New York: Harper and Row, Publishers, 1971) 12–21.

[21] Jefferson, *State of Virginia*, 138.

"cultural conscience" of English-speaking people from the moment they first encountered African people in the sixteenth century?[22] Or did the social and political system of slavery help to create this prejudice, as Edmund S. Morgan suggests?[23] The question of whose thesis is more accurate is beyond our scope. Together, despite their different emphases, Jordan and Morgan demonstrate the peculiarity of slavery in North America. It was integrally tied to a particular brand of anti-African racial thinking with which nineteenth-century moralists were forced to come to terms.

The Intellectual Environment of the Antebellum United States

When nineteenth-century Americans spoke out on slavery (or any other moral problem), they did so in a specific intellectual environment. Americans grappled with the problem of racial slavery in conversation with one or more of three prominent intellectual traditions: Evangelicalism, the American Enlightenment, and Romanticism. None of these traditions, as we shall see presently, was unambivalently proslavery or antislavery, nor were they unambivalently racist or antiracist. While some individuals wielded these traditions as weapons against the idea of racial slavery, others used them for the opposite purpose.

Evangelicalism. The antebellum United States was not lacking in religious diversity. Not all Americans were Christians. Not all Christians were Protestant. In fact, immigration was quickly making

---

[22] Jordan, *White over Black*, 573–82.

[23] Morgan, *American Slavery*, 381, 387, describes how in colonial Virginia racial slavery gradually replaced a system of indentured servitude, which made poor white immigrants the virtual slaves of wealthy white planters. Racial slavery not only provided planters with necessary cheap labor, it also allowed small and large white farmers, who shared a common opposition to monarchical despotism, to affirm a degree of equality: "Neither was a slave. And both were equal in not being slaves" (381). Though it is ironic to the point of self-contradiction, racial slavery undergirded the belief in republican equality that Virginians like Thomas Jefferson and James Madison were to write into the foundational documents of the United States.

the Roman Catholic Church the largest single Christian denomination in the nation. Nevertheless, the plurality of Americans, including Charles Hodge and Horace Bushnell, fit into a group we can define broadly as "Evangelical."

"Evangelicalism" arose in the English-speaking world in the eighteenth century. It was planted in North America in the eighteenth and early nineteenth centuries in the form of two "Great Awakenings." It derived from the Protestant and Reformed traditions of Martin Luther and John Calvin, mediated by German Pietists, English Puritans, and Scottish Presbyterians. It was nurtured by the heartfelt piety of revivalists like Jonathan Edwards and George Whitefield, by the eclectic Arminianism of John Wesley and his followers, and—in Hodge and Bushnell's day—the systematic efforts of Charles Grandison Finney, along with a number of other religious leaders, including countless forgotten preachers who itinerated across the country.[24]

The influence of the Evangelical movement in the antebellum United States was tremendous. Though approximately only one in seven Americans belonged to a church, Evangelical ministers preached regularly to congregations three and four times the number of their churches' membership roles. Evangelical ideas found their way into the letters and diaries of many ordinary Americans,[25] into the curricula of the "common" or public schools Evangelicals helped to organize, into the colleges and theological seminaries they erected, and into the thousands of tracts, journals, and newspapers they

---

[24] For discussions of the Pietist, Reformed, and Wesleyan influences on American Evangelicalism, see Jerald C. Brauer, "Conversion: From Puritanism to Revivalism," *Journal of Religion* 58/3 (July 1978): 227–43; Glenn T. Miller, "God's Light and Man's Enlightenment: Evangelical Theology of Colonial Presbyterianism," *Journal of Presbyterian History* 51/2 (Summer 1973): 97–115; and Paul K. Conklin, *The Uneasy Center: Reformed Christianity in Antebellum America* (Chapel Hill: University of North Carolina Press, 1995) 63–89.

[25] Mark Noll, *A History of Christianity in the United States and Canada* (Grand Rapids: Eerdmans Publishing Company, 1992) 228.

published.[26] According to a number of historians, the piety promoted by the religious revivals of the eighteenth and nineteenth centuries did more to create an American national identity than any other intellectual tradition.[27]

Among the tenets Evangelicals commonly espoused were a high doctrine of biblical authority and an emphasis on the individual's voluntary commitment to Christ, often (but not always) taking the form of a dramatic personal conversion experience. Evangelicals also expected Christians to prove their redemption through moral action.[28] They had, of late, organized for the purpose of demonstrating their redemption more effectively, forming voluntary societies for benevolent purposes.[29]

Despite their sharing certain basic beliefs, Evangelicals were diverse group, lacking a uniform theology or a single denomination.[30] The Evangelical movement included Methodists, Baptists,

---

[26] C. C. Goen, *Broken Churches, Broken Nation: Denominational Schisms and the Coming of the American Civil War* (Macon GA: Mercer University Press, 1985) 34–37.

[27] Ibid., 18–24. See also H. Richard Niebuhr, *The Kingdom of God in America* (New York: Harper and Row, Publishers, 1937; reprint, Middletown CT: Wesleyan University Press, 1988) 126 (page numbers correspond to the reprint edition), and Perry Miller, *The Life and Mind of America: From the Revolution to the Civil War* (New York: Harcourt, Brace & World, Inc., 1965) 6, 7, 11, 14, 47.

[28] One set of Evangelical scholars name their common traits as "biblicism (a reliance on the Bible as ultimate religious authority), conversionism (a stress on the New Birth), activism (an energetic, individualistic approach to religious duties and social involvement), and crucicentrism (a focus on Christ's redeeming work as the heart of essential Christianity)." See Mark Noll, David Bebbington, and George A. Rawlyk, eds., *Evangelicalism: Comparative Studies of Popular Protestantism in North America, the British Isles, and Beyond, 1700–1990* (New York, Oxford: Oxford University Press, 1994) 6.

[29] These included the American Board for Foreign Missions (formed 1810), the American Bible Society (1816), the American Sunday School Union (1824), the American Tract Society (1825), the American Education Society (1826), the American Society for the Promotion of Temperance (1826), the American Home Missionary Society (1826), and many others. See Noll, *History of Christianity*, 169.

[30] Winthrop Hudson, *Religion in America*, 3d ed. rev. (New York: Charles Scribner's Son's, 1981) 135–36.

Presbyterians, Congregationalists, and others.[31] Evangelicals differed over particular matters of theology and style of worship. Hodge and Bushnell, for example, disagreed with the amount of emphasis their fellow Evangelicals placed on the dramatic personal conversion experience.[32] Evangelicals also differed over matters of morality, politics, and slavery.

There was a radically egalitarian dimension to Evangelicalism that formed the basis of Evangelical opposition to slavery.[33] Evangelical piety reinforced the idea that God is no respecter of persons, that all people are created in the image of God and are equally obligated to love their neighbors as themselves, that all people are equally sinful and equally in need of salvation. With its emphasis on voluntarism, lay participation, and lay leadership, Evangelicalism promoted a kind of personal freedom.[34] This theme was reinforced by the biblical story of Israel's liberation from Egyptian slavery and the Mosaic law's prohibition of "man-stealing" (Exodus 21:16).[35] These themes of equality and freedom, which were prominent in the rhetoric of antislavery Evangelicals, may have been

---

[31] Methodists, Baptists, and Presbyterians gained the most members as a result of the "Awakenings." Congregationalism, while not experiencing the same growth in numbers, included a number of important Evangelical leaders, including Edwards and Finney (who was first a Presbyterian and later a Congregationalist). See Edwin S. Gaustad, *Historical Atlas of Religion in America* (New York: Harper and Row, Publishers, 1962) 43, 52, 76, and Goen, *Broken Churches*, 43–63.

[32] Charles Hodge, "Bushnell on Christian Nurture," *BRPR* 19/4 (October 1847): 513–15, 519.

[33] Leonard Sweet, "Nineteenth Century Evangelicalism," in *Encyclopedia of the American Religious Experience*, vol. 2 of *Studies of Traditions and Movements*, ed. Charles Lippy and Peter Williams (New York: Charles Scribner's Sons, 1988) 894–95.

[34] Nathan O. Hatch, *The Democratization of American Christianity* (New Haven: Yale University Press, 1989) 10–16 et passim.

[35] Genovese, *Roll Jordan Roll*, 253; Mason Lowance, ed., *Against Slavery: An Abolitionist Reader* (New York: Penguin Books, 2000) 49–86.

what attracted so many African Americans to the Evangelical denominations in the late eighteenth and early nineteenth centuries.[36]

In Hodge and Bushnell's day, a number of Evangelicals emphasized the radical pole of their tradition by preaching a novel doctrine of "holiness" or "perfectionism." Going against the grain of the traditional Protestant and Reformed views on original sin and total depravity, these "perfectionists" claimed that freedom from sin was within human reach in this earthly life.[37] This optimism about liberation from personal sin at times led to a similar hopefulness about freedom from societal evils. Many Evangelicals who fell under the influence of the holiness movement refused to accept certain evils, such as slavery or war, as inevitable aspects of the natural world. As Finney put it, "War, slavery, licentiousness and all such evils and abominations are necessarily regarded by the saint as great and sore evils, and he longs for their complete and final overthrow." This attitude at times led to utopian social activism, especially against slavery.[38]

---

[36] Albert J. Raboteau, "The Black Experience in American Evangelicalism: The Meaning of Slavery," in *The Evangelical Tradition in America*, ed. Leonard Sweet (Macon, GA: Mercer University Press, 1984) 183.

[37] The doctrine of perfection or "entire sanctification" originally belongs to the Wesleyan branch of Protestantism. Wesley exhorted Christians to aspire to perfection, by which he meant "freedom from voluntary transgression." In the middle of the nineteenth century a number of Methodist lay people, including Phoebe Palmer, claimed to experience entire sanctification and promoted their piety through publications and informal midweek meetings. See Jean Miller Schmidt, "Holiness and Perfection," in *Encyclopedia of the American Religious Experience*, 2:813–16. Three vivid examples of how the holiness doctrine could imply leveling of social differences between sexes and races and opposition to slavery are in William L. Andrews, ed., *Sisters of the Spirit: Three Black Women's Autobiographies of the Nineteenth Century* (Bloomington: Indiana University Press, 1986).

[38] Charles Grandison Finney, quoted in William G. McLoughlin, *Revivals, Awakenings, and Reform: An Essay on Religion and Social Change, 1607–1977*, Chicago History of American Religion, ed. Martin Marty (Chicago: Chicago University Press, 1978) 129. See also Timothy L. Smith, *Revivalism and Social Reform in Mid-Nineteenth Century America* (New York and Nashville: Abingdon Press, 1957) 204–24.

However, Evangelicalism also maintained a socially conservative pole, which at times discouraged an antislavery stance. Not every Evangelical promoted revivalism as a leveling and liberating social force. For some Evangelicals, including those who defended slavery, revivals were at best a means of social control. Revivals put individuals under the ordering influence of religion, and one purpose of religion was to maintain divinely ordained social hierarchies.[39]

Proslavery Evangelicals specifically rejected the novel ideas—the perfectionist doctrines—that empowered other Evangelicals to challenge entrenched social structures like slavery. Instead, they affirmed racial slavery as, at worst, an inevitable tribulation of earthly existence or, at best, a necessary means of social control in a fallen world—definitely not something religious people should be in the business of abolishing. Universal freedom and social equality would be proper, perhaps, in the Garden of Eden or in heaven. But in a sinful world, human society requires the protection of restrictive social institutions like slavery.[40]

Proslavery Evangelicals had ready answers to the biblical arguments of Evangelical opponents of slavery. They argued that God, speaking through Moses, permitted the Israelites to take slaves from among the inhabitants of Canaan (Leviticus 25:44–46). They challenged their opponents to find a specific condemnation of slavery by Jesus or the apostles. They recited the apostle Paul's instructions to Christian slaves to obey their masters (1 Corinthians 7:21; Ephesians 6:5; Colossians 3:22; 1 Timothy 6:1; Titus 2:9), and

---

[39] McLoughlin, *Revivals*, 112–13, 131–38. See also Samuel Davies, *The Duty of Christians to Propagate Their Religion Among Heathens, Earnestly Recommended to the Masters of Negroe Slaves in Virginia. A Sermon Preached in Hanover, January 8, 1757* (London: J. Oliver, 1757) 23, quoted in Andrew E. Murray, *Presbyterians and the Negro—a History* (Philadelphia: Presbyterian Historical Society, 1966) 11.

[40] Donald G. Mathews, *Religion in the Old South* (Chicago: University of Chicago Press, 1977) 168–78; Jenkins, *Pro-Slavery Thought*, 217; James Henley Thornwell, *The Rights and Duties of Masters. A sermon preached at the dedication of a church, erected in Charleston, South Carolina, for the benefit and instruction of the coloured population* (Charleston: Walker and James, 1850) 31.

described how Paul sent the slave Onesemis, whom he baptized, back to Philemon, his Christian master. Proslavery Evangelicals could also interpret the Bible as acknowledging racial differences. Specifically, they could refer to the story of Noah, who curses his son Ham (and/or Ham's son Canaan) to be a "servant of servants" (Genesis 9:25, KJV) for having looked on his father's nakedness. One interpretation of this passage, which makes Africans the descendants of Ham and therefore destined for slavery, had an infamous career as a proslavery argument.[41]

The American Enlightenment. Those who spoke out on antebellum American slavery had to come to terms with another influential intellectual trend, the American Enlightenment—the American version of "the age of Science," a "period of profound intellectual and social change" that began in the late seventeenth century and extended into the nineteenth.[42]

Proponents of the Enlightenment trusted reason to discern the laws by which the physical and social universe ran. They distrusted truth claims based on religious tradition or supernatural revelation. They were optimistic about human nature. They affirmed "the perfectibility of the individual, and the human capability to shape history."[43] Therefore, they had a high regard for intellectual and political liberty, which they affirmed as "natural human rights." Proponents of the American Enlightenment had an extraordinary influence on the American society, and Enlightenment ideals are prominent in the foundational documents of the United States.[44]

---

[41] Benjamin Braude, "The Sons of Noah and the Construction of Ethnic and Geographical Identities in the Medieval and Early Modern Periods," *William and Mary Quarterly*, 3d ser., 14/1 (January 1997): 127; Thomas Virgil Peterson, *Ham and Japheth: The Mythic World of Whites in the Antebellum South* (Metuchen NJ: Scarecrow Press, 1978) passim.

[42] John Corrigan, "The Enlightenment," in *Encyclopedia of the American Religious Experience*, 2:1089.

[43] Ibid.

[44] E.g., the Declaration of Independence: "We hold these truths to be self-evident, that all men are created equal, endowed by their Creator with certain unalienable rights; that among these are life, liberty, and the pursuit of happiness."

These tenets of the Enlightenment—humanism, optimism, and rationalism—often clashed with the traditional Christian doctrines of a God-centered universe, of original sin, and of the necessity for supernatural revelation.[45] Nevertheless, American Evangelicalism and the American Enlightenment were not so opposed to each other that they could not converge. The Protestant tradition was never entirely hostile to reason, nor was every proponent of the Enlightenment hostile to the claims of traditional Christianity.

Some Enlightenment figures took up the task of confirming revealed truths of the Christian tradition with the tools of science. Such was the task of Scottish "Common Sense" philosophers like Thomas Reid. A Presbyterian clergyman, Reid defined science as a "doxological" task. For him, understanding the divine order of the created world was a means of glorifying God.[46] Reid and other proponents of the "Didactic" stream of the Enlightenment had an extraordinary influence on nineteenth century American Protestant clergy, including Charles Hodge and Horace Bushnell (though we shall see that Bushnell tended to rebel against this influence).[47]

Not only did Reid give Evangelicals an orthodox means of "assimilating" the Enlightenment's enthusiasm for science and reason,[48] he also provided them a defense against what they considered the dangerous fringe of the European Enlightenment,

---

[45] Theodore Dwight Bozeman, *Protestants in an Age of Science: The Baconian Ideal and Antebellum American Religious Thought* (Chapel Hill: University of North Carolina Press: 1977) 44.

[46] Ibid., 45–48, 75–80.

[47] Sydney Ahlstrom, "The Scottish Philosophy and American Theology," *Church History* 24/3 (September 1955): 257–72. See also Jack B. Rogers and Donald K. McKim, *The Authority and Interpretation of the Bible: An Historical Approach* (San Francisco: Harper and Row, Publishers, 1979) 235–48; E. Brooks Holifield, *Theology in America: Christian Thought from the Age of the Puritans to the Civil War* (New Haven: Yale University Press, 2003) 173–96; and Mark Noll, *America's God: From Jonathan Edwards to Abraham Lincoln* (Oxford: Oxford University Press, 2002) 93–113, 233–38.

[48] Henry F. May, *The Enlightenment in America* (New York: Oxford University Press, 1976) xvi, 337–57. Ahlstrom, "Scottish Philosophy," 257–72.

represented by David Hume. Hume doubted, among other things, the reliability of human sense perceptions and the human conscience. To many Evangelicals, such skepticism about the human capacity to know what is true and right undermined the universal validity of the gospel. Reid answered Hume by affirming the "innate principles" of the human constitution. Reid conceded that certain assumptions, such as the reliability of the senses or the obligation to do one's duty, could not be proven rationally. However, Reid contended, these "universal and irresistible" human assumptions must be trusted because they form the bases of all knowledge. Reid's affirmation of the reliability of "common sense" left all people open and accountable to the plain "truth," whether that truth proceeded from the Bible or the book of nature. Reid's epistemology was not only useful for Evangelical apologetics, it was a vindication the inductive scientific method of Francis Bacon. It also had a democratic appeal that Americans appreciated. It assumed and emphasized the essential mental and moral similarity of all people. For Reid, the foundation of all human knowledge was a "common" possession.[49]

The American Enlightenment, like American Evangelicalism, was a diverse tradition. It shared with Evangelicalism a radically egalitarian and libertarian branch that was predisposed against slavery. For many proponents of the Enlightenment, intellectual and political liberty was the *sine qua non* of human well-being. Furthermore, just as traditional Christians affirmed a belief in a single human nature, the Enlightenment generally affirmed that all people are essentially similar rational creatures with a fundamentally equal capacity for intellectual improvement and for freedom.[50]

On the basis of these values, many proponents of the Enlightenment opposed African slavery, finding it especially inappropriate in the United States of America, the new nation that was to embody for the world the ideals of liberty and equality. Even

---

[49] Keith Lehrer, *Thomas Reid* (London and New York: Routledge, 1989) 8, 20, 31, 35.

[50] Gossett, *Race*, 34.

Thomas Jefferson, who owned slaves, recognized that the institution contradicted the basic precepts of the Declaration of Independence: that all people are created equal and with a natural right to liberty.[51] Benjamin Franklin, another famous American philosophe, presided over an abolition society and lobbied Congress to end slavery.[52]

However, as was the case with Evangelicalism, the American Enlightenment also had a socially conservative branch, which did not lead all its proponents in an antislavery direction. Among the "natural rights" the philosopher John Locke and his American followers deemed to be essential were life, liberty, and *property*. When the right to property was understood to be in conflict with the rights to life and liberty, it was not certain that the latter two would win out. Defenders of slavery argued that the "common sense" of the American people had deemed African slaves to be legitimate property, and such property rights were not to be tampered with lightly.[53]

Furthermore, despite the fact that Enlightenment ideas fueled a revolutionary war in America, many proponents of the American Enlightenment favored "moderation" in the realm of politics. Many believed that the goal of the statesman, like the goal of the philosopher, should be to harmonize discordant elements. Compromise was preferable to dogmatic pursuit of one's own ends. According to Henry May, this tendency toward moderation and compromise helped to intrench the institution of slavery in the United States. American statesmen who found slavery distasteful compromised with American slave interests. They compromised enough to work an implicit affirmation of the validity of slave property in US Constitution, which limited taxation on imported slaves, postponed the prohibition of slave importations for twenty

---

[51] Jordan, *White over Black*, 430–31.

[52] Ruchames, *Racial Thought*, 206.

[53] Jordan, *White over Black*, 350–51. See also Paul Finkleman, *Slavery and the Founders: Race and Liberty in the Age of Jefferson* (Armonk, New York, and London: M. E. Sharpe, 1996) 62.

years, provided for the recapture of runaway slaves, and designated (for tax purposes) a slave as "three fifths" of a person (Art.1, Sec. 2).[54]

Furthermore, not every proponent of the Enlightenment affirmed its basic anthropological assumption: that all people of all races are essentially similar and fundamentally equal. Some of those who "dared to know" were not to be put off by any form of orthodoxy, even that of the Enlightenment itself. Some members of the radical branch of the Enlightenment claimed that races were inherently different and unequal.

"The most dramatic and unambiguous way to make this point of genetic inferiority before the rise of Darwinism was to argue that whites and Negroes had literally been *created* unequal"; that is, that all races did not have Adam and Eve as ancestors, but were created at different times and are therefore biologically unrelated.[55] Voltaire, unruffled by accusations of blasphemy, was one of the first Enlightenment figures to suggest this hypothesis, using as evidence the races' different appearances and their different states of "civilization and intelligence."[56] This "polygenetic theory" of human origins was elaborated by Lord Kames, the Scottish jurist whose *Sketches of the History of Man* was published in 1774, and Charles White in his 1799 *Account of the Regular Gradation in Man*.[57] Thomas Jefferson, despite his assertion that "all men are created equal," was one of the first Americans to suggest, tentatively, that Africans were a separately created inferior species.[58] The polygenetic origins argument won a great deal of respectability when it was later taken up by the "American school" of anthropologists: Samuel George Morton, Swiss immigrant Louis Agassiz, Josiah Clark Nott, and George Robbin Glidden—all contemporaries of Hodge and

---

[54] May, *Enlightenment in America*, 99–100.
[55] Fredrickson, *Black Image in the White Mind*, 78.
[56] Gossett, *Race*, 45.
[57] Ibid., 47–48.
[58] Jordan, *White over Black*, 435–40.

Bushnell.[59] Though the majority of Southern defenders of slavery rejected this heterodox theory, some employed it in the defense of slavery.[60]

Enlightened opponents of the polygenetic theory argued that the races were not created differently. Rather, racial differences emerged over time as results of environmental causes. The apex of the environmentalist argument in the United States was *An Essay on the Causes of the Variety of Complexion and Figure in the Human Species*, first published in 1787 then revised and republished in 1810. The work was written by Samuel Stanhope Smith, the president of the College of New Jersey (Princeton) and later one of Charles Hodge's teachers. In opposing the polygenetic theory, Smith believed he was defending both religious orthodoxy and Enlightenment science.[61]

Even this enlightened defense of essential human unity and equality was not immune to racial assumptions, however. Smith's dispute with the polygenesists concerned not so much whether the races were different and unequal, but how these differences and inequalities came into being. Smith did not deny that "the Negro" was intellectually inferior; rather, he tried to give an environmentalist explanation for this "apparent" fact.[62] Furthermore, Smith, like many of his contemporaries, blurred the distinction between nature and nurture, holding that children could inherit their parents' acquired traits. One generation's sunburn could be the next generation's racial mark. Smith showed his bias by assuming that black skin was a flaw, a result of poor environmental conditions. He believed that the cultural

---

[59] The career of the "American School" is covered in William Stanton, *The Leopard's Spots: Scientific Attitudes Toward Race in America, 1815–59* (Chicago: University of Chicago Press, 1960) passim.

[60] J. C. [Josiah] Nott, "Nature and Destiny of the Negro," *De Bow's Review* 10/3 (March 1851): 329–32.

[61] Stanton, *Leopard's Spots*, 3–4.

[62] Samuel Stanhope Smith, *An Essay on the Causes of the Variety of Complexion and Figure in the Human Species...*, 2d ed. (New Brunswick NJ: J. Simpson and Company, 1810) 16–17.

elevation of the African would actually effect a change in skin color.[63] Given the ambivalence of Smith's arguments, it is not surprising that not every opponent of polygenesis was antislavery.[64]

Nevertheless, Smith himself, as well as others (including the former slave and abolitionist Frederick Douglass) who criticized the polygenetic theory, saw themselves as defenders of essential human equality and as opponents of slavery.[65] The debate between "polygenesists" and "monogenesists" played significant, though different, roles in Hodge and Bushnell's statements on slavery and race.

Romanticism. A third intellectual tradition was not as pervasive in the United States as were Evangelicalism or the Enlightenment, but its influence grew during the period under discussion. Ahlstrom describes the first quarter of the nineteenth century as a "watershed in the flow of theological influences" to the United States. The predominance of Common Sense philosophy was being challenged by an intellectual trend that was born in Europe and had taken a generation to cross the Atlantic: Romanticism, a literary and philosophical movement promoted by poets like Samuel Taylor Coleridge of England, theologians like Friedrich Schleiermacher of Germany, and many others. This movement was nurtured by the idealism of German philosophers like G. F. S. Hegel and (despite his decidedly passionless prose style) Immanuel Kant.[66]

Romanticism was, in part, a reaction against the dry rationalism of the Enlightenment. Compared to proponents of the

---

[63] Ibid., 204–205, 315–19. This theory was shared by the famous Philadelphia physician Benjamin Rush (Gossett, *Race*, 40–41).

[64] The most prominent opponent of the polygenetic theory during Hodge and Bushnell's day was a Southerner, John Bachman, who defended slavery and argued for the "permanent" inferiority of the African. See J. C. [Josiah] Nott, "Diversity of the Human Race," *DeBow's Review* 10/2 (February 1851): 115.

[65] Stanton, *Leopard's Spots*, 12–14; Frederick Douglass, "An Evaluation of Racial Anthropology," in Ruchames, *Racial Thought*, 478–92.

[66] Sydney Ahlstrom, "Theology in America: A Historical Survey," in *The Shaping of American Religion,* vol. 1 of *Religion in American Life,* ed. James Ward Smith and A. Leland Jamison (Princeton: Princeton University Press, 1961) 235.

Enlightenment, Romantics held less confidence in the perspicuity of objective truth. They placed a higher value on subjective knowledge. For Romantics, imagination and emotion were organs of a truth that was too profound to be grasped by the cognitive intellect.[67] Romanticism also paid a different kind of attention to history. For Enlightenment rationalists, human history was the empirical laboratory for demonstrating eternal principles. Yet nineteenth-century Romantics viewed the drama of history not as a means to extract object lessons of obvious propositions but as an opportunity to witness a mysterious ideal actualizing itself through an organic, evolutionary process.[68]

As was the case with the Enlightenment and Evangelicalism, the relationship between Romanticism and Evangelicalism was complex. Some Evangelicals, like Charles Hodge, rejected Romanticism, with its subjective understanding of truth, as subversive to the authority of Scripture.[69] Others fell under its influence and either renounced or revised their Evangelical beliefs. Some, like the American Transcendentalist Ralph Waldo Emerson, left organized religion behind to follow the Romantic genius down the path of extreme individualism.[70] Others, captivated by the Romantics' emphasis on the organic historical community, renounced individualistic Evangelical piety and drifted in the direction of Roman

---

[67] One historian says that while no one definition is satisfactory, the "best definitions of Romanticism advanced through the years" include something like this "constellation of themes." See George Shriver, "Romantic Religion," in *Encyclopedia of the American Religious Experience*, 2:1103.

[68] Sydney Ahlstrom, *A Religious History of the American People* (New Haven: Yale University Press, 1972) 589. See also Walter H. Conser, *God and the Natural World: Religion and Science in Antebellum America* (Columbia: University of South Carolina Press, 1993) 37–47.

[69] Charles Hodge, "Latest Forms of Infidelity," *BRPR* 12/1 (January 1840): 31–71.

[70] George M. Fredrickson, *The Inner Civil War: Northern Intellectuals and the Crisis of the Union*, 2d ed. (Chicago: University of Illinois Press, 1993) 10–16. Emerson left the Unitarian Church, not an Evangelical denomination. Nonetheless, he set a pattern for breaking from traditional religion that other Americans followed.

Catholicism.[71] However, some found Evangelicalism and Romanticism to be compatible. The two movements had at least one thing in common: both, in contrast to the Enlightenment, upheld the importance of the affections as a source of knowledge.[72] Horace Bushnell, as we shall see, maintained his Evangelical core of beliefs but also participated to an extent in the Romantic critique of the Enlightenment.

Romanticism supplied some opponents of racial slavery with new tactics. For example, Romanticism affirmed emotion—sympathy for poor slaves, for example—as an important indicator for the human conscience.[73] Also, some opponents of slavery adopted a Romantic view of history as a dynamic evolutionary process—a gradual realization of an ideal. Many opponents of slavery understood history to be driven by a universal longing for freedom. Harriet Beecher Stowe's *Uncle Tom's Cabin* is a prime example of the use of Romantic discourse, allied with Evangelical religion, in the battle against African slavery.[74]

Furthermore, idealist hermeneutics, if one was bold enough to employ them, offered a way around the biblical texts that apparently permitted slavery. Rather than laboriously extracting an antislavery meaning from the writings of Paul, one could, as did the Unitarian minister Theodore Parker, simply ditch the authority of Scripture in favor of the authority of subjective experience and base one's

---

[71] This was the path followed by Hodge's friend and colleague, John Williamson Nevin, though he did not actually become a Roman Catholic. See James Hastings Nichols, *Romanticism in American Theology: Nevin and Schaff at Mercersburg* (Chicago: University of Chicago Press, 1961) 192–217.

[72] Harriet Beecher Stowe sometimes combined the language of Romanticism with Evangelical sentiments. See Fredrickson, *Black Image in the White Mind*, 110–12.

[73] Elizabeth B. Clark, "'The Sacred Rights of the Weak': Pain, Sympathy, and the Culture of Individual Rights in Antebellum America," *Journal of American History* 82/2 (September 1995): 463–91.

[74] Fredrickson, *Black Image in the White Mind*, 110–12; Harriet Beecher Stowe, *The Annotated Uncle Tom's Cabin*, ed. Philip Van Doren Stern (New York: Bramhall House, 1964) 560.

antislavery argument exclusively on "our own conscience, the permanent, everlasting oracle of God."[75] Or if one was not quite so bold, one could at least make a distinction between the crude letter of Scripture and its sublime ethical spirit and build a biblical antislavery argument on the basis of the latter authority.[76]

However, as was the case with Evangelicalism and the American Enlightenment, Romanticism had a socially conservative pole that was not necessarily antislavery. For some, Romanticism was a reaction against Enlightenment libertarianism and egalitarianism. For those who drew on the English philosopher Edmund Burke, the impelling genius of history was not the universal yearning for freedom but the yearning for belonging, for stable social institutions.[77] Many Romantics were fascinated with medieval and classical hierarchical cosmologies, organic models that made social inequality part of the natural order. This particular version of the Romantic sensibility was more likely to be enlisted to defend rather than to attack slavery.[78] Southern writers also proved adept at playing on the sentiments of their readers in order to paint a sympathetic picture of slavery as a benevolent and paternal institution. Southern readers could weep over Mary Eastman's proslavery *Aunt Phillis's*

---

[75] Theodore Parker, "The Function and Place of Conscience in Relation to the Laws of Men," in Lowance, ed., *Against Slavery*, 273–90. See also Henry Steele Commager, *Theodore Parker* (Boston: Little, Brown, and Company, 1936) 202: "Did Abraham have 'servants bought with his money,' did Paul say, 'Slaves obey your masters?' That argument had no terrors for him, he put no stock in the inspiration of Scriptures."

[76] This, as we shall see in a later chapter, was Bushnell's tack.

[77] Ahlstrom, *Religious History*, 593–94.

[78] James O. Farmer, *The Metaphysical Confederacy: James Henley Thornwell and the Synthesis of Southern Values*, 2d ed. (Macon GA: Mercer University Press, 1999) 112–13. See also Eugene Genovese, *The Slaveholder's Dilemma: Freedom and Progress in Southern Conservative Thought, 1820–1860* (Columbia: University of South Carolina Press, 1992) 5–8, 66–72.

Cabin almost as much as Northerners could weep over *Uncle Tom's Cabin*.[79]

Furthermore, Romantics tended to turn away from the Enlightenment view of human beings as essentially similar creatures whose chief characteristic was the capacity for reason. Rather, they tended to depict human beings as formed and driven by superrational historic forces. In particular, they tended to embrace "at least implicitly, concepts of inbred national characteristics and genius that could be easily transmuted into concepts of 'racial' superiority."[80]

Such racial thinking is evident in the writings of the German Lutheran pastor Johann Gottfried Herder, a pioneer of Romantic nationalism, who believed that nature "placed the black next to the ape," lacking the "nobler gifts" of humanity.[81] English contemporaries of Herder, historians Sharon Turner and John Pinkerton, proudly delved into their "Teutonic origins" and claimed that the Anglo-Saxon race had an inherent love of freedom, as did American contemporaries of Hodge and Bushnell, William Prescott, Francis Parkman, and John Lothrop Motley. These Anglocentric histories also contained "another, more chilling note—the idea that freedom was the race heritage of the Germanic peoples but perhaps not that of other peoples."[82]

Even those American Romantics who opposed slavery fell under the spell of "Romantic racialism." Parker and Harriet Beecher Stowe depicted the African "genius" as docile and childlike—not necessarily bad qualities, but not the qualities of a self-sufficient people, either.[83] Southerners were adept at depicting this sentimental Negro stereotype as ideally suited for slavery.[84]

---

[79] Mary Eastman, *Aunt Phillis's Cabin; or, Southern Life as It Is* (Philadelphia: Lippincott, Grambo, 1852; reprint, New York: Negro Universities Press, 1968) passim.

[80] Fredrickson, *Black Image in the White Mind*, 97.

[81] Olender, *Languages of Paradise*, 45.

[82] Gossett, *Race*, 86, 88.

[83] Fredrickson, *Black Image in the White Mind*, 100–101.

[84] Eastman, *Aunt Phillis's Cabin*, 119–24.

The Range of Moral Arguments Regarding Slavery

Evangelicalism, the Enlightenment, and Romanticism, three wellsprings of antebellum American moral discourse, provided the vocabulary with which public figures spoke out on slavery. And speak out they did, in great numbers. Circumstances practically required them to do so, particularly after 1830. Well before this time, many Americans questioned whether slavery was compatible with the religious and political ethos of the United States, but a number of factors—Nat Turner's rebellion, the rise of abolitionist agitation, the prospect of westward expansion, and the extension of slavery into new territories—made the 1830s a decade of crisis. Many Americans now felt the issue of slavery had to be decided. Especially vocal were clergy, who made use of the newly invented steam press and the Evangelical publishing industry to proliferate their views.

But neither of these three dominant intellectual traditions— Evangelicalism, the Enlightenment, or Romanticism—predetermined one's policy on slavery. As we have seen, all three could be used to attack or defend slavery. Those who spoke out on slavery, drawing on any combination of these three traditions, formed a broad spectrum of opinion. Yet within this broad spectrum are family resemblances. The arguments cluster around three types—three options that presented themselves to Hodge and Bushnell as they articulated their moral policies on slavery: the emancipationist, the abolitionist, and the proslavery arguments.

The Emancipationist Argument. The emancipationist option was the most common antislavery argument in the United States before 1830. This argument advocated a policy of limited reforms that would ameliorate the cruelties of slavery and pave the way for its gradual abolition. Early in the nineteenth century, this gradualist policy was married to a scheme of African colonization. As the years passed, many (though certainly not all) emancipationists lost their enthusiasm for colonization, but they continued to embrace the principles of gradualism and moderation.

Some of the first emancipationists in America were Quakers, whom many Americans regarded as a political and religious fringe element.[85] But by Hodge and Bushnell's day the emancipationist position had, in the North, moved to the mainstream. The typical public emancipationist of that time was white, male, and Protestant— often an Evangelical clergyman.[86] Some advocates of this position, whose careers overlapped with those of Hodge and Bushnell, were the revivalist Lyman Beecher (father of Harriet Beecher Stowe), Amherst College professor and Congregational minister Samuel Worcester, Reformed Presbyterian minister Alexander McLeod, Baptist pastor and educator Francis Wayland, Congregational minister Leonard Bacon (Bushnell's friend and colleague), Presbyterian minister Robert J. Breckinridge (Hodge's Old School Presbyterian ally), and theologian Archibald Alexander (Hodge's mentor and colleague at Princeton Theological Seminary).

The guiding principle of the emancipationist policy was that slavery was an "evil" but not necessarily a "sin." When emancipationists called slavery an "evil," they generally meant that it was not the kind of social relation for which human beings were originally created. It was coercive. It was divisive. It presupposed a degree of enmity between people and it deprived a group of people of personal liberty. Emancipationists, drawing on the language of the Christian tradition and of the Enlightenment, were willing to acknowledge that all people are essentially equal and that personal liberty is a "natural right."[87] They hopefully predicted that the

---

[85] Ruchames, *Racial Thought*, 77–134.

[86] There are three helpful perspectives on the emancipationist position in *Religion and the Antebellum Debate over Slavery*, ed. John McKivigan and Mitchell Snay (Athens: University of Georgia Press, 1998) 164–245. They are Elizabeth R. Varnon, "Evangelical Womanhood and the Politics of the African Colonization Movement in Virginia," 169–95; Deborah Bingham Van Broekhoven, "Suffering with the Slaveholders: The Limits of Francis Wayland's Antislavery Witness," 196–220; and Hugh Davis, "Leonard Bacon, the Congregational Church and Slavery, 1845–1861," 221–48.

[87] Samuel Worcester et al., "On the Racial Theory of Slavery," in Ruchames, *Racial Thought*, 300–301.

United States, a nation that embodied the ideals of liberty and equality and that bore the sublime influence of Evangelical Christianity, would soon make slavery obsolete.

However, in refusing to label slaveholding a "sin" in all cases, emancipationists acknowledged that ideal human relationships often cannot be realized in a fallen world. While the human race may have originally been created to enjoy liberty and equality, circumstances have made the universal enjoyment of these natural rights impossible. Schooled in the Bible, which contained passages that apparently permit slavery, and schooled in the Didactic Enlightenment, which placed great trust in the innate moral sense of the majority of educated adults, emancipationists balked at branding thousands of respectable, Christian, American slaveholders as criminals. Loyal to the political values of moderation and stability, emancipationists balked at the radical social change that would result from the sudden emancipation of millions of slaves. If emancipationists saw something tragically wrong with slavery as a system, they saw something right, or at least appropriate, about slaveholding in particular circumstances. Slavery was an evil. So was war, but sometimes both were necessary evils. Leonard Bacon, while calling slavery an evil system, still insisted there was such a thing as a "good slaveholder."[88]

In keeping with their moderate evaluation of the evils of slavery, emancipationists advocated a strategy of moderate resistance. They encouraged Christian forbearance toward slaveholders. They sought to appeal to the slaveholders' conscience and reason, to persuade them to manumit their slaves voluntarily. They generally agreed that slaveholders should be remunerated for their loss of slave property. They believed emancipation should happen gradually. They believed slaveholders were morally obligated to prepare their slaves for freedom and to not release them until they were so prepared. To

---

[88] Leonard Bacon to Amos A. Phelps, 29 August 1845, quoted in Hugh Davis, "Bacon, the Congregational Church, and Slavery," in *Religion and the Antebellum Debate*, 226. See also Francis Wayland, *The Elements of Moral Science*, ed. Joseph L. Blau (Cambridge: Belknap Press of Harvard University Press, 1963) 197.

suddenly release millions of slaves would be disastrous for the slaves themselves and for the nation as a whole.[89]

The gradualism of the emancipationists was at least partly based on their racial assumptions. They believed African-American slaves were not, as a whole, ready for freedom because they were of an inferior race. Emancipationists did not doubt that African slaves were human beings or that as human beings they had a qualified claim to liberty and equality with other people. In fact, their belief in the essential unity and equality of the human race was an important factor in their moderate opposition to slavery. Samuel Worcester decried the system that relegated the slave to "a sort of midlink between brute and man."[90] However, for emancipationists, the orthodox tenet of the unity of humankind apparently did not rule out the possibility of some racial differences and a degree of inferior and superior relationships between races. Essential equality did not preclude accidental inequalities. Just as individuals had different and unequal capacities, so might whole groups of people. These typically Protestant, socially conservative, male emancipationists generally accepted that the two sexes, though they shared the same essential human nature, had certain constitutional differences and properly held unequal social roles.[91] They did not rule out a similar inequality between races.

Emancipationists typically used some form of the environmentalist theory to explain the African's "inferiority," but they sometimes blurred the distinction between nurture and nature: Africans had been "degraded" by slavery, oppression, and other disadvantages, including their "barbarous" pagan heritage.[92] Many

---

[89] This was the stance of the Presbyterian General Assembly's statement on slavery in 1818. See above, p. 2.

[90] Worcester, 300. See also Alexander McLeod, "Negro Slavery Unjustifiable," in Lowance, ed., *Against Slavery*, 77; and Wayland, *Elements of Moral Science*, 182–88.

[91] Wayland, *Elements of Moral Science*, 282.

[92] Hugh Davis, *Leonard Bacon: New England Reformer and Antislavery Moderate* (Baton Rouge: Louisiana State University Press, 1998) 79.

emancipationists shared the common distaste for racial intermarriage or "amalgamation" and the common assumption—sometimes expressed explicitly, more often implicitly assumed—that the United States was to be a white man's country.[93] That they could make such assumptions while at the same time decrying the racial prejudice of others might be a sign of hypocrisy, or it might be a sign that a more vicious racism than theirs was extant in their day.

The emancipationists' racial assumptions played into the scheme of African colonization. Samuel Hopkins was one of the first Americans to propose, at the time of the American Revolution, that freed slaves be settled in a colony in Africa established especially for them.[94] Later, the American Colonization Society (first under the leadership of Robert Finley, then that of Ralph Gurley) took up Hopkins's idea. With limited US government aid, the ACS privately founded the colony of Liberia, which received its first settlers in 1822.[95]

Colonizationists believed, among other things, that Liberia would serve as a base of operations for Christian missions in Africa. Former American slaves would help to evangelize and civilize Africa. This was to be God's providential redemption of the evils of the international slave trade. But evangelism was not the only cause that motivated this project. Many saw colonization as a legitimate means of racial segregation—a way to preserve the United States exclusively for the white race.[96]

Some Colonizationists were very forthright in their racial exclusivism, explicitly excusing whites' aversion to dark-skinned people and warning anxiously against the possibility of an American

---

[93] Robert J. Breckinridge, "Colonization and Abolition," *BRPR* 5/3 (July 1833): 287–88, 288–300.

[94] Joseph A. Conforti, *Samuel Hopkins and the New Divinity Movement: Calvinism, the Congregational Ministry, and Reform in New England between the Great Awakenings* (Grand Rapids: Christian University Press, 1981) 146–49.

[95] P. J. Staudenraus, *The African Colonization Movement 1812–1865* (New York: Columbia University Press, 1961) 59–68.

[96] Ibid., viii.

continent teeming with Negroes.[97] In fact, not every colonizationist was at all interested in even the gradual abolition of slavery. Some were slaveholders who supported colonization as a means of ridding the nation of the troublesome presence of free blacks.[98]

Just as often, however, colonizationists advocated separation of the two races as a means of pursuing the greater good of both—an intention that was probably genuinely humanitarian, though based on narrow racial assumptions. The argument generally ran as follows: Africans could not excel in America, where environmental factors were against them; whites' prejudice against Africans, not to mention the Africans' reciprocal hostility, was too deeply intrenched; furthermore, the black "temperament" was better suited to the torrid climate of Africa than the moderate climate of North America. For these reasons, the African American should "use every exertion to reach a land where it is no crime and no dishonor to appear in a coloured skin, a country where no white superiors look down upon the black race, but where they are lords of the soil and rulers of the nation." So wrote Archibald Alexander, Charles Hodge's favorite teacher.[99]

The Abolitionist Argument. Two momentous publications—David Walker's pamphlet *An Appeal to the Colored Citizens of the World* (1829) and the first issue of William Lloyd Garrison's newspaper the *Liberator* (January 1831)—signaled the arrival of a new form of opposition to slavery in the United States: the abolitionist argument.

Walker and Garrison embraced different tactics. Garrison, a white printer and editor, was a strict pacifist who sought to emancipate slaves through a policy of "moral suasion," though his version was much more belligerent in tone than that of the emancipationists. He sought to expose the evils of slavery and galvanize a national moral phalanx against it. Walker, on the other

---

[97] Breckinridge, "Colonization and Abolition," 285.

[98] Staudenraus, *African Colonization Movement*, 29.

[99] Archibald Alexander, *A History of Colonization on the Western Coast of Africa* (Philadelphia: W. S. Martien, 1846) 20.

hand, did not shy from advocating violence in the black struggle for liberation. This free black merchant from Boston, Massachusetts, suggested that such violence might well be the vengeance of heaven: "and believe this," he reassured his African-American readers, "that it is no more harm for you to kill a man who is trying to kill you, than it is for you to take a drink of water when thirsty."[100] However, both men agreed on one goal: the total, unconditional, and immediate abolition of slavery.

Walker, who circulated his *Appeal* by stitching it into the clothing of complicit black sailors, did not live to see the effect his pamphlet would have. He died mysteriously in 1830. However, Garrison himself would work for over thirty years to give the abolitionist argument organizational legs. In 1832 he helped found the New England Antislavery Society and in 1833 the American Antislavery Society. These were the prototypes of hundreds of other abolition societies that formed in the Northern and Border states until the Civil War. Many individuals who did not formally join abolitionist societies advocated abolitionist principles.[101]

Unlike the relatively homogenous emancipationists, the abolitionists were a diverse bunch. Black and white and male and female abolitionists made their views public. Most would claim to be Christians. Many were trained in Evangelical churches. Many left those churches because they did not excommunicate slaveholders, calling the churches "combinations of thieves, robbers, adulterers, pirates, murderers, and, as such…the bulwark of American slavery."[102] Some joined antislavery "comeouter sects." Others left

---

[100] David Walker, *David Walker's Appeal* (New York: Hill and Wang, 1965) 26.

[101] Louis Filler, *The Crusade against Slavery, 1830–1860* (New York: Harper and Row, Publishers, 1960) 48–81.

[102] Abby Kelly, quoted in Wendell Phillips Garrison and Francis Jackson Garrison, *William Lloyd Garrison, 1805-1879: The Story of His Life Told by His Children*, Vol. 3 of 4 (New York: The Century Company, 1889) 29.

organized religion entirely.[103] Some embraced unique, even eccentric belief systems.[104] Many had a high regard for the Bible and made (sometimes strained) exegetical antislavery arguments.[105] Others rejected the authority of Scripture in favor of an enlightened appeal to reason ("The Bible, if Opposed to Self-Evident Truth Is Self-Evident Falsehood") or a romantic appeal to "conscience."[106] Some, like Garrison, rejected the federal Constitution, with its compromises with slavery, as "a compact formed at the sacrifice of the bodies and souls of millions of our [human] race" and called for the Northern states to secede from the Union.[107] Others, like Frederick Douglass, remained faithful to the Constitution "as an antislavery document which, when properly amended, would allow emancipation."[108]

Partly because of such diversity, abolitionism was a loose and fractious movement. The American Antislavery Society split in 1840 after Garrison publicly embraced doctrines of perfectionism, egalitarianism, and libertarianism. Some of his positions (such as his advocacy of complete equality of the sexes) would win praise in later

---

[103] John McKivigan, *The War against Proslavery Religion: Abolitionism and the Northern Churches, 1830–1865* (Ithaca NY: Cornell University Press, 1984) 93–110.

[104] For example, there is the labyrinthine spiritual journey of the abolitionist Angelina Grimké Weld: from Episcopalianism, through Presbyterianism, Quakerism, and Adventism to spiritualism. See Gerda Lerner, *The Grimké Sisters of South Carolina: Pioneers for Women's Rights and Abolition*, new ed. (New York/Oxford: Oxford University Press, 1998) 52–53, 68–70, 103–104, 192–93, 229–30, 259.

[105] Mark Noll, "The Bible and Slavery," in *Religion and the American Civil War*, ed. Randall M. Miller, Harry S. Stout, and Charles Reagan Wilson (New York/Oxford: Oxford University Press, 1998) 43–46.

[106] Henry C. Wright, *Liberator*, 11 May 1848, quoted in Wayne A. Meeks, "The 'Haustafeln' and American Slavery: A Hermeneutical Challenge," in *Theology and Ethics in Paul and His Interpreters: Essays in Honor of Victor Paul Furnish*, ed. Eugene H. Lovering, Jr., and Jerry L. Sumney (Nashville: Abingdon Press, 1996) 251. Parker, "The Function and Place of Conscience in Relation to the Laws of Men," in Lowance, ed., *Against Slavery*, 273–90.

[107] Garrison, *Liberator*, 29 December 1832 excerpted in Lowance, ed., *Against Slavery*, 115. Garrison, *Liberator*, 31 May 1844, excerpted in *William Lloyd Garrison*, ed. Fredrickson, 52–55.

[108] Lowance, ed., *Against Slavery*, xxxi.

decades, but at the time even some of his fellow abolitionists found them extreme and offensive.[109] Despite these conflicts, however, abolitionists continued to agree that slavery was a sin under all circumstances, that the notion of slave property had no moral foundation, and that colonization was a cruel scheme to deport free blacks.[110]

The Proslavery Argument. A third option that presented itself at this time was to defend the institution of slavery, not as a necessary evil but as a positive good, "a great blessing to both races" (according to John Calhoun), something that ought to continue to exist in the United States indefinitely or even permanently.[111]

The origins of the proslavery argument are an item of contention among historians. Some claim that it was a relatively novel argument that developed in the South after 1820 as a reaction to antislavery propaganda. Others locate its origin earlier in American history and in the North, not the South.[112]

However, historians agree that the proslavery argument became louder—more pronounced and less compromising—in the South after 1830.[113] During this period, Southern secular theorists like law

---

[109] Bertram Wyatt-Brown, *Lewis Tappan and the Evangelical War against Slavery* (Cleveland: Press of Case Western Reserve University, 1969) 185–200; McKivigan, *War against Proslavery Religion*, 56–73. Garrison, *Liberator*, 15 December 1837, excerpted in *William Lloyd Garrison*, ed. Fredrickson, 47–51.

[110] William Lloyd Garrison, *Thoughts on African Colonization: or an Impartial Exhibition of the Doctrines, Principles, and Purposes of the American Colonization Society* (Boston: Garrison and Knapp, 1832) 120–21, 141–47; excerpted in Ruchames, *Racial Thought*, 311.

[111] John Calhoun, *The Works of John C. Calhoun*, 6 vols., ed. Richard Cralle (New York: n.p., 1853) 2:630, quoted in Jenkins, *Pro-Slavery Thought*, 80.

[112] Jenkins, *Pro-Slavery Thought*, 65, 73, 76–81, 87–89. Larry Tise locates the proslavery argument's origin in the prerevolutionary Northern colonies, describing it as an aspect of a conservative social ideology that had existed in North America in some form since the first English settlers arrived, an antithetical counterpart to American revolutionary egalitarianism and libertarianism (Larry E. Tise, *Proslavery: A History of the Defense of Slavery in America, 1701–1840* [Athens: University of Georgia Press, 1987] 12–40 and passim.).

[113] Tise, *Proslavery*, 323–46; Farmer, *Metaphysical Confederacy*, 195–96.

professor and economist Thomas Dew, sociologists George Fitzhugh and Edmond Ruffin, and politicians like Calhoun and John Henry Hammond made a similar argument: that human society necessarily restrains individual freedom and that human equality, if it is to be affirmed at all, must be qualified by the exigencies of social existence. "The moment a man opens his eyes in this world," wrote Hammond, "...he exists as *one among many* of his kind, who at once impose upon him Laws from which he has no possible escape, but by ceasing to be and returning to whence he came."[114]

Any functioning society includes inferior and superior relationships. In order for anybody to enjoy freedom, some people have to be deprived of it. Civilization depends on the existence of a class of people who have the leisure to provide intellectual, cultural, and political leadership, and the existence of such a leisured class depends on the existence of a laboring class. Great civilizations in the past depended on slavery for just this reason. Proslavery Southerners of this period rejected the idea of African colonization because it deprived the South of this essential laboring class.[115] To this argument proslavery advocates added that Southern slaves, for whom masters cared for life, were better off than northern "wage slaves" who were discarded into jails and alms houses after they had outlived their usefulness. Finally, they argued that Africans were a "docile" race, ideally suited for slavery.[116]

Southern clergy rallied with these secular writers against Garrisonian abolitionism. James Smylie, Iveson Brooks, Thorton Stringfellow, James Henley Thornwell, Frederick Ross, Robert Dabney, and Benjamin Palmer among many others—armed with

---

[114] John Henry Hammond, "Laws of Nature—Natural Rights—Slavery," MS in a private collection, quoted in Jenkins, *Pro-Slavery Thought*, 129, emphasis original.

[115] Tise, *Proslavery*, 72.

[116] Genovese's *Slaveholder's Dilemma* is a helpful brief summary of proslavery ideology that touches on all these ideas. See also Drew Gilpin Faust's introduction, "The Proslavery Argument in History," in *The Ideology of Slavery: Proslavery Thought in the Antebellum South, 1830–1860* (Baton Rouge: Louisiana State University Press, 1981) 1–20.

proslavery proof-texts from the Old and New Testaments—
denounced what they understood to be the heterodoxy of the
abolitionists, who were "setting up individual notions of justice and
humanity against the morality of the Bible."[117] They blamed the
abolitionists for dragging the church, a "spiritual" institution, into the
muck and mire of political argument (though Southern clergy proved
to be adept at political rhetoric when they felt obliged to defend
slavery).[118] They affirmed the necessity of hierarchical relationships
and social restraint in a fallen world. They argued that Africans
benefited from slavery because the institution rescued them from a
barbarous heathen culture and introduced them to the benefits of
Christianity and civilization.[119] Seeking to sanctify the institution
they affirmed as morally legitimate, Southern clergy also encouraged
the evangelization of slaves and admonished masters to treat slaves
with paternal kindness.[120]

Some Southern clergy also defended slavery on the basis of
Genesis 9, the story of the sons of Noah. By the nineteenth century,
many educated defenders of slavery had dropped the positive
argument that Africans actually bore the curse of Ham and were
therefore divinely destined for slavery.[121] However, they still used this
passage as evidence for the negative argument that it was not contrary
to God's nature to destine a race of people for slavery.[122]

For all this, Southern clergy were still not on the vanguard of
proslavery thought. Schooled in the Evangelical tradition, they were
more accustomed to speak of slavery as a necessary evil than a

---

[117] *Southern Baptist*, 23 October 1850, quoted in Mitchell Snay, *Gospel of Disunion: Religion and Separatism in the Antebellum South* (Cambridge: Cambridge University Press, 1993) 62–63.

[118] Snay, *Gospel of Disunion*, 41.

[119] Ibid., 53–77. See also Mathews, *Religion in the Old South*, 168–78.

[120] Snay, *Gospel of Disunion*, 78–99. See also Mathews, *Religion in the Old South*, 136–50.

[121] Noll, "Bible and Slavery," 62.

[122] See, for example, Robert Dabney, *A Defense of Virginia and through Her of the South* (New York: E. J. Hale and Son, 1867) 101–104.

positive good.[123] When James Smylie of Mississippi first preached his apology for slavery in the early 1830s, his fellow Southern clergy criticized him for failing to describe slavery as a necessary evil.[124] Decades would pass before many Southern clergy could stand firmly behind his positive proslavery arguments. In fact, many clergy never entirely gave up on the idea of gradual abolition; they just kept postponing its appropriate future date.[125] These subtleties in the attitudes of Southern clergy demonstrate that the boundary between the moderate opponents and moderate proponents of slavery was often a hairbreadth. The two groups did differ, however, if only in terms of how long they expected the nation to endure the evils of slavery.[126]

A Conventional Typology. No individual figure, including those we have named, fits exactly into any one of the three proslavery arguments. Historians have argued and will continue to argue over the best way to interpret and categorize antebellum reasoning concerning slavery. However, the typology as a whole is accurate and conventional. Historians agree that the earliest antislavery arguments in the United States usually advocated gradual abolition and colonization, that Garrison and other abolitionists revolutionized antislavery by demanding immediate emancipation, and that the proslavery argument was, if not invented in, then "carried...to its logical conclusion" in the South, in part as a reaction to abolitionism.[127]

---

[123] Anne C. Loveland, *Southern Evangelicals and the Social Order, 1800–1860* (Baton Rouge: Louisiana State University Press, 1980) 187–218.

[124] E. T. Thompson, *Presbyterians in the South, 1607–1861,* vol. 1 of 3 (Richmond VA: John Knox Press, 1961) 343.

[125] Genovese, *Slaveholder's Dilemma,* 59.

[126] Drew Gilpin Faust, "Evangelicalism and the Meaning of the Proslavery Argument," *Virginia Magazine of History and Biography* 85/1 (January 1977): 3–17. My discussion of the views of Charles Hodge might help to define the boundary between the most moderate emancipationist and the most moderate proslavery argument.

[127] Tise, *Proslavery,* 346.

Most importantly, this was how Hodge and Bushnell read the situation. As they began to speak publicly on slavery, they located themselves on a spectrum with two extremes: the left calling slaveholding a sin in all circumstances, the right calling slavery a permanent and positive good. Hodge and Bushnell also acknowledged a middle ground—a policy of gradual abolition and colonization, an older argument that was currently being assaulted by novelties from the left and right.[128] As we shall see presently, Hodge tried to buttress and defend this older orthodoxy with the authority of Scripture. Bushnell, on the other hand, tried to create a new middle ground. He sought to articulate a novel alternative to all three positions and, in so doing, used a novel language that brought with it a new set of possibilities and problems.

---

[128] Horace Bushnell, *The Census and Slavery, Thanksgiving Discourse, Delivered in the Chapel at Clifton Springs, New York, November 29, 1860* (Hartford: L.E. Hunt, 1860) 17–20; Charles Hodge, "Slavery," *BRPR* 8/2 (April 1836): 268–69.

2

Charles Hodge:
Slavery and Race

Writing in 1871, after the United States had settled the matter of slavery through a long and bloody war, professor Charles Hodge reflected on his public statements on the subject, which he had made over three decades.

He was pleased to find that he had "from first to last" maintained a consistent position, something similar to the "emancipationist" position described in the previous chapter. That is, Hodge maintained that slavery *per se* (meaning involuntary servitude in the most abstract sense) was morally permissible. But he opposed the particular inhumane practices that were associated with slavery in the United States. He supported humanitarian reforms that he believed would have led not only to the gradual abolition of slavery but to racial equality in American civil society: "the gradual elevation of the slaves to all the rights of free citizens." Hodge even quoted his first major article on slavery (published in 1836) in order to demonstrate that this had always been his position. Furthermore, Hodge asserted, his position had always been based on clear biblical principles. The first question he always asked himself when "any matter, either of doctrine or of morals, came under discussion" was, "What saith the Lord?"[1]

---

[1] Charles Hodge, "Retrospect of the History of the Princeton Review," *BRPR* index ed. (1871): 17.

Not all of Hodge's readers, in his or in later days, have agreed with Hodge's self-assessment.[2] Some claim that Hodge was actually proslavery.[3] Some say that his position changed from proslavery to antislavery over time.[4] Other historians challenge Hodge's claim to be a proponent of racial equality, saying he affirmed the commonplace white supremacist attitudes of his day.[5] Some doubt Hodge's claim that his policy was based on plain biblical principles,[6] saying he relied on other authorities: his own conservative

---

[2] Peter J. Wallace, "The Defense of the Forgotten Center: Charles Hodge and the Enigma of Emancipationism in Antebellum America," *Journal of Presbyterian History* 75/3 (Fall 1997): 165–77. Wallace, in describing Hodge as an "emancipationist," basically affirms Hodge's understanding of himself as a consistent albeit moderate opponent of slavery.

[3] Larry E. Tise, *Proslavery: A History of the Defense of Slavery in America, 1701–1840* (Athens: University of Georgia Press, 1987) 282.

[4] This last group includes many of Hodge's Southern contemporaries, who depicted him as a traitor to their cause, as well as recent historians, who have a number of ways of describing how Hodge changed his views and why. David Murchie, "From Slaveholder to American Abolitionist: Charles Hodge and the Slavery Issue," in *Christian Freedom: Essays in Honor of Vernon C. Grounds*, ed. Kenneth W. M. Wozniak and Stanley J. Grenz (Lanham MD: University Press of America, 1986) 127–52, and John W. Stewart, *Mediating the Center: Charles Hodge on American Science, Language, Literature, and Politics*, Studies in Reformed Theology and History 3/1 (Princeton: Princeton Theological Seminary, 1995) 85, depict Hodge as going through a process of moral evolution. Hodge gradually moved from either a "naive" emancipationist position or even a "proslavery" position to a more definite antislavery position over time, though he himself was not entirely conscious of this movement. Allen Guelzo, "Charles Hodge's Antislavery Moment," in *Charles Hodge Revisited: A Critical Appraisal of His Life and Work*, ed. John W. Stewart and James Moorhead (Grand Rapids: Eerdmans Publishing Company, 2002) 317, basically depicts Hodge as waffling on slavery and employing a scholastic distinction between "slavery *per se*" and slavery as it was practiced in the U.S. in order to cover his inconsistency.

[5] Mark Noll, "The Bible and Slavery," in *Religion and the American Civil War*, ed. Randall M. Miller, Harry S. Stout, and Charles Reagan Wilson (New York/Oxford: Oxford University Press, 1998) 63.

[6] At least one twentieth-century critic allows that Hodge was trying to be consistently biblical, though this modern writer sees Hodge's biblicism itself as narrow-minded and blameworthy. See Penrose St. Amant, "The Rise and Early Development of the Princeton School of Theology" (Ph.D. diss., University of Edinburgh, 1952) 190, 195–96.

temperament[7] or the moral intuition and innate reason (and the unexamined prejudices) of his readers.[8] Some suggest that Hodge, who knew many slaveholders and dabbled in slaveholding himself, simply provided an ideological defense of himself, his peers, and the institutions that claimed his loyalty.[9]

Hodge's policy on slavery was indeed complicated. It was not entirely free from prejudice, self-interest, and short-sightedness. For these reasons, his views are open to diverse interpretations. Nevertheless, Hodge's self-assessment in 1871 was essentially correct. He did in fact maintain a basically consistent policy on African-American slavery. He was indeed a moderate opponent of slavery, despite his opposition to the abolitionists' program of immediate emancipation. Hodge opposed slavery on the basis of a genuine, though qualified, belief in racial equality. This is so despite the fact that he personally harbored racial prejudices. Finally, though Hodge's stance on slavery was the product of many factors, no factor was more important or more basic than his theological commitments, especially his understanding of the Bible as the source of divine truth. This is not to say that Hodge's was the only biblically based view on slavery. But Hodge's policy was definitely shaped by his understanding of the authority and meaning of the Bible. His theological method was part of a general religious vision that cannot be reduced to an ideological defense of himself or his race and class.

This chapter will explicate all these arguments with their respective qualifications. First, we will place Charles Hodge's views on slavery in context by examining the salient points of his biography, his theology, his institutional loyalties, and his own slaveholding. The rest of the chapter will analyze Hodge's important writings on slavery

---

[7] William S. Barker, "The Social Views of Charles Hodge (1797–1818): A Study in Nineteenth-century Conservatism," *Presbyterion: Covenant Seminary Review* 1/1 (Spring 1975): 7, 22.

[8] Noll, "Bible and Slavery," 63.

[9] Glenn Alden Hewitt, *Regeneration and Morality: a Study of Charles Finney, Charles Hodge, John W. Nevin, and Horace Bushnell* (Brooklyn: Carlson, 1991) 83; Guelzo, "Hodge's Antislavery Moment," in *Charles Hodge Revisited*, 317.

and race, using the five ethical terms that were defined in the first chapter.[10]

We will close with a discussion of a brief passage in Hodge's first major article on slavery (1836), the same passage Hodge quoted in 1871 to prove his consistency. This passage was so ambivalent that even Hodge himself, thirty-five years later, apparently missed an important subtlety. However, we shall see that this very ambivalence is proof of the power of the theological beliefs that shaped Hodge's statements on slavery and race. It is evidence that his theological commitments challenged and set limits on his own racial prejudices.

Charles Hodge: Biography and Beliefs

Charles Hodge was born in Philadelphia, Pennsylvania, on December 28, 1797. He was the fifth child of Mary Blanchard Hodge and Hugh Hodge, a physician who died when Charles was only seven months old. All of Charles's older siblings died before he was born except his brother Hugh Lennox Hodge. In his unfinished autobiography, Charles remembered Hugh (who later became a physician) as "a guardian," saying, "I never slept out of his arms until I was eleven or twelve years old."[11]

The family lived in Philadelphia for the first part of Charles's childhood, then Mary Hodge moved with her sons to Princeton, New Jersey. For a time the widowed mother drew a "comfortable income" from her father-in-law Andrew Hodge's commercial interests. When that source dried up, the family was reduced from a state of gentile comfort to a state of gentile poverty. Mary Hodge supported her children by taking in boarders and laundry while still managing to teach her sons the Westminster Catechism, which they repeated to their pastor Ashbel Green.[12]

---

[10] See above, pp. 11-14.

[11] Charles Hodge, quoted in Archibald Alexander Hodge, *The Life of Charles Hodge, by His Son, Alexander A. Hodge* (London: T. Nelson, 1880) 11.

[12] Ibid., 9–10.

Hodge, on profession of faith, became a communing member of the Presbyterian Church of Princeton in 1815. He went on to graduate from the College of New Jersey that year and then from Princeton Theological Seminary in 1819. There Hodge developed what would be a life-long filial affection for his professor, Archibald Alexander, who had already tutored the young Hodge in Greek.[13] After a brief stint as a supply preacher, Hodge began his half-century professional tenure at the seminary, uninterrupted except for a two-year study leave in Germany (1826–1828).[14] While at Princeton Hodge wrote a number of books, founded and edited a journal, the *Biblical Repertory and Princeton Review*, and taught thousands of students. Hodge was married twice (first to Sarah Bache in 1822 and after her death to Mary Hunter Stockton in 1852). He had eight children with Sarah. Two of his sons, Archibald Alexander Hodge and Casper Wistar Hodge, became theologians themselves.

More than one scholar has used the term "naive" to describe Hodge's attitude toward American slavery.[15] Hodge, who remembered using profane language only once in his life, after stubbing his toe when he was thirteen or fourteen years old ("I am thankful that no similar experience ever occurred to me," he wrote),[16] did seem to be something of an innocent. Other well-attested aspects of Hodge's personality were his gregariousness,[17] his love of order and routine,[18] his erudition,[19] his industriousness,[20] and his penchant

---

[13] A. A. Hodge, *Life of Charles Hodge*, 18.

[14] E. Brooks Holifield, "Hodge, the Seminary, and the American Theological Context," in *Charles Hodge Revisited*, 105.

[15] Stewart, *Mediating the Center*, 85; Wallace, "Defense of the Forgotten Center," 169.

[16] Charles Hodge, quoted in A. A. Hodge, *Life of Charles Hodge*, 11, 13–14.

[17] Stewart, *Mediating the Center*, 9–11; A. A. Hodge, *Life of Charles Hodge*, 364–67, 528, 565, 616.

[18] Richard J. Carwardine, "The Politics of Charles Hodge," in *Charles Hodge Revisited*, 256. A. A. Hodge, *Life of Charles Hodge*, 236, 241–42, 253.

[19] Stewart, *Mediating the Center*, 11–13.

[20] Carwardine, "Politics of Charles Hodge," in *Charles Hodge Revisited*, 266. A. A. Hodge, 32–33, 42–43, 56, 63, 91, 100–101.

for peace-making.[21] This last quality stood in stark contrast to his often polemical writing style.[22] Hodge confessed that at times in some of his articles in the *Princeton Review* his love of truth took precedence over his Christian forbearance.[23]

Hodge the Theologian. The overriding personal factor that shaped all of Charles Hodge's moral stances, including his views on slavery, was that he was a theologian—one of the first full-time academic theologians in the United States.[24] Hodge became known as the "Princeton theologian" who "immortalized the school's thought" in his writings (many of which are still in print to this day);[25] these works include his biblical commentaries on Romans (1835, revised 1836 and 1864), Ephesians (1856), and 1 and 2 Corinthians (1857 and 1858); the *Constitutional History of the Presbyterian Church in the United States* (1839–1840, two volumes); his devotional volume *The Way of Life* (1841); *Systematic Theology* (1872–1874, three volumes); many articles in the *Princeton Review*; and his last book, *What Is Darwinism* (1874). Hodge's posthumously published *Conference Papers* (1878) were a collection of his Sunday afternoon lectures to Princeton seminarians.

Preserver and Adapter of Tradition. Hodge, the self-avowed "conservative," denied that there was anything original about the "Princeton theology" he taught. He saw himself as doing nothing more than representing an essentially homogenous Reformed tradition that was taught to him by his pastors and professors (and his mother), formulated by the Westminster Assembly and the Synod of Dort, delineated with precision by scholastics like Francis Turretin,

---

[21] Carwardine, "Politics of Charles Hodge," in *Charles Hodge Revisited*, 283; Stewart, *Mediating the Center*, 13–14.

[22] James Turner, "Charles Hodge in the Intellectual Weather of the Nineteenth Century" in *Charles Hodge Revisited*, 41–43; Stewart, *Mediating the Center*, 9.

[23] Charles Hodge, "Retrospect," 4.

[24] Holifield, "Hodge," in *Charles Hodge Revisited*, 103–104.

[25] W. Andrew Hoffecker, *Piety and the Princeton Theologians: Archibald Alexander, Charles Hodge, and Benjamin Warfield* (Grand Rapids: Baker Book House, 1981) 45.

rooted in the theology of John Calvin, Ulrich Zwingli, and Augustine, and ultimately based on the Bible, which, Hodge believed, was dictated by God.[26]

Hodge affirmed the classic Reformed doctrine of a transcendent, sovereign, and personal God.[27] He understood the human race to be created in the divine image but guilty of and corrupted by original sin.[28] He believed that God had, from the beginning of time, designated the "elect" for eternal salvation and the "reprobate" for eternal damnation.[29] Hodge believed in a divine-human Jesus Christ who, through his death and resurrection, redeemed the elect from the powers of sin and death.[30] Hodge described Christ's atoning work with the legalistic "federal" or "covenant" theology of the seventeenth-century scholastic Turretin.[31] Hodge trusted the Holy Spirit to inspire and preserve the faith of the elect, gathering them into the church: an "invisible" communion of genuine saints encased in an outward "visible" institution, which is distinguished by the teaching of right doctrine and obedience to divine law. Finally, Hodge awaited the second advent of Christ, the resurrection of the dead, God's final judgment, and the establishment of God's kingdom

---

[26] Mark A. Noll, *The Princeton Theology, 1812–1921: Scripture, Science, and Theological Method from Archibald Alexander to Benjamin Breckinridge Warfield* (Phillipsburg NJ: Presbyterian and Reformed Publishing Company, 1981) 25–30.

[27] Charles Hodge, *Systematic Theology*, 3 vols. (New York: Charles Scribner, 1871; reprint, Grand Rapids: Eerdmans Publishing Company, 1997) 1:376.

[28] Charles Hodge, *Systematic Theology*, 3 vols. (New York: Charles Scribner, 1871; reprint, Grand Rapids: Eerdmans Publishing Company, 1997) 2:96–98, 192 (page numbers correspond to the reprint edition).

[29] Ibid., 535–45.

[30] Hodge *Systematic Theology*, 1:531–32; Charles Hodge, *Systematic Theology*, 3 vols. (New York: Scribner, Armstrong and Company, 1872; reprint, Grand Rapids: Eerdmans Publishing Company, 1997) 3:545, 563–64 (page numbers correspond to the reprint edition).

[31] Noll, *Princeton Theology*, 27–30. Hodge, *Systematic Theology*, 2:192–226; 563–91. For Turretin's theology, see John Walter Beardslee, III, "Theological Development at Geneva under Francis and Jean Alphonse Turretin (1648–1737)" (Ph.D. diss., Yale University, 1956) 29–33, 276–83, 499–518; Hodge, *Systematic Theology*, 3:259–71.

at the end of time.[32] In these ways Hodge was, as he claimed to be, generally in conformity with the mainstream of Reformed Christianity.

Of course, Hodge and the other Princetonians inevitably left their own imprint on the tradition they inherited. Perhaps as an accommodation to nineteenth-century American optimism,[33] they, like many other American Calvinists, reversed Calvin's grim ratio of elect to reprobate, saying that ultimately many more would be saved than lost. Hodge also claimed that all children who die in infancy, "baptized or unbaptized, born in Christian or in heathen lands, of believing or unbelieving parents," are immediately and unconditionally saved.[34]

The Princetonians were especially influenced by a particular branch of the Enlightenment, the "Didactic Enlightenment," that is, the Common Sense philosophy of Thomas Reid and his followers. Two important and interrelated elements of Hodge's theology were his theological method, which included a very high doctrine of biblical authority, and his doctrine of human nature—that is, his "anthropology"—which emphasized the essential unity of humankind. As we shall see, Hodge articulated these two doctrines with a balance of Reformed Protestant orthodoxy and Common Sense philosophy. Furthermore, both these doctrines had a decisive influence on his views on slavery.

Hodge's Institutions. Hodge's stance on slavery was partially influenced by the institutions to which he belonged. Like many Calvinists, he affirmed the necessity of stable religious, political, and

---

[32] Hodge, *Systematic Theology*, 3:837–60.

[33] See Earl W. Kennedy, "From Pessimism to Optimism: Francis Turretin and Charles Hodge on 'the Last Things,'" in *Servant Gladly: Essays in Honor of John W. Beardslee the Third*, ed. Jack D. Klunder (Grand Rapids: Eerdmans Publishing Company, 1989) 104–16, and "An Historical Analysis of Charles Hodge's Doctrines of Sin and Particular Grace" (Ph.D. diss., Princeton Theological Seminary, 1968) passim.

[34] Hodge, *Systematic Theology*, 1:26. See also Kennedy, "An Historical Analysis," 257–61.

educational institutions—structures that bind societies together, maintain order, define duties, and transmit traditions. Three very influential institutions in Hodge's life were the Presbyterian Church, the Federalist political tradition, and Princeton Theological Seminary.

From his baptism to his death, Hodge identified with the Presbyterian Church in the United States of America, even serving as moderator of its (Old School) General Assembly of 1846. This mostly white (Scotch-Irish and English),[35] relatively wealthy,[36] Calvinist and Evangelical denomination was defined by its distinctive polity. Unlike the Congregationalists (who entrusted decision-making power to the membership of each local congregation) and unlike the Roman Catholics (who invested similar power in a self-perpetuating hierarchy), Presbyterians located the balance of power in the "presbytery," the college of theologically-educated ministers. The ministry, who were elected by lay people, were organized into a graded series of church courts with rotating leadership, the highest adjudicatory being the national General Assembly, which met

---

[35] In Hodge's day there were a were a number of relatively small English-, German-, and Dutch-speaking Presbyterian bodies, but the largest was Hodge's Presbyterian Church (U.S.A.). See D. G. Hart and Mark Noll, "The Presbyterians: A People, a History and an Identity," in *Dictionary of the Presbyterian and Reformed Tradition in America*, ed. D. G. Hart (Downers Grove IL: InterVarsity Press, 1999) xxi–xxii. At least one influential African-American Presbyterian minister of the antebellum period, Theodore Wright, was educated at Princeton Seminary. See Andrew E. Murray, *Presbyterians and the Negro—a History* (Philadelphia: Presbyterian Historical Society, 1966) 30–39, 43–45.

[36] Timothy L. Smith, *Revivalism and Social Reform in Mid-Nineteenth Century America* (New York and Nashville: Abingdon Press, 1957) 26. Hodge admitted "with great reluctance...that the Presbyterian Church in this country is not a church of the poor." See "Preaching the Gospel to the Poor," *BRPR* 43/1 (January 1871): 86. Nevertheless, Hodge was not a despiser of wealth or wealthy people. Though not particularly wealthy himself, Hodge expected property to command a degree of deference, privately taking the position that only men of property should be allowed to vote (A. A. Hodge, *Life of Charles Hodge*, 233). On the professionalization of the Presbyterian clergy, see Lefferts Loetscher, *Facing the Enlightenment and Pietism: Archibald Alexander and the Founding of Princeton Theological Seminary* (Westport CT: Greenwood, 1983) 138–49.

annually.[37] This connectional system balanced a high regard for official authority with the primacy of the individual conscience.

In Hodge's day the Presbyterian Church in the USA was divided. In 1838, after years of conflict, the "Old School" and "New School" factions split into two denominations, each with its own General Assembly, not to be reunited (in the North) until 1869.

Charles Hodge hated disunity in the church, but when push came to shove he sided with the Old School, which upheld presbyterian polity and the traditional Calvinist doctrines of divine sovereignty, human depravity, the gratuitous nature of salvation in Christ, and predestination. Hodge remained a staunch supporter of the Old School his whole life, opposing the more progressive evangelical New School, which bore the influence of New England. Many of the New School's members found their way into the western US presbyteries as a result of the 1801 "Plan of Union," which allowed for close cooperation between Presbyterians and Connecticut Congregationalists in evangelizing the west. New Schoolers were sympathetic to New England's more independent congregational form of polity. They were also influenced by the activist, revival-oriented "New Haven theology" of Yale Professor Nathaniel Taylor, who emphasized human free will and apparently rejected the traditional Calvinist ideas of total depravity and predestination.[38]

---

[37] John Leith, "Presbyterianism, Reformed," in *Encyclopedia of Religion*, 16 vols., ed. Mircea Eliade et al. (New York: MacMillan Publishing Company, 1987) 11:523–24.

[38] George M. Marsden, *The Evangelical Mind and the New School Presbyterian Experience* (New Haven: Yale University Press, 1970) 7–30, 45–52, 57–58, 219–223; Lefferts Loetscher, *The Broadening Church: A Study of Theological Issues in the Presbyterian Church since 1869* (Philadelphia: University of Pennsylvania Press, 1957) 1–5; Holifield, "Hodge," in *Charles Hodge Revisited*, 107–14; Hodge, "Retrospect," 20–27. See also Nathaniel William Taylor, "*Concio ad Clerum*: A Sermon," in *Theology in America: The Major Protestant Voices from Puritanism to Neo-Orthodoxy*, ed. Sydney Ahlstrom (Indianapolis: Bobbs-Merril Company, 1967) 211–49. There has been a difference of opinion, in Taylor's day and later, as to whether he was actually as "Arminian" as his critics said he was; see E. Brooks Holifield, *Theology in America: Christian Thought from the Age of the Puritans to the Civil War* (New Haven: Yale University Press, 2003) 352–61.

Slavery was also a factor, though not the major factor, in the Old School/New School division. In keeping with their activist orientation and their relatively optimistic view of human nature, New Schoolers were often deeply involved in Evangelical efforts toward social reform, including the temperance and antislavery movements. Many New School Presbyterians were sympathetic with abolitionism. Southern Presbyterians, who tended to be proslavery, also tended to favor the traditional Calvinism of the Old School. Northern Old Schoolers were not necessarily friends of slavery but were uncomfortable with what they perceived to be the radical doctrines of Garrisonian abolitionism, especially when these teachings found their way into Presbyterian pulpits.[39]

Though the correlation between Old School and New School and proslavery and antislavery Presbyterians was a loose one, it was tight enough to form a temporary alliance. At an Old School convention preceding the 1837 General Assembly (at which Charles Hodge was not present), a contingent of Southerners led by George Baxter of Virginia agreed to support Old Schooler Robert Breckinridge's plan to gain control of the denomination by excising the Plan of Union Synods. At the same meeting, Northern Old Schoolers who opposed slavery agreed to keep those opinions to themselves.[40] This was to be a decisive step towards the denominational division of 1838. It is significant, however, that despite this alliance both "schools" continued to have internal conflicts over slavery, even after the division.[41]

---

[39] Marsden, *Evangelical Mind*, 95–97.

[40] E. T. Thompson, *Presbyterians in the South, 1607–1861*, vol. 1 of 3 (Richmond VA: John Knox Press, 1961) 394.

[41] The preceding interpretation of the role slavery played in the New School/Old School division is essentially that of E. T. Thompson in *Presbyterians in the South*. Marsden also adopts Thompson's explanation. Historians have differed in their interpretations of these events. Marsden's *Evangelical Mind* includes a "Historiography of the Causes of the Division of 1837–1838" (250–51). Thompson and Marsden marshal convincing evidence that the Old School/New School division was not simply (or even mainly) a battle over slavery but was the result of a confluence of political, social, and theological factors. A more recent article, Chris

Another institution that claimed Hodge's loyalty was the Federalist political tradition. Hodge wrote proudly, "every drop of blood in our veins is of the old federal stock."[42] Federalists were "classical republicans" (as opposed to "liberal republicans" like Thomas Jefferson). While they were not opposed to individual freedom, Federalists believed that a free republic could only flourish within limits. They "valued religion, education, and law as the means of maintaining a harmonious and controllable social order." They believed in a strong federal union, limited democracy, and gradual and controlled social progress managed by strong government institutions, churches, and influential benevolent voluntary societies, all staffed by members of a pious, educated and propertied elite.[43] For Hodge, who expressed his political views privately in letters to his brother and publicly in his journal articles,[44] "Federalism" was more of a politically conservative intellectual tradition than a political

---

Padgett's "Evangelicals Divided: Abolition and the Plan of Union's Demise in Ohio's Western Reserve," in *Religion and the Antebellum Debate over Slavery*, ed. John McKivigan and Mitchell Snay (Athens: University of Georgia Press, 1998) 249–72, also assigns the division of the Presbyterian Church to a convergence of causes including theological conflicts, quarrels over slavery, and generational difference between older, more moderate and deferential Evangelicals and "younger, more aggressive Evangelicals" (265). However, Padgett focuses less on conflicts at the General Assembly and more on those between Presbyterians in Ohio's Western Reserve, a Plan of Union synod.

[42] Charles Hodge, "The Church and the Country," *BRPR* 23/2 (April 1861): 333.

[43] Carwardine, "Politics of Charles Hodge," in *Charles Hodge Revisited*, 257.

[44] A. A. Hodge, 230–34, 343–51, 393–96, 462–66, 485–88. See also Carwardine, "Politics of Charles Hodge," in *Charles Hodge Revisited*, 247–97. Privately Hodge often vented his federalist ire at President Andrew Jackson and his Democratic party. When the state of Georgia, with Jackson's support, sent the Cherokee Indians marching on the "trail of tears" to Oklahoma, Hodge forgot his usual inclination to support established authority, saying, "Verily, I think I could join a rebellion with a clear conscience." See Charles Hodge to Hugh Hodge, 1 October 1831, quoted in A. A. Hodge, *Life of Charles Hodge*, 217. Publicly Hodge showed Federalist inclination in his opposition to Sunday mails, his support of other Sabbatarian legislation, and his support of religious education in public schools. See Charles Hodge, "Sunday Mails," *BRPR* 3/1 (January 1831): 86–134, and "The Sunday Laws," *BRPR* 31/4 (October 1859): 733–67.

party. Hodge still took pride in his brand of Federalism even after the Federalist party dissolved in the 1820s. Hodge became a Whig and then, when the Whig party dissolved in 1856, a Republican.[45]

Federalism, like so many other American intellectual traditions, was ambivalent toward slavery. While one historian finds the Federalist model of a unified, hierarchically ordered, stable society to be an important element of the proslavery argument,[46] others find countervailing antislavery tendencies in Federalism. At least some Federalists purported that their model of controlled social progress would lead to the progressively wider enjoyment of personal freedom and the gradual extinction of slavery.[47]

Presbyterianism and Federalism converged in the particular ethos that was formed at Princeton—the college and (most importantly for Hodge) the seminary. Princeton Theological Seminary, one of the earliest graduate schools of any kind in the United States, was founded in 1812 by Ashbel Green and Archibald Alexander in order to provide advanced professional training of ministers. While the seminary did not exist until Hodge was eighteen years old, it was as much in his blood as it could be. Its founders were his childhood mentors. The seminary educated him, supported him, and provided a platform for his views throughout his entire career.

While the seminary was never officially affiliated with the College of New Jersey (which would become Princeton University), the two institutions were, for most of the nineteenth century, "joined in spirit" with "interlocking boards, shared concerns, and their common location."[48] The college and the seminary also shared a

---

[45] Carwardine, "Politics of Charles Hodge," in *Charles Hodge Revisited*, 258–59, 264, 274–79.

[46] Tise, *Proslavery*, 233–37.

[47] Carwardine, "Politics of Charles Hodge," in *Charles Hodge Revisited*, 279. See also Eric Foner, *Free Soil, Free Labor, and Free Men: The Ideology of the Republican Party before the Civil War* (Oxford/New York: Oxford University Press, 1970) 73–102, and Linda K. Kerber, *Federalists in Dissent: Imagery and Ideology in Jeffersonian America* (Ithaca NY: Cornell University Press, 1970) 23–66.

[48] Noll, *Princeton Theology*, 12–21.

common intellectual foundation, one that was built by the college's vigorous fifth president, John Witherspoon, during the era of the American Revolution—the "Princeton synthesis" of Calvinist Evangelical piety, Enlightenment science, and Federalist politics.[49] Like the other institutions that influenced Hodge, Princeton Seminary combined a love of freedom with a love of order, but it did not prescribe a definite policy on slavery. The "Princeton synthesis" was an intellectual foundation that could produce both the famous abolitionist Elijah Lovejoy and the Southern evangelist and defender of slavery Charles Colcock Jones, both students and admirers of Charles Hodge.[50]

As we have seen, each of these three institutions—the Presbyterian Church, the Federalist political tradition, and Princeton Theological Seminary—was ambivalent toward slavery. Partly for this reason, Hodge's membership in these establishments did not predetermine his views on the subject. However, these institutions did inculcate in Hodge certain habits and values that helped him form and pursue a general vision for society. In this way they influenced, though they did not determine, his views on slavery.

Hodge, in keeping with the values of these three institutions, balanced a qualified social egalitarianism with a similarly qualified elitism. He balanced a qualified love of personal liberty with a similarly qualified regard for formal authority. He believed that egalitarianism should be tempered by deferential social customs—a regard for the authority of those who possessed merit, experience, education, and wealth. He believed that individual freedom should be tempered by a regard for the common good, which was to be maintained by the rule of law, by strong government institutions, by

---

[49] Mark Noll, *Princeton and the Republic, 1768–1822* (Princeton: Princeton University Press, 1989) 32–53, 140–50, 283–88. Noll describes how different leaders within the Princeton community emphasized different poles of the "synthesis," sometimes resulting in conflicts.

[50] D. Blake Touchstone, "Charles Colcock Jones (1804–1863)," in *Dictionary of the Presbyterian and Reformed Tradition in America*, 134. Murray, *Presbyterians and the Negro*, 99.

(to a limited extent) influential voluntary societies, and by Protestant churches.[51]

As we shall see, three elements of Hodge's social vision played particularly important roles in his views on slavery: his love of institutional unity, his respect for distinct spheres of power and responsibility, and, most importantly, his belief in individual and social "improvement."

Hodge the Slaveholder. One cannot discuss Hodge's writings on slavery without acknowledging his personal connections to the institution. Slavery was not an abstract idea in nineteenth-century New Jersey. Since Colonial times New Jersey's economy had depended on the labor of African slaves. The state's 1804 Act for the Gradual Emancipation of Slavery did not even affect slaves born before the fourth of July of that year; they were expected to remain slaves for life. Children of slaves born after that date were to be "free" in name but remained essentially the property of their owners—to be used, bought, and sold just as their parents were—until they were twenty-one years of age for females or twenty-five for males.[52] Consequently, slaves labored in New Jersey well into the nineteenth century.

It is no surprise, then, that Hodge had close contact with a number of slaveholders, even at Princeton Seminary.[53] Most

---

[51] Carwardine, "Politics of Charles Hodge," in *Charles Hodge Revisited*, 249–58.

[52] Graham Russell Hodges, *Slavery and Freedom in the Rural North: African Americans in Monmouth County, New Jersey, 1665–1865* (Madison NJ: Madison House, 1997) 129, 135–36.

[53] Professor Samuel Miller was the son of a slaveholder and a slaveholder himself, though he was troubled by the institution and argued for its gradual abolition. See Samuel Miller, Jr., *Life of Samuel Miller*, 2 vols. (Philadelphia: Claxton, Remsen, and Haffelfinger, 1869) 1:91–94. Archibald Alexander hailed from a Virginia slaveholding family, though he also found the institution distasteful and sought its gradual abolition through his work with the American Colonization Society. See Loetscher, *Facing the Enlightenment*, 56, 83–84, 181.

significantly, Hodge himself was a slaveholder.[54] At least, he employed those nominally free "paupers of the state" (slaves' children born after 1804) to perform domestic labors and help him cultivate his 6-acre truck garden.[55] According to his letters, Hodge paid 75 dollars in 1828 for Henrietta, a "sixteen-year-old who has five years to serve."[56] Hodge also referred to other servants by their first names: John, Cato, and Hetty—all apparently African American, though their civil status is not clear.[57] In 1834 a slave woman, Lena, was somehow attached to Hodge's household. She probably belonged to

---

[54] For assessments of Hodge as a slaveholder, see Guelzo, "Hodge's Antislavery Moment," in *Charles Hodge Revisited*, 308–109; Murchie, "From Slaveholder to American Abolitionist,"127–52; and David Murchie, "Morality and Social Ethics in the Thought of Charles Hodge" (Ph.D. diss., Drew University, 1980) 294–343.

[55] An Act for the Gradual Abolition of Slavery, facsimile in Hodges, *Slavery and Freedom*, 129; A. A. Hodge, *Life of Charles Hodge*, 228.

[56] Charles Hodge to Hugh Hodge, 12 December 1828, papers of Charles Hodge, box 9, folder 3, Firestone Library, Princeton University, Princeton NJ (hereafter cited as PCH-FLPU).

[57] Charles Hodge to Hugh Hodge, 18 March 1829, PCH-FLPU, box 9, folder 3. Hodge wrote, "We wrote to New York, for Hetty and Cato, of whom you have heard Sarah speak of so often and with so much regret at her not being able to keep last summer. They have promised to come the first of April. Cato we are to give 100 dollars a year and Hetty a dollar a week. This seems high. But this is all the wages we shall have to pay. At present we are to give Henrietta a dollar and John fifty cents and his clothes which is the same as giving him a dollar. I then have to hire all our wood cut and all our gardening by the day, which experience has taught us is the most expensive way of living. We have thought it best therefore to get a man whose wages will not probably amount to as much as we should have otherwise have to pay. For we certainly pay more than fifty dollars when we have a boy. Henrietta we are very sorry to part with and she would stay, did we urge it, but prefers going, and we are glad she does because it would be expensive to keep her...." I interpret this to mean that Hodge is arranging to hire free servants to replace Henrietta and John, who are children of slaves. This would be the simplest explanation for why the 1830 census, which Guelzo cites, reports a free black male and a free black female living in the Hodge household. Guelzo interprets the same letter differently to mean that Hodge is planning to rent slaves from their owner to replace free workers. Guelzo believes the census mistakenly referred to Henrietta as "'free colored,' either because the census taker miscategorized her, or because she was not actually bound for life" (Guelzo, "Hodge's Antislavery Moment," in *Charles Hodge Revisited*, 308–309).

Hodge's mother, who was living with him at the time.[58] That year Hodge tried to purchase "the time" of Lena's son but returned him to his former owner, a Mr. Rice, when he found "the poor little fellow" to be "in consumption" with an expectation that he would "not live six months."[59]

What kind of slaveholder was Hodge? How did he treat the people who labored for him? How did the fact that Hodge owned slaves shape his public statements on slavery? We cannot know with certainty the answers to these questions. Our knowledge of his practice of slaveholding is minimal. Hodge never referred to his own slaveholding in his public articles. However, one must risk the conclusion that his practice of slaveholding was consistent with his theory of the morality of slavery.

Hodge described slavery as a potentially benign though less-than-ideal system of labor—an institution that, given the proper circumstances, could and should be peacefully and gradually phased out of society. Rightly or wrongly, Hodge probably saw himself as a benign, temporary employer of slave labor. He only purchased the "time"of his servants, a limited number of years. Lena would have been legally a slave for life, but she belonged to Hodge's mother. Hodge appears to have been a relatively lenient, albeit paternalistic, slaveholder. His household was not a plantation like the one in rural Maryland described by Frederick Douglass, in which dozens of slaves of all ages and sexes were crowded into one-room, bedless cabins to be roused early in the morning by "the driver's horn" and forced to work far into the night or suffer brutal physical punishment.[60]

---

[58] Louise Stevenson, e-mail message to author, 27 September 2000. Dr. Stevenson's statement is based on her reading of Hodge's correspondence.

[59] Charles Hodge to Hugh Hodge, 9 January 1834, PCH-FLPU, box 9, folder 5. Murchie transcribes this letter in "From Slaveholder to American Abolitionist," 151–52.

[60] Douglass, *Narrative of the Life of Frederick Douglass* (Boston: Anti-Slavery Office, 1845; reprint, New York: Dover Publications, Inc., 1995) 6–7 (page numbers correspond to the reprint edition). Such cruel treatment was not typical of the slaveholding culture in New Jersey at the time (Hodges, *Slavery and Freedom*, 152–57, 203–10). This is not to say that abuse of slaves did not occur in New Jersey.

Hodge, who spoke of his domestic servants in friendly and familiar terms,[61] appears to have paid Henrietta wages and respected her wish to leave his household.[62] It is probable that among the "various sufficient weighty considerations" that induced Hodge to purchase Lena's son was a desire to unite the boy with his mother.[63]

Of course, it would be wrong to understand Hodge's dabbling in slavery as a pure act of kindness. Hodge would not have employed bonded labor were it not advantageous to him. He may have had a genuinely benevolent reason for purchasing Lena's son, but he did not hesitate to return him to his previous owner when he discovered the boy had tuberculosis and was therefore damaged property. However, Hodge's motivations for returning him were probably not entirely mercenary either. He may have been concerned about the risk of spreading contagion to his own family, and he had reason to believe that the boy would receive decent care from the Rice family.[64]

Unfortunately, we do not have firsthand testimony of what Hodge's slaves thought of him. We do not know whether Lena was freed or died in bondage. Nor do we know what became of the rest of Hodge's servants, nor whether Hodge still employed bonded labor when he published his first major article on the subject in 1836. We

---

Hodges reports how one "aged black" celebrated the passage of the Thirteenth Amendment in 1865: "Adam Johnson, formerly claimed by the Forman family of Freehold, was in his cups when he took up a stout stick, and recalling a 'trouncing' given him during servitude, pounded his old master's grave with a vengeance" (ibid., 204). Hodge, who was physically handicapped for part of the time that he held slaves (A. A. Hodge, *Life of Charles Hodge*, 228) did not mention punishing his servants. Even when he defended involuntary servitude, Hodge did not defend the right of owners to physically punish their slaves. In fact, he called for legal protection for slaves against the "insults and oppression of the whites" (Charles Hodge, "Slavery," *BRPR* 8/2 (April 1836): 278).

[61] When Cato praised Hodge's toddler son, Wistar, as the "smartest fellow…I ever saw," Hodge reported it proudly to his brother (Charles Hodge to Hugh Hodge, 1 October 1831, quoted in A. A. Hodge, *Life of Charles Hodge*, 217).

[62] Charles Hodge to Hugh Hodge, 9 March 1829, PCH-FLPU, box 9, folder 3.

[63] Charles Hodge to Hugh Hodge, 9 January 1834, PCH-FLPU, box 9, folder 5.

[64] This is how Stevenson interprets Hodge's actions (Louise Stevenson, e-mail message to author, 27 September 2000).

do know that his antislavery opponents did not throw Hodge's slaveholding in his teeth. On the contrary, the *Presbyter*, the organ of the Old School antislavery faction, called Hodge "an antislavery man at heart."[65] It was not Hodge's personal slaveholding that bothered his antislavery opponents but his moral views on the subject, which are the subject of the remainder of this chapter.

Hodge on Slavery and Race

In "Slavery" (1836), his first major article on the subject, Charles Hodge introduced elements of a general moral policy that he would explicate the next thirty-five years. Using the ethical terms we defined in our first chapter, we can explore the "theological method," the "normative principles," the "anthropological assumptions," and the "predominant loyalties" of Hodge's policy toward slavery by focusing (especially but not exclusively) on this 1836 article. We will then analyze Hodge's "circumstantial considerations" as he explicated these themes in changing historical contexts over the next three decades.

Theological Method

A theologian's "method" is that individual's understanding of the authoritative sources of divine truth. Hodge emphasized the importance of method in his articles on slavery as much as in his general theological works. Central to Hodge's theological method was a high regard for the authority of Scripture. He made it known at the outset of his earliest argument on slavery in 1836 that "we recognize no authoritative rule of truth and duty but the word of God."[66]

Hodge, like many of his fellow Evangelicals, believed that the Bible contained a clear, coherent, and consistent message. The Bible

---

[65] Editorial, "The Assembly of 1863 on Slavery," *Presbyter* (23 September 1863), quoted in Vander Velde, *The Presbyterian Churches and the Federal Union, 1861–65* (Cambridge: Harvard University Press, 1932) 165.

[66] Hodge, "Slavery," 275.

does not contradict itself. It does not lie. It does not err on any subject. Anyone with common sense can grasp its meaning. It contains the necessary truths of salvation and rules for how a Christian should live out his or her entire life.[67]

Hodge used the vocabulary of Thomas Reid's Common Sense realism to articulate his doctrine of biblical authority. This epistemology placed great trust in the reliability of the senses, in the objectivity and perspicuity of truth, and in the inductive method as a means of arriving at the truth. Hodge, who understood biblical interpretation to be a rational process, saw the Bible itself as a eminently reasonable document: the Bible was a catalogue of objective "facts" that were so plain, so consistent, and so perspicuous that one could not doubt its truth without rebelling against one's own innate rational and moral sense.[68]

Some critics have charged that Hodge's confidence in human reason and common sense at times superseded his belief in the Bible.[69] However, despite his many appeals to the innate reason and commonsense assumptions of his readers,[70] Hodge was still a biblicist. He believed that the Bible contained divinely revealed truths that unaided reason could not ascertain. He believed that the Bible

---

[67] Noll, "Bible and Slavery," 47.

[68] For the influence of Common Sense philosophy on Charles Hodge, see Noll, *Princeton Theology*, 30–33; Noll "Charles Hodge as an Expositor of the Spiritual Life," in *Charles Hodge Revisited*, 181–216; Jack B. Rogers and Donald K. McKim, *The Authority and Interpretation of the Bible: An Historical Approach* (San Francisco: Harper and Row, Publishers, 1979) 238, 384; Hodge, *Systematic Theology*, 1:9–10; and Charles Hodge, *The Way of Life*, ed. Mark Noll (New York/Mahwah NJ: Paulist Press, 1987) 53.

[69] Noll lists some of these critics—Abraham Kuyper, Thomas Lindsay, and others—in *Princeton Theology*, 41–45. Noll believes that Hodge is generally less guilty of this thinking than some of his contemporaries (ibid., 165–66). However, Noll holds that in Hodge's writings on race, Hodge essentially drops his belief in the authority of Scripture in favor of appeals to common sense, with morally disastrous consequences; see "Bible and Slavery," 63–65; "Charles Hodge as an Expositor," in *Charles Hodge Revisited*, 201–202; and *America's God: From Jonathan Edwards to Abraham Lincoln* (Oxford: Oxford University Press, 2002) 414–20).

[70] E.g., Charles Hodge, "Abolitionism," *BRPR* 16/4 (October 1844): 545.

contained mysteries, especially the mystery of God's Incarnation in Jesus Christ that can be "known" but not "understood" or "comprehended" by reason. Just as a natural scientist can know a great deal about the phenomenon of electricity without being able to explain exactly what electricity is, the theologian can affirm a number of biblical mysteries without being able to explain them thoroughly.[71] Hodge insisted, both in his general writings and in his writings on slavery, that the Bible has a higher authority that trumps human reason and intuition: "Men are too nearly upon a par as to their powers of reasoning and ability to discover truth to make the conclusions of one mind an authoritative rule for others. It is our object, therefore, not to discuss slavery upon abstract principles but to ascertain the scriptural rule of judgement and conduct in relation to it."[72]

Principles

In the Bible, Hodge found positive and negative principles that would inform and set parameters on his policy on slavery. In ethical discourse, "principles" are the rules that direct one's behavior.

Hodge was a "deontological" ethicist. That is, for Hodge, living a moral life was primarily a matter of following the correct rules, which he defined in the strictest terms as divine "laws." It was paramount for Hodge that his moral policy on slavery be in accordance with divine law. A disastrous moral policy would be one that forsakes right principles, even for the sake of a good end.[73] Hodge would have been appalled by the utilitarianism of the twentieth-century "situation ethics" of Joseph Fletcher, who claimed

---

[71] Hodge, *Systematic Theology*, 1:50.
[72] Hodge, "Slavery," 275.
[73] Ibid., 274.

that in a given situation, any rule might be broken for a loving purpose.[74]

For Hodge, it followed from the biblical doctrine of a transcendent, sovereign, and personal God that the moral life is chiefly a matter of obedience to divine laws.[75] God is the great law-giver. God's will is the basis for moral law. Only the will of God can "bind the conscience" and "regulate the conduct of men." Human laws are authoritative and only authoritative in so far as they are in accordance with the will of God. Hodge, in keeping with his Common Sense reliance on intuition and reason, affirmed that the divine will is "revealed in the constitution of our nature," but, in keeping with his biblicism, he affirmed that it is "more fully and clearly in the written Word of God."[76]

For Hodge, two kinds of obedience to divine law are necessary. One must do what the law requires and, just as importantly, one must not presume to make "that sin which God does not forbid; and that obligatory which God has not commanded." According to Hodge, many kinds of behavior are in themselves "indifferent," neither forbidden nor required by Scripture. Rather, such behaviors are appropriate or inappropriate only according to circumstances. Furthermore, the individual Christian, not the church as a whole, has the responsibility to assess circumstances and decide whether and how to engage in such behavior: "No man has the right to decide that question for other men." This right to judgment is the heart of "Christian freedom." Hodge claimed that Christians often err in being more prohibitive than the Bible, labeling certain activities—such as dancing and drinking alcohol—as necessarily sinful in all cases without regard for circumstances.[77] Hodge used similar

---

[74] James F. Childress, "Situation Ethics," in *Westminster Dictionary of Christian Ethics*, ed. Childress and John Macquarrie (Philadelphia: Westminster Press, 1986) 586.

[75] Hewitt, *Regeneration and Morality*, 80–83.

[76] Hodge, *Systematic Theology*, 3:260, 266.

[77] Ibid., 263–65.

logic in his arguments with abolitionists about the morality of slaveholding.

A Negative Principle. What the Bible does not forbid is permitted. This regulative authority of the Bible was the basis of the negative principle that pervaded all Hodge's public statements on slavery. Hodge could find no specific condemnation of slavery or slaveholding in the Bible, either in the Old Testament or the New. Consequently, he insisted over and over again that slaveholding was not a sin in itself, not a *malum in se*. Slavery, which Hodge defined as involuntary servitude in the most general, abstract terms ("the obligation to labor for the benefit of the master, without the contract or consent of the servant"[78]) was one of many forms of social organization that "belong in morals to the *adiaphora*, to things indifferent. They may be expedient or inexpedient, right or wrong, according to circumstances."[79] From this position, Hodge opposed all attempts to making sweeping condemnations of all forms of slaveholding.

Some of Hodge's contemporaries argued that the idea of slave property was necessarily an affront to God-given human dignity because it reduced human beings to the status of things. Hodge responded by distinguishing "property" from "things."

To say that slave was a master's "property," according to Hodge, only meant that the master has a right to the slave's labor. Hodge argued that one may regard a human being as property without necessarily regarding him or her as less than human, a "brute" or a "thing." Hodge, using the patriarchal language of his day,[80] said that

---

[78] Hodge, "Slavery," 279.

[79] Ibid., 286.

[80] Hodge believed that men and women share the same essential human nature, but he was no feminist. Unfortunately we will not be able to explore in depth Hodge's understanding of gender differences. For a thorough exploration of this topic, see Louise Stevenson, "Charles Hodge, Women and Womanhood, and Manly Ministers," in *Charles Hodge Revisited*, 159–79, and Ronald Hogeland, "Charles Hodge, the Association of Gentlemen and Ornamental Womanhood: 1825–1855," *Journal of Presbyterian History* 53/3 (Fall 1975): 239–55.

a man may legitimately have "property in his wife" or "in his children" but this does not mean he may treat them as "things." He may only use them "according to the nature which [God] has given them."[81] Whether someone is a slave for life (as opposed to a limited time) or whether he or she is bought, sold, or given away does not affect the argument, according to Hodge. These are only the terms by which the slaveholder might dispose of the slave's labor. They do not necessarily reduce the slave "property" to the status of a "thing."[82]

Nor does the fact that a slave's "children are under the same obligation of service as the parent" reduce the slave to inhuman status. The hereditary character of slavery does not even depend on the concept of slave property, according to Hodge, but rather on a particular hierarchical organization of society in which "children take on the rank, or the political and social condition of the parent." Hodge insisted that he did not claim that such a hierarchical organization of society was good or bad, but simply that it did not affect his argument that the idea of slave property does not necessarily deny the humanity of the slaves.[83]

In Hodge's mind, the great mistake made by many opponents of slavery was their failure to make a distinction "between slaveholding in itself considered, and its accessories at any particular time and place." Hodge admitted that many Southern slave laws, those "which forbid the instruction of slaves; which interfere with their marital and parental rights;" and "which subject them to the insults and oppression of whites" were "in the highest degree unjust," but "slavery may exist without any one of these concomitants."[84] Hodge acknowledged that slaveholding was wrong under certain circumstances, but he insisted that slavery is not *necessarily* a sin and certainly not in itself grounds for excommunication from the

---

[81] Hodge, "Slavery," 292–93.
[82] Ibid., 293–94.
[83] Ibid.
[84] Ibid., 278

Christian church. To say the opposite is to say that the Bible is wrong.

Hodge had personal motivations for not condemning slaveholding as a sin under all circumstances, particularly the fact that he owned slaves. Nevertheless, he stood on firm ground when he made this argument. Hodge lacked the one thing he needed to condemn slavery as a sin in all cases—a text, in the Old Testament or the New, saying that involuntary servitude, or perpetual involuntary servitude, or hereditary involuntary servitude, or owning, or buying, or selling servants was wrong in itself.

In fact, abolitionists, despite their early efforts to prove that the biblical terms for "servant"('*ebed* in Hebrew and *doulos* in Greek) did not connote "slave,"[85] grew progressively less comfortable with basing their arguments on chapter-and-verse expositions of the Bible. Some simply denied the authority of the Bible.[86] Others, either consciously or unconsciously, dropped the commonsense literalist method of interpreting Scripture in favor of a more selective hermeneutic. They emphasized broad biblical principles, such as the law of love, rather than particular passages of the Bible that permitted

---

[85] Wayne A. Meeks, "The 'Haustafeln' and American Slavery: A Hermeneutical Challenge," in *Theology and Ethics in Paul and His Interpreters: Essays in Honor of Victor Paul Furnish*, ed. Eugene H. Lovering, Jr., and Jerry L. Sumney (Nashville: Abingdon Press, 1996) 233; J. Blanchard and N. L. Rice, *A Debate on Slavery Held in the City of Cincinnati, on the First, Second, Third, and Sixth Days of October, 1845, upon the Question: Is Slave-Holding in Itself Sinful, and the Relation between Master and Slave, a Sinful Relation?* (Cincinnati: Wm. H. Moore, 1846) 336, quoted in J. Albert Harrill, "The Use of the New Testament in the American Slave Controversy: A Case History in the Hermeneutical Tension between Biblical Criticism and Christian Moral Debate," *Religion and American Culture: A Journal of Interpretation* 10/2 (Summer 2000): 151. The 1835 antislavery statement of the Synod of Kentucky followed this tack: "How can we expect to find in scripture, the words 'slavery is sinful,' when the language in which it is written contained no term which expressed the meaning of our word slavery?"—to which Hodge responded with another rhetorical question, "Does the gentleman mean to say the Greek language could not express the idea that slaveholding is sinful?" ("Slavery," 281).

[86] Wright, *Liberator*, 11 May 1848. Noll, *America's God*, 387–88.

slavery. They also emphasized certain passages of the Bible more than, and sometimes over and against, others. They took a critical approach to the Bible "long before German critical scholarship became a seminary fashion." Thus the history of biblical interpretation in antebellum America suggests that if Hodge intended to adhere to the commonsense, literalist approach to Scripture for which he was famous, he could not condemn slavery as a sin in itself, even if he wanted to.[87]

However, this negative principle did not leave Hodge completely hemmed into a proslavery position. If slavery, according to Hodge, was not necessarily wrong, neither was it necessarily right. Because slavery was "a thing indifferent," Hodge was under no obligation to defend it as a natural, essentially good, or permanent institution. The Bible does not prescribe slavery, or any other particular form of organization, for all societies in all times and places.[88]

Positive Principles. Furthermore, the Bible teaches a number of positive "principles of justice and love." These principles do not necessarily preclude slavery. However, if left "to produce their legitimate effects in ameliorating the condition of all classes of society," they generally lead to less restrictive and more egalitarian forms of social organization.[89] The "sacred writers did not regard slaveholding as in itself sinful," but they did "condemn all unjust or unkind treatment on the part of masters toward their slaves."[90] Even slaves have certain basic human rights according to Hodge. Hodge asserted that if Southerners reformed their practice of slavery in order to honor the basic rights of slaves, the result would be the

---

[87] Timothy Smith, 217. See also Harrill, "Use of the New Testament," 174, and Robert Bruce Mullin, "Biblical Critics and the Battle over Slavery," *Journal of Presbyterian History* 61/2 (Summer 1983): 223 ("[T]he exegetical theory of both Andover and Princeton...proved unable to deal successfully with the question of the Bible and slavery").

[88] Hodge, "Slavery," 302.

[89] Ibid., 275.

[90] Ibid., 280.

gradual abolition of slavery. Hodge's understanding of basic human rights will become clearer as we discuss his anthropological assumptions. Likewise, Hodge's theory that the humane treatment of slaves would lead to the abolition of slavery will become clearer as we learn more about his predominant loyalties and his interpretation of historical circumstances.

Anthropological Assumptions: The Unity of Humankind

Throughout his career, Hodge presupposed and affirmed an "anthropology" (a doctrine of human nature) that emphasized the essential unity of humankind. He claimed that all human beings share the same essential nature, are descended from the same original couple, and are culpable of the same original apostasy; moreover, all are offered the same salvation in Christ. Not all will accept salvation, of course. The Holy Spirit only enables those whom God has so predestined to be saved through faith. But God's elect consists of all kinds of people. No race will be excluded from ultimate salvation.[91]

The doctrine of human unity was ingrained in Hodge's theological method. For him, the unity of humankind was a biblical "fact," clearly stated in Scripture, and an essential component of God's plan of salvation. Furthermore, the Common Sense epistemology on which Hodge based his doctrine of biblical authority presumed this unity. All people perceive the same truth and, at least on a natural level, are affected by it in the same way. Hodge would say that all people are constitutionally capable of recognizing the truth as truth. Even those who reject the truth revealed in Scripture only do so by rebelling against their own innate rational and moral sense. The fact that some people respond to biblical truth with saving faith and others do not is because of the mysterious operation of the Holy Spirit, not because truth is ambiguous, or because people are constitutionally different, and certainly not because of racial

---

[91] Hodge, *Systematic Theology*, 2:77–91, 362, 364, 3:810–11.

differences. The perspicuity of truth requires that all people share the same intellectual and moral nature.[92]

Hodge based his plea for the humane treatment of slaves on this anthropological assumption. Slaves merit humane treatment, Hodge constantly reminded his readers, because they are human beings. Slaves "are men," wrote Hodge; "their color does not place them beyond the operation of the gospel."[93] Hodge did not believe that all people have an equal claim to personal freedom. However, he did believe that all human beings, including slaves, have basic rights: the right to marry and raise a family, the right to receive religious and academic education, the right to acquire property, and the right to be protected from abuse. Hodge charged slaveholders with the special responsibility of protecting the basic rights of their dependants. Divine law required that slaveholders treat slaves as human beings.[94]

---

[92] Rogers and McKim, *Authority and Interpretation*, 284. Joel L. From explores the tensions involved in combining a Common Sense notion of the perspicuity of truth and the Reformed doctrine of predestination in "The Uniform Operations of Grace: Nature, Mind, and Gospel in Early Nineteenth Century Evangelicalism," *Fides et Historia*, combined issue 37/2 (Summer/Fall 2005); 38/1 (Winter/Spring 2006): 137–50.

[93] Ibid., 305.

[94] Hodge, "Slavery," 303–304; Charles Hodge, "West India Emancipation," *BRPR* 10/4 (October 1838): 604–605. Hodge defended these rights on the basis of "common sense," on his intuitive sense of right ("Abolitionism," 575–76) but he trumped his argument with biblical language (1 Timothy 5:18; Mark 10:9). It was "the gospel...which teaches that the labourer is worthy of his hire, and that a fair compensation must in all cases be made to him; which forbids the separation of those whom God has joined in marriage; which requires all appropriate means to be used for the intellectual and moral improvement of our fellow men, and especially that free access should be allowed them to the word of God, and to all the means of grace." See Charles Hodge, "American Board," *BRPR* 21/1 (January 1849): 50. In his *Systematic Theology*, Hodge derived certain basic human rights from the Ten Commandments. He argued for the sanctity of marriage and the family on the basis of the fifth commandment ("Honor thy father and thy mother") and the seventh commandment, which prohibited adultery. He argued for the sanctity of property rights on the basis of the eighth commandment, which prohibits stealing (3:349, 376–78, 421).

Furthermore, because Hodge believed in the basic similarity and equality of all people, he could not accept slavery as a permanent American institution—not because it limited human freedom but because it was based on racial differences and assumed that these differences were permanent, essential, and insuperable. Hodge criticized Southern proslavery writers not because they defended slavery at all but because they wished to perpetuate racial slavery indefinitely, and they did so because they wrongly presumed "the essential inferiority of the Negro race."[95]

Hodge defended the doctrine of human unity most vigorously in his arguments against the polygenetic theory of human origins—the idea, then being promoted by the "American school" of ethnologists, that Africans and Europeans were separately created species.[96] Hodge explicitly associated this new heterodox theory with the attempt to perpetuate the institution of racial slavery in the United States: "It is quite certain that the new doctrines which would hold the black people in perpetual slavery to the whites, do rest at bottom upon a diversity of origin and species in the human race." It did not matter to Hodge that these same proslavery Southerners "would be the last to admit any such diversity."[97] Whether or not they admitted it, they were de facto polygenesists. In Hodge's mind, to accept racial slavery as a permanent American institution would be to deny the essential humanity of black people.

Racial Differences and Inequalities. This is not to say that race meant nothing to Hodge. For him, as for many of his contemporaries, the essential unity of humankind did not rule out the possibility of accidental differences between individuals and between whole races. Hodge, who took the stories of Genesis literally, believed that all people were members of the same biological family.

---

[95] Charles Hodge, "The Church and the Country," *BRPR* 23/2 (April 1861): 346–47.

[96] Charles Hodge, "The Unity of Mankind," *BRPR* 31/1 (January 1859): 103–49; Charles Hodge, "Diversity of Species in the Human Race," *BRPR* 34/3 (July 1862): 435–64. See also Hodge, *Systematic Theology*, 2:78–91.

[97] Hodge, "Diversity of Species," 112.

But Hodge, who was a student of ethnologist Samuel Stanhope Smith, believed that over time environmental factors created racial differences that were virtually innate: "separation and the protracted operation of physical and moral causes" have given each race "its peculiar and indelible type." Hodge, like Smith, mixed nature and nurture together by assuming that children could inherit parents' acquired characteristics.[98]

For Hodge, racial differences inevitably resulted in superior and inferior relationships. Hodge believed that in the United States (though not necessarily elsewhere), blacks were temporarily "inferior" to whites, meaning that for the most part they were not currently competent for freedom or civil equality with white Americans. On the basis of these supposed differences and inequalities, Hodge excused a good deal of racial discrimination and even a degree of racial oppression (including racial slavery as a temporary institution).[99]

Nevertheless, Hodge could not accept that the black and white races were *so* different, or that the black race was *so* inferior, that blacks should be permanently destined for slavery in America. For Hodge this would be too gross a violation of a basic Christian principle, the doctrine of human unity. The greatest irony of his policy toward slavery is that the same factor that made slavery a legitimate temporary measure—race—also made it unacceptable as a permanent social institution.

---

[98] Charles Hodge, "Emancipation," *BRPR* 21/4 (October 1849): 587. This "fact" was so obvious to Hodge that as late as 1871, in his *Systematic Theology*, he used it as proof of the plausibility of a more abstract theological concept, the idea of universal hereditary depravity: "No process of discipline or culture can transmute a Tartar into an Englishman, or an Irishman into a Frenchman. The Bourbons, the Hapsburgs, and other historical families, have retained and transmitted their peculiarities for ages. We may be unable to explain this, but we cannot deny it. …There is nothing therefore in the doctrine of hereditary depravity out of analogy with providential facts" (2:255).

[99] Hodge, "Emancipation," 591, 595. Noll, "Bible and Slavery," 62–63; Hodge, "Slavery," 297.

Human Unity: a Higher Authority. Hodge's understanding of race was complex and open to misinterpretation, but it becomes clearer if we understand it in light of his theological method. Hodge's racial assumptions were based on one source of knowledge. His belief in human unity was based on another, higher authority. Hodge's racial assumptions were based on his "common sense," his reason, his intuition, his observations of people and society, and the trusted judgments of others. Hodge's belief in the essential unity and equality of humankind was based explicitly on the Bible, on the biblical doctrine of creation and the universal scope of the gospel. Mark Noll correctly points out that Hodge did not use the Bible to justify his assertions of African inferiority.[100] Hodge refrained from doing so, not because he forgot his high doctrine of biblical authority but because he knew the Bible would not support his racial assumptions.[101]

Hodge's belief in the unity of humankind was also based on the "Common Sense" school, but in a more fundamental way than his racial assumptions were. Hodge's racial theories were based on his observations. The unity of humankind was a basic epistemological presupposition Hodge needed in order to accept his observations and judgments, including those about race, as reliable. All people must be essentially similar and essentially equal because all people perceive the same truth, and the truth affects them in essentially the same way. This was a fundamental tenet of Hodge's theory of knowledge in general and of his doctrine of biblical authority in particular.[102]

Because it was based on a higher authority, Hodge's belief in the unity of humankind was of a higher order than his racial assumptions. For him the essential similarity and equality of the human race was an article of faith, whereas assumptions about racial differences and

---

[100] Noll, "Bible and Slavery," 62–65, and *America's God*, 420.

[101] In fact, Hodge labeled as "monstrous" the theory that Africans, as the descendants of Ham, were cursed and destined for slavery (the popular racist interpretation of the ninth chapter of Genesis). See Charles Hodge, "Short Notices," *BRPR* 34/2 (April 1862): 368.

[102] Rogers and McKim, *Authority and Interpretation*, 284.

inequalities were more like opinions. Hodge's belief in the unity of the human race did not preclude his assuming that particular races were different and unequal, but it did set limits on those assumptions.

In Hodge's various references to race, even at times (as we shall see at the end of this chapter) in the convoluted nature of his grammar, his belief in essential human unity vied with his racial theories. It is not always clear in each case which side won the conflict. But Hodge's belief in essential human unity was the winner to the extent that he rejected racial slavery as a permanent American institution. Furthermore, Hodge based this rejection explicitly on the Bible. He was shocked that "men who receive the Bible as the word of God, can be readily persuaded that he has doomed the black race to be the perpetual slaves of the white."[103]

Predominant Loyalties:
Unity, Freedom, and Improvement

In ethical discourse "predominant loyalties" are ends: the good(s) a moral agent pursues, the cause(s) that motivate the agent, the goal(s) the agent keeps in sight. Hodge's policy on slavery was guided by his vision for a Christian society, one that grew out of his theological convictions and his abiding loyalty to the institutions that nurtured him. As we have seen, it was a social vision that balanced a love of freedom with a love of order.

One important concern that played a role in Hodge's views on slavery was maintaining unity within and among the institutions that were supposed to preserve the common good, particularly the Presbyterian Church and the Federal union. Hodge was also concerned with protecting the relative independence of each institution and its members. Like many American conservative Christians, he saw no inconsistency between the idea of separation of church and state and the idea that American society should be guided

---

[103] Hodge, "Church and Country": 346–47.

by Christian principles.[104] He believed that individual Christians, the institutional church, and the civil government each play a role in building and maintaining a Christian society. However, Hodge did maintain that each entity must work within its respective sphere. As we shall see, during the long period of time in which he wrote on slavery Hodge was concerned with protecting the distinct rights and duties of each entity from unjust interference from the others.

The element of Hodge's social vision that played the most important role in his views on slavery was the idea of "improvement." This concept was the basis of his belief that the humane treatment of slaves would lead gradually to abolition. Hodge argued that if masters treated slaves properly, according to those "principles of justice and love" taught by Christ and the apostles, the result would be that slaves would "improve" intellectually, morally, and materially to the point that they would no longer be fit for slavery; this would, in some way, lead to their actual freedom.[105]

The goal of "improving" individuals and society was one Hodge shared with many Evangelicals of the Federalist/Whig political persuasion,[106] but it was not just a value Hodge picked up from his contemporary political culture. It was part of a general religious vision. Improvement was a concept that allowed Hodge to apply biblical themes, such as divine providence and the promised temporal blessings of God, to contemporary experience.[107] It was a theme of his general theological writings, though he often used different language to express it.[108] The capacity and desire for improvement was, according to Hodge and many other Common Sense thinkers, a

---

[104] Charles Hodge, "The Relation of Church and State," *BRPR* 35/4 (October 1863): 691–93, and "Sunday Laws," 757–60.

[105] Hodge, "Slavery," 275–80.

[106] Daniel Walker Howe, *The Political Culture of the American Whigs* (Chicago: University of Chicago Press, 1979) 20.

[107] Hodge, "Slavery," 303–304.

[108] He described sanctification by the Holy Spirit as the gradual transformation of the "whole" person: "The mind becomes more and more enlightened, the will more submissive to the rule of right, and the affections more thoroughly purified." See Hodge, *Way of Life*, 210.

universal value—a basic aspect of the human "mental anatomy."[109] Improvement was also part of Hodge's personal experience; his diary, letters, and autobiography show his efforts to improve himself.[110] When one understands Hodge's commitment to improvement in this way, his program for "improving" the African-American people appears less condescending and more a projection of his autobiography.

For Hodge, improvement was a holistic concept. To "improve" is to grow in all aspects of one's life: to know more, to behave better, and to have more wealth. To improve is to become more competent and capable of personal liberty. Hodge described improvement as a moral imperative for individuals and society.[111] The "grand principle of the gospel," he suggested, is "that every man is bound to promote the moral, intellectual, and physical improvement of his fellow men." Society is obligated to provide to all its members access to the "means of improvement," the "most precious of all human rights."[112] And as it does so, society itself improves, becoming collectively more wealthy, educated, and pious.

Improvement was a synthetic concept that allowed Hodge to reconcile certain tensions in his social vision. It was a means of reconciling his love of social order with the value he placed on freedom and equality. The idea of improvement allowed Hodge to depict society as moving through various forms of polity on an upward path to a progressively wider dispersion of freedom. It allowed him to depict restrictive social institutions (like slavery) as temporary educational tools that prepare people for the responsible

---

[109] Peter J. Diamond, *Common Sense and Improvement: Thomas Reid as a Social Theorist* (Frankfurt am Main: Peter Lang, 1998) 15.

[110] Carwardine, "Politics of Charles Hodge," in *Charles Hodge Revisited*, 266–68; A. A. Hodge, *Life of Charles Hodge*, 32–33, 42–43, 56, 63, 91, 100–101, 225–28. Charles D. Cashdollar, "The Pursuit of Piety: Charles Hodge's Diary, 1819–1820," *Journal of Presbyterian History* 55/3 (Fall 1977): 267–83.

[111] Charles Hodge explicates his understanding of improvement in "Slavery," 299–305; "West India Emancipation," 639–44; and "Emancipation," 601–607.

[112] Hodge, "Slavery," 302; "Emancipation," 603.

use of freedom and that could eventually be discarded. Improvement allowed Hodge to reconcile the apparent biblical sanction of slavery with his own hopes for its gradual abolition.[113]

Improvement also allowed Hodge to reconcile his racial assumptions with his basic belief in human equality—to reconcile what he considered the apparent "fact" of African "inferiority" with the egalitarian implications of the biblical doctrine of the unity of humankind. Hodge accepted the ideas of African inferiority and African slavery only because he believed these were conditions that could be altered by improvement. Conversely, he held that those who wished to perpetuate racial slavery indefinitely stood in the way of improvement. Perpetuating slavery was, for Hodge, tantamount to a parent refusing to let a child become an adult.[114]

It was Hodge's commitment to "improvement" as a means to the goal of abolishing slavery that distinguished him most clearly from proslavery Southern clergy.

It is understandable that some critics label Charles Hodge as "proslavery." There was a reason why E. N. Elliot published Hodge's 1836 article "Slavery" along with Hodge's 1851 article "Civil Government" in his famous volume of propaganda, *Cotton Is King and Proslavery Arguments*.[115] There was a reason why many of Hodge's Southern friends and former students considered him an ally in the sectional conflict over slavery. Hodge could sound very similar to proslavery Southerners when he attacked abolitionism as a dangerous doctrine and described slavery as a potentially benign institution.[116] Similarly, proslavery Southern clergy could sound a good deal like

---

[113] Hodge, "Slavery," 275–80.

[114] Ibid., 303.

[115] Stewart writes, "The details of the circumstances surrounding the permission to print Hodge's essays remain shrouded by the lack of manuscript evidence. Apparently, Hodge was offended at their reprinting..." (*Mediating the Center,* 82).

[116] Hodge, at least once, echoed a classic proslavery argument, that wage laborers (in England, not the U.S.) were often in worse condition than Southern slaves, so those who employ free labor (in England) ought to refrain from passing judgement on the South. See Hodge, "Abolitionism," 576–77.

Hodge when they advocated some of the same humanitarian reforms of slavery that Hodge did: legal protection of slave marriages and families, protection against harsh punishments, religious instruction of slaves, and even teaching slaves how to read.[117]

Nevertheless, there were also important differences between Hodge and his Southern clerical counterparts that both he and they recognized. E. N. Eliot implicitly recognized them when he edited portions out of Hodge's "Slavery" before publishing it in *Cotton Is King*. Hodge's former students and old friends from the South recognized them when, in 1860, they attacked him as a traitor, an "abolitionist," and a "black Republican."[118] Hodge only gradually became aware of how much he differed from Southern Presbyterian ministers like James Henley Thornwell. While Hodge saw religious instruction of slaves as part of a program of improvement that would lead toward emancipation, Thornwell wrote, "Our design in giving [slaves] the gospel is not to civilize them, not to exalt them into citizens or freemen, it is to save them."[119]

Hodge was not a defender of what Eugene Genovese identifies as a particularly Southern worldview, one that made slavery the

---

[117] James O. Farmer, *The Metaphysical Confederacy: James Henley Thornwell and the Synthesis of Southern Values*, 2d ed. (Macon GA: Mercer University Press, 1999) 219.

[118] George McNiell, *North Carolina Presbyterian*, 19 January 1861, quoted in Richard J. Carwardine, *Evangelicals and Politics in Antebellum America* (New Haven: Yale University Press, 1993) 317; Charles Colcock Jones, quoted in Charles Hodge, "Church and Country," 332; Rev. W. M. Cunningham to C. C. Jones, 18 February 1861, published in Robert Manson Myers, *The Children of Pride: A True Story of Georgia and the Civil War* (New Haven: Yale University Press, 1972) 645.

[119] James Henley Thornwell, *The Rights and Duties of Masters. A Sermon Preached at the Dedication of a Church Erected in Charleston, South Carolina, for the Benefit and the Dedication of the Coloured Population* (Charleston: Walker and James, 1850) 50–51. Hodge gave Thornwell's published sermon, which contained this quote, a positive review but made no direct reference to its content. He apparently assumed at the time that he and Thornwell were in agreement—that Thornwell also saw evangelism of slaves as a step toward emancipation. See Charles Hodge, "Short Notices," *BRPR* 22/4 (October 1850): 680. As the years passed, Hodge and Thornwell's differences became more pronounced.

cornerstone of society and even of civilization.[120] More specifically, Hodge saw the end of American slavery on the near horizon and welcomed the imminent demise as a sign of "improvement," an indicator of the moral progress of individuals and of American society as a whole, while Southern clergy seemed willing to postpone the end of slavery indefinitely.[121]

But *how*, one might ask Hodge, would "improvement" lead to the end of slavery? How would the slave's becoming more competent for freedom lead to the slave's actual freedom? Hodge offered different explanations for how this might happen as he responded to changing circumstances over the thirty-five year period he wrote on slavery.

Circumstances

At the beginning of his career and at the end, Charles Hodge offered strikingly different scenarios for the abolition of slavery and for the future of former slaves. In 1836, Hodge attacked "abolitionists" as wrongheaded disturbers of the churches and the nation. He argued that Northerners did not have the power or the right to forcefully abolish slavery in the South. He supported gradual emancipation

---

[120] Eugene Genovese, "Larry Tise's *Proslavery*: An Appreciation and a Critique," *Georgia Historical Quarterly* 72/4 (1988): 674, 678. Eugene Genovese and Elizabeth Fox-Genovese, "The Culture of the Old South," in Eugene Genovese, *The Southern Front: History and Politics in the Culture War* (Columbia: University of Missouri Press, 1995) 51–78.

[121] Southern clergy often postponed the appropriate date for abolition indefinitely, but not necessarily forever; see Eugene Genovese, *The Slaveholder's Dilemma: Freedom and Progress in Southern Conservative Thought, 1820–1860* (Columbia: University of South Carolina Press, 1992) 59. Hodge acknowledged this subtlety in the Southern clergy's defense of slavery. See Hodge, "Church and Country," 347: "We never supposed that [they were] so forgetful of the limits of the human mind, as to undertake to say what would be the duty of men in reference to slavery a thousand years hence." However insignificant this subtlety was from the slave's point of view, it did indicate that many Southern clergy were hesitant to sign on to the more intrenched proslavery arguments of more secular Southern theorists like George Fitzhugh and Edmond Ruffin. Nevertheless, Hodge could not justify the desire to perpetuate slavery, either "permanently" or "indefinitely."

through the voluntary manumission of slaves and implicitly supported African colonization as a means of racial segregation after emancipation. In the 1860s, Hodge attacked proslavery theology as a shameful dogma, blaming the death and destruction of the Civil War on the Southern defense of slavery. He supported the total legal abolition of slavery in the United States. He also, with qualifications, expressed the hope for a biracial, integrated American civil society. It is not surprising that many of Hodge's critics accuse him of inconsistency.

However, it is more accurate to say that Hodge consistently maintained the same general concerns over the thirty-five year period he wrote on slavery: He sought to avoid the "errors" of both the abolitionists and the new proslavery advocates. He believed in distinguishing the rights and duties of individual Christians, the institutional church, and the civil government. He tried to remain consistent with biblical and constitutional principles (as he understood them). And he believed in having a just and workable plan for the future of former slaves after emancipation. While Hodge expressed these concerns in different ways, adapting to changing circumstances, he remained within the relatively flexible boundaries of the policy his theological method, principles, anthropological assumptions, and predominant loyalties allowed. In so doing, Hodge indicated the degree to which his theological commitments, particularly his theological method, shaped his views on slavery.

The Enemy: From Abolitionism to Proslavery Ideology. Hodge always tried to walk a line between what he considered to be two novel errors: the error of the Garrisonian "abolitionists," who called slavery a sin under all circumstances and demanded immediate unconditional abolition, and the error of the emerging proslavery thinkers who considered slavery a "positive good" and sought to preserve it indefinitely. Changing circumstances caused Hodge to adjust his understanding of which ideological enemy presented the graver danger to the unity and well-being of the church and the nation.

Hodge's earlier writings on slavery (before 1850) suggest that he clearly believed that the doctrine of "abolitionism" presented a greater threat to national unity, and especially ecclesiastical unity. Hodge was especially concerned with the ways abolitionism threatened the peace of the church. In fact, most of his early major articles on slavery were responses to ecclesiastical conflict over the issue, either between Old School and New School Presbyterians ("Slavery," 1836), between two prominent Old School clergymen ("Abolitionism," 1844),[122] or within the interdenominational American Board of Commissioners for Foreign Missions ("American Board," 1849).[123] In these articles Hodge strived to "seek for truth, and utter it in love." Hodge believed that abolitionists erred in pursuing an essentially good cause, the extinction of slavery, according to wrong principles.[124] He clearly believed that by countering what he considered abolitionist errors with right principles and proper policies he would help ameliorate such conflicts that threatened to sever the church and even the nation.

Even during this early period, however, Hodge demonstrated that he was not a proponent of slavery. In 1838 he reported on the gradual abolition of slavery in the West Indies, suggesting hopefully that something similar might happen in the United States.[125] As moderator of the 1846 General Assembly, Hodge supported a resolution that tacitly affirmed the antislavery statement of the General Assembly of 1818.[126] Late in 1849, Hodge came out in support of an amendment to the newly-adopted constitution of Kentucky, which, had it passed, would have gradually abolished slavery in that state. Hodge even argued that the plan should have been extended in order to emancipate more slaves.[127]

---

[122] Murray, *Presbyterians and the Negro*, 110.

[123] Hodge, "American Board," 1–42.

[124] Hodge, "Slavery," 274; and "Abolitionism," 547.

[125] Hodge, "West India Emancipation," 606–607 et passim.

[126] Charles Hodge, "The General Assembly," *BRPR* 18/3 (July 1846): 422.

[127] Hodge, "Emancipation," 582–86, 592.

Nevertheless, before 1850 Hodge understood abolitionism to be the more dangerous error than proslavery. At this time Hodge believed that proslavery advocates were a negligible minority of secular thinkers, that most Americans (and certainly most Presbyterians) hoped for the eventual abolition of slavery.[128] To him the defenders of slavery posed less of a threat than those who opposed slavery in the wrong way.

Though Hodge never retracted or even fully ceased repeating his criticism of abolitionism, he gradually turned his aim toward the proslavery error, the "counter ultraism, which regards slavery as the normal social state, and therefore strives to prevent the Christian improvement of the servile class, in order to prevent their ultimate possible preparation and fitness for emancipation."[129] This position, Hodge had always believed, was, like the abolitionist doctrine, unbiblical and morally wrong. A number of events convinced Hodge that this error was also an immanent threat to peace, not only of the church but of the nation.

Hodge worried about the political gains defenders of slavery had made in the 1850s. He actually argued that the Fugitive Slave Act of 1850, which allowed federal marshals to deputize any person to help capture and return a runaway slave, was morally defensible.[130] But privately, in letters to his brother, Hodge disapproved when the congressional Kansas-Nebraska Act of 1854 repealed the Missouri Compromise, which for thirty years had prohibited slavery in the territories north of 36 degrees 30 feet border. He also disapproved when Justice Roger Brook Taney, in the famous Dred Scott Decision of 1858, decided that slave property was protected by the Fifth Amendment and that slaveholders were entitled to keep their slaves anywhere in the United States or its territories.[131] Finally, it became

---

[128] Charles Hodge, "The General Assembly [1846]," 424.

[129] Charles Hodge, "Short Notices," *BRPR* 29/4 (October 1857): 723.

[130] Charles Hodge, "Civil Government," *BRPR* 23/1 (January 1851): 125–59.

[131] Carwardine, "Politics of Charles Hodge," in *Charles Hodge Revisited*, 276.

clear to Hodge that in order to defend slavery the South actually would secede from the Union, a move Hodge abhorred.

It also became clear to Hodge that he could no longer dismiss the "positive good" proslavery argument as a marginal secular opinion. More and more Presbyterian ministers were embracing this ideology. Hodge was not totally inaccurate when (in 1861) he referred to the Southern clerical defense of slavery a set of "new doctrines."[132] The "positive good" proslavery argument took time to develop, and it took time for most Southern clergy to sign on to it. Antebellum diaries of numerous Southern evangelicals describe a process of conversion. They moved from understanding slavery as a necessary evil to seeing it as something like a positive good.[133] Events such as the emergence of Garrisonian abolitionism drew out the implications of the Southern defense of slavery. The full flowering of the proslavery argument was in itself a historical event, an altered circumstance to which Hodge was obliged to respond.

In 1861 Hodge responded by criticizing the New Orleans pastor Benjamin Palmer for implying in his famous *Thanksgiving Sermon* that "the trust reposed in the South is to…perpetuate the inferiority and dependence of four millions of human beings and their descendants indefinitely."[134] Also in 1861, Hodge opposed James Henley Thornwell's view that slavery was rooted in "*the universal custom of mankind*"[135] and that it "goes of right, as a matter of course, into every state and kingdom of the earth in which it is not specially

---

[132] Hodge, "Diversity of Species," 437.

[133] Anne C. Loveland, *Southern Evangelicals and the Social Order, 1800–1860* (Baton Rouge: Louisiana State University Press, 1980) 187–218. Dabney wrote that he and many other Virginians once would have abolished slavery, but "We have investigated the subject, and we find emancipation more dangerous than we had before imagined" (Robert L. Dabney to G. Woodhouse Payne, 20 January 1840, quoted in Farmer, *Metaphysical Confederacy*, 206). It took even more time for Southern clergy to sign on to the idea of Southern secession. Both Thornwell and Dabney opposed it at first, but both died loyal to the Confederacy (Farmer, *Metaphysical Confederacy*, 247, 272).

[134] Hodge, "Short Notices [1861]," 169, 170, 171.

[135] Thornwell, quoted in Hodge, "Church and Country," 350, emphasis original.

prohibited." Hodge instead called slavery a "municipal" institution that should only exist where it is positively permitted by law.[136]

Hodge blamed the evils of the Civil War on the Southern ideology that sought to preserve slavery indefinitely. In his view the Southern rebellion was "an unrighteous effort to establish a government whose cornerstone is slavery."[137] At the close of the war, Hodge condemned proslavery theology with as strong a language as he ever used against abolitionism: "It is enough to humble the whole Christian world to hear our Presbyterian brethren in the South declaring that the great mission of the Southern church was to conserve the system of African slavery. Since the death of Christ no such dogma stains the record of an ecclesiastical body."[138]

Spheres of Responsibility. Another of Hodge's constant concerns was distinguishing the rights and duties of individual Christians, the institutional church, and the civil government. Hodge believed that each entity should play a role in building and maintaining a Christian society but that each must work within its respective sphere, using different powers, accepting different responsibilities, and acknowledging different limits. Over the years, Hodge saw the boundaries between these spheres of responsibility threatened in different ways from different quarters and sought to respond appropriately. Just as he tried to strike a balance between the extremes (as he saw them) of abolitionism and proslavery, he also sought to strike a balance between the extremes (as he saw them) of an inappropriately intrusive church and a church with no moral voice in society at all.

Hodge argued that on matters *adiaphora*—that is, on matters that are not directly prescribed or proscribed by the Bible—the appropriate choices are to be made in each context by the individual Christian acting according to his or her conscience. On these matters

---

[136] Hodge, "Church and Country," 350–51.

[137] Charles Hodge, "England and America," *BRPR* 34/1 (January 1862): 150, 157.

[138] Charles Hodge, "President Lincoln," *BRPR* 37/3 (July 1865): 439.

individual Christians have a right and a duty to make informed judgments, to express informed opinions, and even to make use of their "access to the public ear" in order to persuade others.[139] However, the church, acting as a body with the power to discipline its members, does not have a right to make sweeping judgments on these matters. One of Hodge's difficulties with abolitionists was that he believed they expected the church to "bind the conscience" of individual Christians by enforcing obedience to a particular political policy with the threat of excommunication.[140]

Hodge was especially nervous when the church gave political directives to its members. Like other Calvinists, he believed that the church as an institution had a right and a duty to enjoin obedience to the civil government, as did the apostle Paul (Romans 13). This conservative, almost feudal view of civil authority undergirded Hodge's argument that Northerners should obey the Fugitive Slave Law.[141] Even so, Hodge acknowledged a number of political choices individual Christians could make about the proper *way* to obey civil authority. Also, even Hodge allowed, there were occasions when one must disobey civil law in order to obey the will of God. Hodge argued that these particular political choices must be decided by each individual. The church, as an institution, must not dictate them.[142]

Hodge was often misunderstood and ran into conflict because he did not expect the church, as an institution with the power to discipline its members, to enforce the political opinions he expressed as an individual. In 1861, in a widely read article and pamphlet, Hodge condemned Southern secession as "a breach of faith, and a violation of the oaths by which that faith was confirmed" and "a crime, the heinousness of which can only be imperfectly

---

[139] Charles Hodge, "The State of the Country," *BRPR* 33/1 (January 1861): 1

[140] Charles Hodge, "The General Assembly of 1836" *BRPR* 8/3 (July 1836): 441; Charles Hodge, "The General Assembly" *BRPR* 33/3 (July 1861): 550.

[141] Hodge, "Civil Government," 125–40.

[142] Ibid., 143–54. See also Charles Hodge, "The General Assembly [1861]": 558–59.

estimated."[143] However, at the Old School Presbyterian General Assembly of the same year, Hodge refused to sign on to the Gardiner Spring Resolutions, which enjoined Presbyterians "to strengthen, uphold, and encourage, the Federal Government in the exercise of all its functions under our noble Constitution."[144] Hodge disappointed his Northern colleagues in the clergy, who had praised him for his patriotism. They tried to persuade him to change his mind by repeating back to him his own words from "The State of the Country." Still, Hodge found the resolution "wrong and out of place" at the General Assembly. It was like compelling Christians "to sing the Star Spangled Banner at the Lord's table." He believed that the General Assembly, which at the time represented both Southern and Northern Presbyterians, lacked a biblical mandate to decide whether Southerners owed their primary allegiance to the federal government or to the state governments.[145]

However, while Hodge advocated restraint at the General Assembly, he did not advocate quietism. To say that *some* social and

---

[143] Hodge, "State of the Country," 32.

[144] Presbyterian Church in the U.S.A. [Old School], *Minutes of the General Assembly* (Philadelphia: n.p., 1861) 16:329–30, quoted in Velde, *Presbyterian Churches*, 58.

[145] Charles Hodge, "The General Assembly," *BRPR* 33/3 (July 1861): 544, 549–50. Hodge protested that he would have willingly signed on to a statement similar to the Spring Resolutions if it only it were framed as an expression of the sentiments of those present at the assembly ("*The members of this Assembly*") rather than as a moral pronouncement of the Presbyterian Church as a whole ("*This General Assembly*"). Ibid., 559, 565. Similarly, Hodge did not expect the General Assembly to repeat or enforce his personal judgement against the proslavery theology of the likes of Palmer and Thornwell. The General Assembly should not formally condemn "the extreme Southern views on this subject," but it should not sanction them either. See Hodge, "Church and Country," 376. After the war, Hodge opposed a resolution of the 1865 General Assembly that required every Southern minister who held "the system of Negro slavery in the South" to be "a divine institution" to confess and renounce this error before being accepted into the Northern Old School communion. See Charles Hodge, "The General Assembly," *BRPR* 37/3 (July 1865): 505. This policy of restraint on Hodge's part may have also been part of a quixotic hope for averting the sectional division of the Old School Presbyterian Church, which actually occurred in December 1861. See Hodge, "Church and Country," 322.

political questions were beyond the church's jurisdiction did not mean that all of them were. While one wishes he defined their boundaries more clearly, Hodge did argue that there were areas of political concern where the church as an institution had a right and a duty to give specific guidance. Hodge attacked James Henley Thornwell's argument that the church had no right to condemn the international slave trade or to commend the American Colonization Society or interfere in any other matters of "worldly policy." This was Thornwell's doctrine of "the spirituality of the church," which was to be the cornerstone of his proslavery argument.[146] Hodge called it "poison" that would "reduce the church to a state of inanition, and [deliver] her bound hand and foot to the power of the world."[147]

Hodge allowed a church body more freedom to give specific political guidance when the constituency it represented was less politically diverse. Hodge did in fact approve of a resolution of the 1862 Old School General Assembly that enjoined loyalty to the Federal government. He argued that the General Assembly was now free to do so because the Southern branch had broken off to form their own denomination and the question of whether one owed loyalty to the state or the federal government was not an issue.[148] The context was similar in 1864, when Hodge, along with the General Assembly, called on Presbyterians to support the total abolition of slavery.[149]

From Voluntary Manumission to Legal Emancipation. From the 1830s to the 1860s, Hodge supported different strategies for abolishing slavery ranging from encouraging slaveholders to free their slaves voluntarily to supporting federally mandated emancipation. Throughout this time, Hodge tried to work consistently within what he understood to be biblical principles, particularly the negative principle that slaveholding is not necessarily

---

[146] Farmer, *Metaphysical Confederacy*, 188–89.
[147] Charles Hodge, "The General Assembly" BRPR 31/3 (July 1859): 617.
[148] Charles Hodge, "The General Assembly" BRPR 34/3 (July 1862): 516.
[149] Stanley Matthews, quoted in Hodge, "General Assembly [1862]," 543.

a sin in all circumstances. He also understood himself to be consistently working within the limits of the United States Constitution. However, Hodge believed that political changes during this time period made changes in strategy both possible and necessary.

In 1836 Hodge encouraged Southern slaveholders to treat their slaves humanely so that they might "improve" and become more competent for freedom. He implied that masters ought to compensate slaves monetarily for their labor so that slaves could gradually purchase their freedom. However, he did not advocate any governmental system for encouraging or regulating this process. He assumed that slaveholders would manumit their slaves voluntarily.[150]

In advocating this moderate—even mild—emancipationist strategy, Hodge believed he was working within the limits not only of the Bible but also of the Constitution. He believed that Northern states lacked the legal authority to prohibit slavery in the South: "for all the purposes of legislation on this subject, Russia is not more a foreign country to us than South Carolina." The responsibility for emancipating slaves, and even for reforming the practice of slavery in the South, belonged to Southern slaveholders and legislators. Similarly, in 1851, when Hodge encouraged Northerners to obey the Fugitive Slave Law, he again understood himself to be working within the limits of biblical principles as well as within the limits of the US Constitution, which permitted slaveholders to cross state lines to retrieve runaway slaves.[151]

However, Hodge did not believe that the right to hold slaves as property was absolute. He believed that the appropriate civil authority might compel emancipation when slavery is no longer conducive to the common good. Hodge demonstrated this belief when he supported the plan to end slavery in Kentucky in 1849.

---

[150] Hodge, "Slavery," 303.
[151] Ibid., 271. Hodge, "Civil Government," 128–29.

In so doing, Hodge did not (as one abolitionist, Lewis Tappan, had hoped) change his general moral views on slavery.[152] Rather, Hodge worked within the limits of the principles and assumptions that had guided his policy on slavery in the past. The Kentucky plan of which Hodge approved did not violate the overarching negative principle of his general policy on slavery. It did not assume that slavery was a sin *per se*, only that African slavery "ought not to be made perpetual"; it should not be a permanent American institution.[153] The plan was also within the limits of the US Constitution as Hodge understood it. It was written by Kentuckians and submitted for approval to the Kentucky legislature, not imposed on the state from the outside.

Years later, the Civil War and its aftermath caused Hodge to embrace a new scenario for the abolition of slavery. Whereas in the past Hodge had argued that slaveholders or the legislatures of slaveholding states should take the initiative in emancipating slaves, he now allowed that the federal government could impose emancipation on the South as a military necessity. According to Hodge, Northerners were fighting not directly for the abolition of slavery but to preserve the Union. Hodge conceded, however, that the US president might properly order the general emancipation of slaves as a means of expediting the war.[154]

In 1863 Abraham Lincoln's Emancipation Proclamation freed Southern slaves on the grounds of military necessity. Northern

---

[152] Lewis Tappan to Charles Hodge, 25 November 1849, PCH-FLPU, box 19, folder 1.

[153] Hodge, "Emancipation," 583, 603.

[154] Charles Hodge, "The War," *BRPR* 35/1 (January 1863): 153. See also Charles Hodge, "Short Notices," *BRPR* 33/4 (October 1861): 758. Hodge accepted the prospect of the "immediate and universal emancipation of the slaves" with anxiety at first (in 1862). He preferred that emancipation should be preceded by "a system of moral, intellectual, and social culture of the blacks, as would render their transition from slavery to freedom as certain and as healthful as the transition from childhood to manhood." Yet he warned that "the South may render [immediate] emancipation indispensable and inevitable." Charles Hodge, "The General Assembly," *BRPR* 34/3 (July 1862): 521.

border states soon followed suit by emancipating their slaves. Finally, the thirteenth amendment to the Constitution prohibited slavery in the United States. Even before this process of abolition was complete, Hodge, along with the General Assembly of 1864, encouraged Presbyterians to support the civil government by "laboring honestly, earnestly, and unweariedly in their respective spheres for this glorious consummation," the total abolition of slavery.[155]

For a number of conservative Old Schoolers (who had previously attacked abolitionists), signing on to the General Assembly's 1864 resolution against slavery was a humbling experience: "I was wrong sir," confessed the respected New York pastor Dr. Gardiner Spring.[156] Hodge felt no such contrition. He saw himself as being consistent with the same negative principle he had stated so many times before and which he here repeated: that slaveholding is not in all circumstances sinful. If he now approved the total legal abolition of slavery in the United States, he did so because recent events had made his approbation appropriate. The special circumstances of the Civil War had made "the continuance of the system of slavery among us…'incompatible with the preservation of our own liberty and independence,' as a nation."[157]

The Civil War had apparently given the federal government the right to abolish slavery and to override the states' rights to keep it. This development Hodge not only accepted but celebrated as the effect of divine providence. The God of Israel, who for mysterious reasons had hardened the heart of Pharaoh against the petition of Moses, also used the stubbornness of the South to serve divine ends. The South's "[r]esistance to the constitutional limitation of slavery to the States in which it already existed, resistance to all plans of gradual emancipation, the insane purpose to dissolve the Union and

---

[155] Stanley Matthews, quoted in Hodge, "General Assembly [1862]," 543.

[156] Anonymous, "Position Defined," *Presbyter*, 13 July 1864, quoted in Velde, *Presbyterian Churches*, 128.

[157] Charles Hodge, "The General Assembly," *BRPR* 36/3 (July 1864): 550. Hodge is quoting the General Assembly's antislavery resolution.

overthrow the general government in favor of this system, have led to its sudden overthrow."[158]

From Colonization to an Integrated Society. Over the decades Hodge took different positions concerning the future of former slaves after emancipation. For many years he supported different forms of the colonization scheme, the plan to resettle former slaves in Liberia. However, he eventually dropped colonization and looked forward to former slaves integrating into American civil society.

Hodge's changing views on colonization do not necessarily demonstrate his philosophical inconsistency but they do reveal the tension, which we have previously discussed, between his racial prejudices on the one hand and his belief in the essential similarity and equality of all people on the other. As we have seen, Hodge's belief in essential human unity set limits on but did not absolutely preclude some racial assumptions. These assumptions undergirded his advocacy of colonization, but his belief in essential human unity prevented him from ever ruling out other possibilities for the future of former slaves.

Hodge first favored the idea of African colonization, at least in part because he believed that separating the races in this way was the best way to deal with what he saw as their differences and inequalities. In a footnote in his 1836 article "Slavery," Hodge extolled colonization as "one of the noblest enterprises of modern benevolence."[159] Hodge, who had served as an officer in the New Jersey auxiliary of the American Colonization Society[160] and who had published a number of articles in the *Princeton Review* by other authors in favor of African colonization,[161] apparently understood

---

[158] Hodge, "President Lincoln," 440. The direct analogy to Pharaoh's hardened heart is mine, not Hodge's.

[159] Hodge, "Slavery," 305n.

[160] P. J. Staudenraus, *The African Colonization Movement 1812–1865* (New York: Columbia University Press, 1961) 85.

[161] Erastus Hopkins, "African Colonization," *BRPR* 5/2 (April 1833): 257–80; Robert Breckinridge, "Colonization and Abolition," *BRPR* 5/3 (July 1833): 281–305;

resettlement in an African colony to be the best prospect for former slaves. However, even by 1839, as we shall see, Hodge stopped short of ruling out the possibility of a future racially integrated American civil society.

Over the years Hodge upheld the scheme of colonization in different forms, adjusting it to different contexts. Whereas previously he had implicitly approved of colonizing former slaves only "with their consent,"[162] in 1849, in an article titled "Emancipation," Hodge approved of a plan for forcefully "expatriating" or deporting Kentucky's freed slaves to Liberia.[163] Hodge was not advocating forced emigration of former slaves as a general rule. He approved of it as an aspect of a particular plan for the emancipation of slaves in Kentucky. A definite plan for large-scale emancipation required a definite plan for dealing with the social changes emancipation would bring. Hodge made it clear that he did not approve of forcing all free blacks to emigrate, only those slaves who would be made free by the proposed legislation. He argued that slaves did not have the right to set the terms of their own manumission and that removal to Africa would be a reasonable price to pay for freedom.[164] In any case, the argument was moot because the proposal for emancipating Kentucky's slaves, along with its plan for deporting them, failed to be ratified by the legislature.

Nevertheless, it is indeed disturbing to see Hodge approve, for frankly racial reasons, of a policy that would have forced thousands of native-born Americans to resettle in Africa. Hodge argued that both the black and white races could not hope to flourish as social equals in the United States. He warned that the more politically powerful white race would oppress the weaker black race out of existence. He even disapproved of the idea of "amalgamation" or interracial

---

and Archibald Alexander, "History of the American Colony in Liberia," *BRPR* 12/2 (April 1840): 205–25.

[162] Hopkins, "African Colonization," 268.
[163] Hodge, "Emancipation," 594–601
[164] Ibid., 597–601.

marriage (an opinion he later contradicted).[165] Ironically, Hodge's most explicit affirmation of a plan for emancipation to date contained his most rigid construal of racial differences and his most explicit statement of African inferiority.[166] Hodge's 1849 article demonstrates the extent to which the traditional doctrine of the unity of humankind allowed for theories of racial differences and inequalities. It also demonstrates how Hodge's racial prejudices and his belief in essential human unity vied for control of his policy toward slavery.[167]

Eventually, however, when circumstances made colonization on a grand scale impossible to justify, Hodge was prepared to drop it in favor a different scenario for the future of former slaves.[168] Previously Hodge had imagined colonization as an orderly process that would accompany gradual emancipation. Now the general emancipation of Southern slaves had suddenly occurred in a way he did not originally expect. Hodge apparently did not consider the deportation of millions of newly free people, some of whom had taken up arms to serve their country, to be a moral or practical option.[169]

---

[165] Ibid., 594–95. Hodge later affirmed a racially mixed marriage as a legitimate Christian marriage; see *Systematic Theology*, 3:379.

[166] Hodge, "Emancipation," 588.

[167] Ibid., 603.

[168] As late as 1862, Charles Hodge, "Short Notices," *BRPR* 34/3 (July 1862): 557 endorsed Princeton Professor Alexander McGill's argument for "the colonization of the black race to a land that is their own," though Hodge no longer approved the idea of *forcing* former slaves to emigrate. See Charles Hodge, "The General Assembly," *BRPR* 34/3 (July 1862): 523. After Southern slaves were actually freed in 1863, however, Hodge completely dropped the policy of colonization as a means of separating the two races. When Hodge mentioned colonization again, he was simply rehearsing his argument against Thornwell's doctrine of the spirituality of the church, arguing that the church as a body can in principle approve of it insofar as it was a Christian mission project. But Hodge no longer seriously proposed it as a means of racially purifying the nation. See "General Assembly [1864]," 562–63; "The Princeton Review on the State of the Country and of the Church" *BRPR* 37/3 (July 1865): 645; "The General Assembly [1866]," 431.

[169] Hodge, "General Assembly [1864]," 542, implicitly recognized the military service tendered by former slaves when quoting the General Assembly's report against slavery of 1864: The "highest executive authorities…have enlisted those formerly held as slaves to be soldiers in the national armies."

In 1865 Hodge affirmed in principle that former slaves should become full citizens of the United States. The right to vote "cannot justly be made dependent on the color of the skin or any other adventitious difference," he argued.[170] Hodge, who was by no means a supporter of Thaddeus Stevens and "radical reconstruction," set no deadline for when political enfranchisement of former slaves should happen, saying that they first needed to be prepared for it: "It is a dictate of common sense that no man, whether white or black, has a right to exercise any privilege for which he is not qualified."[171] Hodge tacitly leant his support to the Northern Old School mission to evangelize and educate the freedmen, presumably as part of a program of "improvement" that would help them assimilate into American civil society.[172] Integration into American society had always been a possibility, though not Hodge's favorite possibility, for the future of former slaves. Now Hodge accepted it, however apprehensively, as God's gracious will and sought to face the "inevitable difficulties and sufferings" that accompanied such social change "as comprehended in the design of God."[173]

Did Hodge Change His Mind? As Hodge responded to changing circumstances over the years, he made himself vulnerable to the charge of inconsistency. Both the antislavery *Presbyter* and the proslavery *Southern Presbyterian Review* chided him for refusing to admit that he had converted from a proslavery to an antislavery position.[174] More recent scholars have also argued that Hodge, either consciously or unconsciously, changed his position on slavery over time.[175]

---

[170] Hodge, "President Lincoln," 456–57.

[171] Ibid., 457.

[172] Hodge, "General Assembly [1865]," 463–67.

[173] Hodge, "President Lincoln," 440.

[174] Editorial, "The Biblical Repertory," *Presybter*, 3 August 1864, quoted in Velde, *Presbyterian Churches*, 136. John B. Adger, "Northern and Southern Views on the Providence of the Church," *Southern Presbyterian Review* 16 (1866): 406, quoted in Wallace, "Defense of the Forgotten Center," 174.

[175] Ibid., 68, n. 4.

Certainly not every single one of Hodge's later statements on slavery agrees with his earlier ones. The mature Hodge was more severe in his description of the actual cruelties of Southern slavery and allowed the church as an institution more freedom to criticize Southern slave laws than the younger Hodge.[176] Nevertheless, his change in perspective, even if he was not fully aware of it, did not render him completely inconsistent. Hodge did not stay still for thirty years. He moved. Perhaps he was, as some claim, not entirely conscious of this.[177] Nevertheless, Hodge's general policy toward slavery allowed for movement.

One factor that gave Hodge room to maneuver was his belief in divine providence. For those not schooled in Calvinism, it is easy to underestimate how sincerely Hodge and his contemporaries believed in the mysterious personal power that drove history. While human beings act in history, pursuing their own ends and acting according to their own free will, God is "everywhere present, upholding all things by the word of his power, and controlling, guiding, and directing the action of second causes, so that all events occur according to the counsel of his will."[178] Human motivations are often very properly different from divine purposes in history.

The providence of God effected emancipation in a different way than Hodge originally expected. Similarly, God had providentially opened up a future for former slaves in America that Hodge did not predict. Hodge did not therefore become convinced that he should have advocated a different policy from the beginning, or even that he

---

[176] In 1838 Hodge doubted the reliability of abolitionists' descriptions of slavery ("West India Emancipation," 613). In 1865 Hodge cited Fanny Kemble's *Journal of a Residence on a Georgia Plantation in 1838–1839* as an authority, a "Dantesque vision of slavery" that others dismissed as fiction ("President Lincoln," 438–39). See John Anthony Scott, "Kemble, Francis Anne (1809–1893)," in *Dictionary of Afro-American Slavery*, ed. Randall M. Miller and John David Stout (New York: Greenwood Press, 1988) 382–83. Kemble was an unlikely authority for Hodge for four reasons: she was an abolitionist, a woman, a divorcee, and an actress. Also, compare Hodge, "General Assembly [1864]," 562 with "Abolitionism," 580.

[177] Stewart, *Mediating the Center*, 85.

[178] Hodge, "President Lincoln," 435.

should have made different predictions. He could only pursue the abolition of slavery in the best way his lights would allow. The Lord of history could use a different method to pursue abolition, and in so doing could create a new set of circumstances laden with new possibilities. New circumstances require that one adjust one's bearings, not that one toss out one's charts and compass, nor even that one apologize for following a different course in the past. So Hodge celebrated the demise of slavery and braced himself to accept the trials along with the blessings of providence, seeing it as his "province to do what is right" and "God's to overrule the results."[179]

Perhaps because of his openness to God's transcendent providence, Hodge always left room for more than one scenario for the end of slavery and the future of former slaves. Even in 1836, when Hodge advocated abolition through the gradual voluntary manumission of slaves, he still suggested other ways abolition might occur. Even a massive servile insurrection, though horrible, might have a place in God's providence. "The South," he wrote, "must choose between emancipation by the silent and holy influence of the gospel…or abide the issue of a long continued conflict with the laws of God."[180] Also in 1836, even as Hodge suggested that he favored some form of racial segregation (preferably African colonization) following the demise of slavery, he could not rule out the possibility a different scenario—as we shall see when we examine a particularly ambivalent passage of Hodge's "Slavery."

An Ambivalent Passage: Race and Theological Method

Hodge's beliefs permitted him to develop a relatively flexible policy on slavery, but was it too flexible—so flexible that it lacked substance? Did his theological method allow him to say whatever he was politically motivated to say?

Hodge had ample political motivation, both for his early antiabolitionist rhetoric and his later antislavery rhetoric. When in

---

[179] Hodge, "Slavery," 305n.
[180] Ibid., 304.

1836 Hodge denied that slaveholding was in itself a crime, he exonerated himself and his friends.[181] By the end of the Civil War, the minority radical antislavery wing of the Old School Presbyterian Church had converted "the whole Church to its policy." Hodge was in a position of proving to this newly converted church that he was not proslavery.[182]

Clearly Hodge was not immune to self-interest or political pressure. He was adept at interpreting the Bible to suit his temperament and to defend himself, his class, his race, and the institutions to which he was loyal.[183] Nevertheless, Hodge's theological method was not simply a front for his political attitudes. It included a deference to the authority of Scripture that set limits on his own interests and prejudices. This deference is best demonstrated by a brief ambivalent passage on race in his first major article on slavery in 1836; this passage is worth quoting in full. At the close of the article, Hodge made his case that the "improvement" of slaves should and would lead to the gradual abolition of slavery. He then addressed a concern of those who "objected" to the idea of gradual abolition because "if the slaves are allowed so to improve as to become freemen, the next step in their progress is that they should become citizens." Hodge answered:

> We admit that it is so. The feudal serf, first became a tenant, then a proprietor invested with political power. This is the natural progress of society, and it should be allowed thus freely to expand itself, or it will work to its own destruction. If a tree is not allowed to grow erect in its natural shape, it will become crooked, knotted and worthless, but grow it must. This objection would not be considered of any force, if the slaves in this country were not of a different race than their masters. Still

---

[181] Guelzo, "Hodge's Antislavery Moment," in *Charles Hodge Revisited*, 308.

[182] Velde, *Presbyterian Churches*, 29. Hodge was consciously defensive in "The Princeton Review on the State of the Country and of the Church," 627–57.

[183] Hewitt, *Regeneration and Morality*, 83.

they are men; their color does not place them beyond the operation of the principles of the gospel, or from under the protection of God. We cannot too frequently remember that it is our province to do what is right, it is God's to overrule the results.

Attached is a footnote:

If the fact that the master and slave belong to different races, precludes the possibility of their living together on equal terms, the inference is, not that the one had a right to oppress the other, but that they should separate. Whether this should be done by dividing the land between them and giving rise to distinct communities, or removal of the inferior class on just and wise conditions, it is not for us to say. We have undertaken only to express an opinion as to the matter in which the bible directs those, who look to it for guidance, to treat this difficult subject, and not to trace out a plan to provide for ulterior results. It is for this reason, we have said nothing of African colonization, though we regard it as one of the noblest enterprises of modern benevolence.[184]

The question that comes to mind immediately on reading this passage is, did Hodge here support the political enfranchisement of former slaves or not? He at first seemed to support it, then he seemed to suggest that racial differences between blacks and whites precluded it, but he still did not seem to want to rule it out. Nor did he wish to rule out segregation or African colonization. This raises the question, why was Hodge not more clear?

Sadly, this passage is not what some readers take it to be, a simple statement of Hodge's approval of the political

---

[184] Hodge, "Slavery," 304–305.

enfranchisement of former slaves.[185] The argument against former slaves becoming citizens "would not be considered of any force," wrote Hodge, "if the slaves in this country *were not* of a different race than their masters" (emphasis added). For Hodge, the fact that slaves *were* of a different race than their masters was a problem.

Hodge himself missed some subtleties in this passage when he referred to it thirty-five years later in his "Retrospect of the History of the Princeton Review" (1871). In order to prove his own consistency over the years on slavery, Hodge quoted the passage in question, but not all of it. He quoted the first part, which affirms that the movement from slavery to freedom to full citizenship is the "natural progress of society," which "should be allowed freely to expand itself," just as a tree should be "allowed to grow erect in its natural shape." But he did not include the next few sentences, which contain ambivalent language about problems created by racial differences between slaves and masters in the United States, and which hint at the propriety of racial segregation. Writing in 1871, Hodge interpreted himself simply to mean that in 1836 he predicted and approved of "the gradual elevation of the slaves to all the rights of free citizens."[186] One might argue that Hodge ought to have known what he meant, but even his own interpretation does not adequately explain the phrase "*if the slaves in this country were not* of a different race from their masters." Much less does it explain Hodge's fear of racial "amalgamation" and his plan to "expatriate" former slaves in 1849.

Hodge's real meaning in 1836 was that racial differences between slaves and masters, though real and problematic, did not excuse slaveholders from treating slaves humanely. Hodge believed that humane treatment would lead to the "improvement" of slaves and the eventual end of slavery. He allowed that a further result *might* be the full enfranchisement of former slaves as American citizens. In

---

[185] Stewart, *Mediating the Center*, 77; Wallace , "Defense of the Forgotten Center," 172.

[186] Hodge, "Retrospect," 17.

1836 Hodge personally did not see this latter scenario as likely or even desirable.[187] Therefore, in a footnote, he indirectly leant his support to colonization as a means of providing for the welfare of former slaves and the good of the United States.

Even so, Hodge could not allow himself to rule out the *possibility* of an integrated biracial society. So he argued that *even if* the humane treatment of slaves led to their acquisition not only of freedom but also of full citizenship in the United States, slaveholders were still morally obligated to treat slaves humanely. Decades later Hodge condensed this convoluted line of reasoning to say simply that he always favored the political enfranchisement of former slaves. Perhaps his memory of his own thoughts of thirty years earlier failed him. Perhaps he misinterpreted himself for some other reason.

The ambiguity of the last paragraph of "Slavery" stems from the general complexity of Hodge's understanding of race and its connection to his theological method. The different components of his view of race, with their different authoritative bases, are all present in this statement.

In 1836 Hodge was not attracted to the idea of a biracial, integrated society. He was so repelled because he understood the two races to be different and unequal. Hodge based this judgment on his intuition, reason, observations of society, and the judgments of others. Such authorities merited respect from Hodge, though not the same respect as the Bible.

But Hodge also held to the doctrine of the essential unity of the human race. This belief was grounded in Scripture itself and on the fundamental epistemological assumptions that were basic to his doctrine of biblical authority. There were ethical implications to this essential truth that Hodge could not compromise. His belief in the unity of the human race set limits on the implications of his theories of racial diversity and inequality. Hodge had to remain open to the possibility of a biracial, integrated society, even if he disliked the prospect. In 1871 Hodge apparently forgot he ever had any distaste

---

[187] Hodge, "Slavery," 297.

for such a prospect. Perhaps the political context of 1871 made such forgetting convenient. Nevertheless, Hodge would not have a statement to misinterpret in 1871 had he not been compelled to make one in 1836.

The very ambiguity of the statement of 1836 testifies to the efficacy of Hodge's theological method. His method caused him real problems. He could not make it conform to his prejudices. In his 1836 statement, Hodge's intuitive belief in racial inequality vied with his biblically grounded belief in essential racial equality. If the latter belief did not win hands down, it at least achieved a partial victory. Hodge's deference to the authority of Scripture, the same deference that prevented him from condemning slavery as a sin *per se*, also forced him to be open not only to the future abolition of slavery but to the future political enfranchisement of former slaves. That Hodge could do so in the midst of what appears to be a proslavery tract was, according to one historian, "a double somersault of dizzying proportions."[188] Hodge's deference to the authority of Scripture may have even set limits on his personal racism.

All this is to prove part of our original thesis, that Charles Hodge's particular constellation of theological method, normative principles, anthropological assumptions, and predominant loyalties enabled and inspired his defense of involuntary servitude per se. This same constellation also enabled and inspired his moderate opposition to slavery as it was practiced in the United States. Hodge's opposition to slavery may seem weak compared to that of Garrison, or even some of Hodge's more moderate Presbyterian colleagues. However, we should remember that such moderate opposition to slavery, perhaps more than the "squalling of the Garrisonians," was what "prevented most Northerners from settling idly down beside slavery, and which, once disunion and blood-letting had set the table, allowed abolition to become a national goal."[189]

---

[188] Guelzo, "Hodge's Antislavery Moment," in *Charles Hodge Revisited*, 314.
[189] Ibid., 324.

This is not to say that Hodge's statements on slavery are morally satisfying. Twentieth-century historians are right to call African-American slavery a crime against humanity. And while it was being perpetrated, Hodge coolly speculated that slavery was not a *malum in se* and confidently assessed the relative inferiority of the Negro. In 1836, while Hodge published his first major article on slavery, Harriet Jacobs, a runaway slave from North Carolina, was hiding from her abusive master in a crawl space above a shed attached to her grandmother's home. There Harriet remained, night and day, in a garret "only nine feet long,...the highest part three feet high" while "rats and mice ran over [her] bed"; here she waited seven years for the chance to leave the state with her two children. While Hodge, at Princeton, was encouraging whites and blacks to obey the Fugitive Slave Law, in nearby Philadelphia, Pennsylvania, Harriet Jacobs was terrified to discover that her former master, encouraged by the new law, had sent slave catchers to track her down.[190]

Surely there was another way of understanding slavery, one that did not reject the authority of Scripture but captured more of the injustice, oppression, and agony of slavery as it actually existed in the United States. Perhaps a more empathetic understanding was present in the experiential, aesthetic theology of Horace Bushnell, the subject of the next chapter.

---

[190] Harriet Jacobs, *Incidents in the Life of a Slave Girl: Written by Herself*, ed. Jean Fagan Yellin (Cambridge: Harvard University Press, 1987) 114, 148, 191.

3

Horace Bushnell: Slavery and Race

For over thirty years, in his statements on slavery and race, Horace Bushnell consistently combined an odd set of ideas: rigorous opposition to African-American slavery and predictions of African-American extinction.

In his relatively early and comparatively direct support of abolition, in his public opposition to the Fugitive Slave Law and the Kansas-Nebraska Act, and in his support of immediate suffrage for former slaves, Bushnell showed himself to be a stronger opponent of slavery than Charles Hodge. At the same time, however, Bushnell predicted that the black race would fail to thrive and would eventually die out on the American continent. Charles Hodge, though a weaker opponent of slavery, did not make such bleak predictions, at least not with Bushnell's consistency. Bushnell repeated this racial extinction theory from the 1830s until the eve of the Civil War.

But what about afterwards? Did the war itself and its outcome cause Bushnell to change this odd combination of ideas? Did he, after the Civil War, drop his racial extinction theory in favor of a more hopeful prospect for the African-American people?

For an answer to this question, scholars have turned to a single intriguing but obtuse postwar essay, "Of Distinctions of Color." The problem is that the essay is so obtuse that scholars cannot seem to agree about what it says any more than they can agree about Bushnell's views on race in general. While most agree that Bushnell was always at least a moderate opponent of slavery, they disagree over his attitude toward race and especially whether this attitude changed after the Civil War. Some depict Bushnell as consistently racist, citing "Of Distinctions of Color" as evidence.[1] Others, who say that Bushnell gradually became less racist over time, also cite the essay to prove their point.[2] Still others question why Bushnell was so "circuitous" and difficult to understand when he spoke of race.[3] Scholars also disagree about the *basis* for Bushnell's views on slavery and race. Some say they were part of a consistent and coherent theological orientation.[4] Some describe them more as accidental aspects of his social background.[5]

As was the case with Hodge, Bushnell's views on slavery and race were complicated and open to different interpretations. Nevertheless, Bushnell maintained a consistent position. Not only was he an unswerving opponent of slavery (even though he criticized the style

---

[1] Barbara M. Cross, *Horace Bushnell, Minister to a Changing America* (Chicago: Chicago University Press, 1958) 41–49; George M. Fredrickson, *The Inner Civil War: Northern Intellectuals and the Crisis of the Union*, 2d ed. (Chicago: University of Illinois Press, 1993) 44–45; Charles C. Cole, Jr., "Horace Bushnell on the Slavery Question," *New England Quarterly* 23/1 (March 1950): 20.

[2] Robert L. Edwards, *Of Singular Genius, of Singular Grace: A Biography of Horace Bushnell* (Cleveland: Pilgrim Press, 1992) 257–58; Ralph E. Luker, "Bushnell in Black and White: Evidences of the 'Racism' of Horace Bushnell," *New England Quarterly* 45/3 (September 1972): 412–13, 417. Robert Bruce Mullin, *The Puritan as Yankee: A Life of Horace Bushnell*, with a forward by Allen C. Guelzo (Grand Rapids: Eerdmans Publishing Company, 2002) 225–26.

[3] Louis Weeks, "Horace Bushnell on Black America," *Religious Education* 68/1 (January–February 1973): 41.

[4] Howard A. Barnes, *Horace Bushnell and the Virtuous Republic*, American Theological Library Monograph 27 (Metuchen NJ: Scarecrow Press, 1991) 34; Mullin, *Puritan as Yankee*, 214; David W. Haddorf, *Dependence and Freedom: The Moral Thought of Horace Bushnell* (Lanham MD: University Press of America, 1994) 50.

[5] Fredrickson claims that Bushnell's opposition to slavery was part of his "New England chauvinism" rather than a real concern for the well-being of slaves. Edwards and Weeks describe some of Bushnell's unfortunate statements on race as an aberration from his generally prophetic theological stance (Fredrickson, *Inner Civil War*, 46; Edwards, *Singular Genius*, 260; Weeks, "Bushnell on Black America," 41).

and tactics of abolitionists like Garrison), but Bushnell also consistently held out a dismal picture for the future of the African-American people. Even after the Civil War he qualified and adjusted but never renounced his prediction that Africans would become extinct on the American continent.

The dissonance of Bushnell's combination of ideas is jarring. Nevertheless, both his opposition to slavery and his negative statements about the African race were parts of a coherent social vision. This vision was the product of many factors, but it was thoroughly grounded in his broader theological commitments, especially his open-ended theological method and his organic anthropology. The different theological commitments of Bushnell and Hodge were at the root of their differences on race and slavery. This chapter argues this point.

The first part of this chapter will place Horace Bushnell's views on slavery in context by examining aspects of his biography, his theology, and his institutional loyalties. The remainder of the chapter will analyze Bushnell's important writings on slavery and race, using the five ethical terms we have used previously, and compare his views to those of Charles Hodge. Finally, we will return to the problems raised by Bushnell's ambivalent essay "Of Distinctions of Color." Like Hodge, Bushnell revealed important aspects of his attitude toward race in a single, widely misunderstood essay. As was the case with Hodge, it is the essay's ambiguity itself that is instructive. The essay is difficult to understand because it was grounded on and driven by a complex set of theological commitments. It demonstrates how the same theological factors that led to Bushnell's opposition to slavery also permitted and encouraged his deprecation of the African race.

Horace Bushnell: Biography and Beliefs

Horace Bushnell was born on April 14, 1802, in Bantam Falls, Litchfield County, Connecticut, the first child of Ensign Bushnell and Dotha Bishop Bushnell. After the birth of his first sibling in

1805, the family moved a few miles west to New Preston, where Horace grew up—working on his father's farm and in his wool-carding and cloth-dressing business, attending school, and exploring the nearby woods. From his youth, Bushnell was athletic and energetic, though as an adult he suffered from long bouts of bad health. He was generally boisterous and cheerful, though he was also thoughtful and given to periods of brooding. He loved nature and was later to help build a municipal park in Hartford that still bears his name. He was interested in mechanics and was later to hold two US patents. He was close to his mother, who determined from her son's earliest years that he should become a minister.[6]

Bushnell's mother was raised an Episcopalian and his father a Methodist. Bushnell was baptized in the Episcopal Church, the only congregation in Bantam Falls. In New Preston, once again offered only one option, the family attended the local Congregational church. Here Bushnell was nurtured in New England Calvinism. He learned the Westminster Catechism and on Sundays listened respectfully to sermons on "Free will, fixed fate, foreknowledge absolute, Trinity, redemption, special grace, eternity."[7] Bushnell's Methodist father, who was never comfortable with their pastor's emphasis on predestination, sometimes expressed his irritation around the Sunday dinner table, but he was quickly silenced by "a begging-off look" from Mrs. Bushnell, who wanted their children to see clergy treated with respect.[8] Respect for religious authority, however, apparently did not create a mentally stultifying atmosphere at the Bushnell household: "No hamper was ever put on our liberty

---

[6] Edwards, *Singular Genius*, 4–20.

[7] Horace Bushnell, "The Age of Homespun," in *Work and Play; or Literary Varieties* (New York: Charles Scribner, 1864) 387.

[8] Horace Bushnell, quoted in Ernest Trice Thompson, *Changing Emphases in American Preaching: The Stone Lectures for 1943* (Philadelphia: Westminster Press, 1943) 11.

of thought and choice."[9] Bushnell seems to have been born to be an independent and comprehensive religious thinker.

As a teenager, while working on his father's carding machine, Bushnell wrote ("a sentence or half a sentence at a time") a treatise on the ninth chapter of Romans in which he accepted the doctrines of election and predestination but called the apostle Paul mistaken or inconsistent in wishing himself accursed for the sake of his brethren. Thus he demonstrated at an early age his capacity for challenging tradition—not only strict Calvinism but the Bible itself. Despite this early foray into heterodoxy, Bushnell became a communing member of the Congregational church two years later in 1821, vowing "to be the Lord's, in an everlasting covenant never to be broken."[10] He then entered Yale College, setting his sights on a career in ministry.

At Yale, perhaps as a result of his exposure to new ideas and the discipline of academic inquiry, Bushnell entered a period of religious skepticism. "Unbelief, in fact," he later reminisced, "had become my element."[11] After graduating in 1827, he temporarily abandoned his earlier vocation to ministry and sought a secular profession. He tried and failed at teaching grammar school, enjoyed some success as a journalist, and finally settled on law. He returned to Yale in 1829 to study at the newly established law school and join the faculty as a tutor of undergraduates.

The winter that Bushnell finished his course work and passed his examinations, a revival swept the Yale campus. Bushnell, the doubter, resisted until all his fellow tutors had been converted. He found his intellectual difficulty with the traditional doctrine of the Trinity to be a stumbling block. Logic seemed to shatter the mysterious doctrine "all to pieces" for him. "But," he said, "I am glad I have a heart as

---

[9] Horace Bushnell, quoted in Mary Bushnell Cheney, *Life and Letters of Horace Bushnell* (New York: Harper and Brothers, Publishers, 1880) 30.

[10] Ibid., 20–21.

[11] Ibid., 32. Yale did, however, encourage piety in its students with mandatory chapel services and other religious exercises. Scholars offer different possible reasons for the young Bushnell's period of religious skepticism (see Mullin, *Puritan as Yankee*, 37–44).

well as a head. My heart wants the Father; my heart wants the Son; my heart wants the Holy Ghost—and one just as much as the other. My heart says the Bible has a Trinity for me, and I mean to hold by my heart." Bushnell characteristically, if this account is to trusted,[12] saw faith as a matter of the heart triumphing over the head. The validity of affective knowledge in matters of faith would continue to be an important theme for him.

After this second conversion, Bushnell reassumed his vocation to ministry and entered the Yale Divinity School. There he studied under the famous linguist Josiah Gibbs, who nurtured Bushnell's lifelong interest in philology. He also studied under theologian Nathaniel Taylor, who was then engaged in his project of "disencumbering" Calvinism by modifying the traditional doctrines of predestination and total depravity (and, in so doing, gaining enemies among conservative New England Congregationalists as well as Scotch-Irish Old School Presbyterians).[13]

Taylor welcomed open discussion in his classroom but was perplexed to find Bushnell always on "t'other side" of whatever argument he was trying to make.[14] Bushnell was not put off by his teacher's departures from traditional Calvinism but by his Common Sense rationalism. Just as much as Charles Hodge, perhaps even more so, Taylor emphasized the importance of logical coherence and clarity in theology. Nothing excited Taylor's scorn more than theologians who were "too lazy to make definitions."[15] Bushnell,

---

[12] This account is actually from the memory of Bushnell's friend Robert McEwen, writing to Mary Apthorp Bushnell, n.d., quoted in Cheney, *Life and Letters*, 55–56.

[13] Vincent Harding, *A Certain Magnificence: Lyman Beecher and the Transformation of American Protestantism, 1775–1863* (Brooklyn: Carlson Publishing, 1991) 137–54. See also Sidney Mead, *Nathaniel William Taylor, 1786–1858: A Connecticut Liberal* (Chicago: University of Chicago, 1942) 95–127, 222–32.

[14] Cheney, *Life and Letters*, 62.

[15] Nathaniel Taylor, quoted in Theodore Thorton Munger, *Horace Bushnell: Preacher and Theologian* (Boston: Houghton, Mifflin and Company, 1900) 101.

though he yet lacked the language to express his frustration, found this rationalistic emphasis stifling to his heartfelt piety.

Bushnell found some relief from his teacher's dry logic in the pages of *Aids to Reflection*, written by the opium-eating Romantic genius of England, Samuel Taylor Coleridge. This volume had enamored many of Bushnell's peers since it was first published in America in 1829. Dense and difficult as it was, it helped Bushnell find a vital and satisfying language to express his faith. Bushnell was drawn to Coleridge's conception of religious language as a kind of poetry that expressed heartfelt truths too mysterious to be forced into precise formulas. It helped him conceive of Christian faith not primarily as adherence to a set of doctrines but as "a life." Afterwards Bushnell was to consider *Aids to Reflection* more important to him than any other book, save the Bible.[16]

Upon completing the divinity course at Yale, Bushnell accepted a call to pastor North Church in Hartford in 1833, the same year he married Mary Apthorp, with whom he would have four daughters and a son. Bushnell spent his entire career at North Church and by all evidence was deeply loved by his congregation. When his health failed him, the church paid for two lengthy sabbaticals during which he traveled to Europe (1845–1846) and the American West (1856). The church stood by him through a long and bitter heresy controversy (1849–1852). When he retired in 1859, the church continued to call him their "minister at large" until his death in 1876. Bushnell also became a popular preacher and speaker and a prolific writer, publishing a number of sermons, articles, major theological works (*Christian Nurture* [1847, revised 1861], *God in Christ* [1849], *Nature and the Supernatural* [1858], *The Vicarious Sacrifice* [1866], *Forgiveness and Law* [1874, republished with supplementary notes, 1877]), and other books.

However, Bushnell's time at North Church was not without trials. He weathered a number of conflicts and crises including intracongregational squabbles, his failure to produce what

---

[16] Edwards, *Singular Genius*, 37–38.

contemporary evangelicals would recognize as a religious revival, the deaths of two children, and accusations of heresy. Finally, Bushnell, like many Americans, had his faith tested by the national sin of slavery and the agonies of the Civil War. All these experiences contributed to his development as a theologian.

Bushnell the Theologian. Sydney Ahlstrom has called Horace Bushnell "the father of American religious liberalism." Indeed, a generation of liberal Protestant leaders in the United States, including Theodore Thorton Munger and Washington Gladden, looked to him as a progressive hero who revised Christian tradition to make it relevant to the modern world. Bushnell did not cast off past traditions indiscriminately, however. He was a "mediator" of past and present, who, more so than the later generation of American liberal Protestant preachers, "sought to retain the critical and dialectical elements in Protestantism." Bushnell has also been described as a "tinkerer" who used Yankee ingenuity to adjust Puritan theology to a changing world.[17]

Bushnell, like Hodge, was trained in the Reformed theology of John Calvin—albeit a particular version of this theology, one that was mediated and modified by New England Congregationalism. Bushnell inherited not only seventeenth-century Puritanism but an Evangelical revivalist tradition that manifested itself in the eighteenth century in the aesthetic sensibilities of Jonathan Edwards, then later in the "benevolence"-centered morality of Samuel Hopkins,[18] and

---

[17] Sydney Ahlstrom, "Theology in America: A Historical Survey," in *The Shaping of American Religion,* vol. 1 of *Religion in American Life,* ed. James Ward Smith and A. Leland Jamison (Princeton: Princeton University Press, 1961) 279–85; Munger, *Preacher and Theologian,* passim; Washington Gladden, "Horace Bushnell and Progressive Orthodoxy," in *Pioneers of Religious Liberty in America,* ed. Samuel A. Eliot (Boston: American Unitarian Association, 1903) 227–63; H. Richard Niebuhr, *The Kingdom of God in America* (New York: Harper and Row, Publishers, 1937; reprint, Middletown CT: Wesleyan University Press, 1988) 193–94 (page numbers correspond to the reprint ed.); Mullin, *Puritan as Yankee,* 17.

[18] Joseph A. Conforti, *Samuel Hopkins and the New Divinity Movement: Calvinism, the Congregational Ministry, and Reform in New England between the Great Awakenings* (Grand Rapids: Christian University Press, 1981) 109–24, 175–90.

most recently in the activism of Nathaniel Taylor.[19] Bushnell worked within the basic framework of his tradition: presuming the existence of a personal God, the human need for salvation, Jesus Christ as the Incarnation of God and the mediator of grace, the importance of the worshiping community, and the goal of a Christian society. However, Bushnell articulated these traditional doctrines in surprisingly new language.

Bushnell did not share Hodge's penchant for systematizing. Partly out of habit and partly on principle, Bushnell did not approach theology as a purely logical science. He wrote in a free-flowing, evocative style. He looked at religious problems from a variety of angles, now arguing logically, now gushing poetically. He did not resolve all the logical contradictions in his writings or work out all the connections between his ideas. A reader who favors logical consistency would find Bushnell's writings incomplete, though not necessarily incoherent. Bushnell's writings invite the reader to draw out their implications, to explicate the connections between his ideas, to find possible solutions to the problems they raise.

As does the thought of Charles Hodge, Bushnell's theology shows the influence of a particular trend of contemporary American intellectual culture. As we have seen, Hodge was especially influenced by the "Didactic Enlightenment," that is, the Common Sense philosophy of Thomas Reid and his followers. Bushnell, on the other hand, stood at the "watershed in the flow of theological influences" to the United States. He shared, to an extent, in the Romantic reaction against the dry rationalism of the Enlightenment. The Romantic movement, compared to the Didactic Enlightenment, was less confident in the perspicuity of objective truth, placing higher value on subjective knowledge, imagination, and emotion. Also, while Common Sense philosophers assumed and emphasized the essential

---

[19] Williston Walker, *A History of the Congregational Churches in the United States*, American Church History 3 (New York: Christian Literature Company, 1894) 1–30, 56–124, 254–61, 279–86, 288–92, 355–61. For a thorough description of the diverse and often divisive theological heritage of Congregationalism and Bushnell's place within it, see Mullin, *Puritan as Yankee*, passim.

mental and moral similarity of all people of all races, Romantics, though they did not necessarily reject the traditional doctrine of a single universal human nature, emphasized the mysterious organic influences that bind particular peoples together and give each people its distinct character.[20]

Bushnell drew inspiration from several sources (from Jonathan Edwards to Nathaniel Taylor to Coleridge to Catholic mystic Madame Guyon to French philosopher Victor Cousin) and cannot be forced into an intellectual pigeonhole.[21] Nevertheless, many themes of Bushnell's thought show the influence of Romanticism. As we shall see, two are especially important to his theology as a whole and to his statements on slavery and race: his theological method, which included a dynamic and mysterious understanding of the nature of religious truth, and his anthropology, which included an organic understanding of human society.

Bushnell's Institutions. Bushnell, like Hodge, affirmed the necessity of stable institutions to bind society together, define duties, transmit traditions, and form human character. The most influential of all social institutions, according to Bushnell, was the family. As we shall see in our discussion of *Christian Nurture*, the family was, for Bushnell, the model and the main artery for the influence of other institutions such as the church and the state.[22] Two other aspects of Bushnell's personality sum up his other institutional loyalties: he was a Congregationalist and he was a New Englander.

Just as Hodge's frame of reference for understanding the Christian church was Presbyterianism, Bushnell's was Congregationalism. Like the Presbyterian Church, the Congregational "Way" was defined by its particular polity. Bushnell, who was not dogmatic in matters of polity any more than in matters

---

[20] Ibid., 45, 49–50.

[21] H. Shelton Smith, *Horace Bushnell, Twelve Selections* (New York: Oxford University Press, 1965) 26–39; Mullin, *Puritan as Yankee*, 128–29.

[22] Horace Bushnell, *Christian Nurture* (New York: Charles Scribner, 1861; reprint, Grand Rapids: Baker Book House, 1979) 90–122 (page numbers correspond to the reprint edition). See also Barnes, *Virtuous Republic*, 32–43.

of doctrine, did not consider Congregationalism the only legitimate church polity. Nevertheless, his lifelong participation in Congregationalism had ingrained in him certain habits of thinking about the structure of the church and society in general, particularly a habit of valuing both individual autonomy and mutual accountability.[23]

Unlike the Presbyterian system, which located the balance of power in the college of ministers (organized into a graded series of church courts), the Congregationalists located power in each local congregation. The members of a single congregation had the power to call ministers, write covenants, and make most of the decisions regarding the discipline of their members and ministers. A local Congregational church in Bushnell's day could run its own affairs with very little interference from outside.[24]

This is not to say that Congregational churches were entirely disconnected from each other. Even while maintaining a degree of autonomy, local churches sought to extend Christian fellowship and establish lines of mutual accountability. New England clergy occasionally gathered in synods, which formalized relationships between different congregations and produced general statements of faith.[25] The Congregational churches in Connecticut were especially inclined to establish systems of accountability. In 1708 they affirmed the Saybrook Platform, which set up a system of "consociations," or standing councils, made up of clergy and lay people from each of the churches in a given district. A consociation could, under certain conditions, discipline lay people and clergy of member congregations, and in such cases its decision was to be "final."[26] In theory, the polity of Congregational churches in Connecticut was virtually identical to

---

[23] Horace Bushnell, "Christian Comprehensiveness," in *Building Eras in Religion* (New York: Charles Scribner's Sons, 1881) 424–29.

[24] John Von Rohr, *The Shaping of American Congregationalism* (Cleveland: Pilgrim Press, 1992) 291–94.

[25] Walker, *History of Congregational Churches*, 162.

[26] Saybrook Platform, in Williston Walker, *The Creeds and Platforms of Congregationalism* (New York: Charles Scribner's Sons, 1893) 504.

Presbyterianism: the college of clergy, rather than the local congregation, had higher authority. In practice, the consociations rarely disciplined a minister. Power to discipline resided chiefly in the local congregations.[27]

Some of Bushnell's opponents sought, through the consociation system, to try him for heresy for statements he made in his book *God in Christ* and for his subsequent defense of those statements in a sequel, *Christ in Theology*.[28] When it appeared his opponents might succeed, Bushnell's congregation, evidently with his approval, broke relations with the North Hartford Consociation in 1852. However, Bushnell subsequently tried to mend fences with one of his chief opponents, Joel Hawes, pastor of First (Congregational) Church in Hartford. Thus Bushnell, throughout this episode, tried to balance both values of the Congregational system: the autonomy of the local congregation and the importance of extending fellowship between congregations and clergy.[29]

To belong to the Congregational Church had social, economic, and ethnic implications. As was the case with the Presbyterians, Congregationalists were generally relatively well-off. Also, with important exceptions, Congregationalists were of Anglo-Saxon heritage. Finally, though the number of Congregational churches in the American West was growing rapidly in Bushnell's day, Congregationalists were, for the most part, New Englanders.[30] When Congregationalists looked proudly back to their Pilgrim ancestors, they celebrated the founding not only of a religious institution but of

---

[27] Edwards, *Singular Genius*, 120.

[28] Ibid., 120–35. The Bushnell controversy was one of the "great theological donnybrooks of mid-nineteenth-century America" (Mullin, *Puritan as Yankee*, 151–79).

[29] Cheney, *Life and Letters*, 335–37.

[30] H. Richard Niebuhr, *The Social Sources of Denominationalism* (New York: Henry Holt and Company, 1929) 147–54. For an interesting reflection on African-American Congregationalism, see Stephen G. Ray, "The Remembrance of Integrity: African-American New England Congregationalists and the Politics of History," in *PRISM: A Theological Journal of the United Church of Christ* 14/1 (Spring 1999).

a godly society that was to serve as a model for old England and the world.

For Bushnell and for many others, New England was more than just a geographic location. It was a culture. To be a New Englander meant to share in a common history, to participate in a matrix of social institutions, and to espouse a particular set of values. Bushnell associated New England with strong educational institutions, with relatively democratic political and religious institutions that encouraged participation and individual freedom, with strict morality and piety tempered by a high regard for the individual conscience, with tightly knit communities—families, churches, and towns—that fostered mutual care and concern, and with a work ethic born out of life and labor on family farms.[31] Though Bushnell spent his career in Hartford, a commercial city, he looked back nostalgically to the agrarian village as the ideal community for cultivating moral character.[32] In helping to build the Hartford municipal park that still bears his name, Bushnell was seeking to bring some of the values of the farm and the village to the city: a healthy dose of the beauties of nature and the amity of the village green.[33]

Bushnell's interpretation of New England's values and institutions differed from those of some of his contemporaries, not to mention those figures of the past whom he lauded. Nevertheless, this regional pride (or chauvinism) was shared by many other New Englanders. For Bushnell and for others, American history began with the Pilgrims, and the New England values of freedom and mutual accountability were the values that created the United States and would make it a great nation.[34]

---

[31] Horace Bushnell, "The True Wealth or Weal of Nations," in *Work and Play*, 43–77; Bushnell, "Age of Homespun," in *Work and Play*, 374–408; Mullin, *Puritan as Yankee*, 11–17, 30.

[32] Barnes, *Virtuous Republic*, 25–29.

[33] Edwards, *Singular Genius*, 171–82.

[34] Joseph Conforti discusses the development of the New England regional identity in the nineteenth century in *Jonathan Edwards, Religious Tradition and American Culture* (Chapel Hill: University of North Carolina Press, 1995) 36–61,

It is a telling irony that despite the importance Bushnell placed on institutions, he himself was not much of a joiner. While his *Christian Nurture* became a classic text of the American Sunday school movement, Bushnell himself had little to do with the American Sunday School Union or any similar evangelical voluntary organization.[35] Bushnell seemed to abhor being hemmed into a predictable identity. In politics, he often spoke and wrote like a Whig, yet he called himself a Democrat up until the late 1850s, when he joined Lincoln's Republican party.[36] This irony was more than just a personal quirk. It grew out of a basic tension between two important values of his social orientation: unity and stability on the one hand and individual spontaneity and creativity on the other. Bushnell was similar to Hodge in that when he spoke about institutions, he combined a love of order with a love of freedom.

For Bushnell, institutions maintained order by defining social obligations. He believed that each individual is born into a web of institutions, of human relationships and moral obligations.[37] We do not choose most of the institutions to which we belong. We are also limited in how we define our roles within institutions. Despite his reputed theological liberalism, Bushnell adhered to some socially conservative notions.[38] For example, Bushnell laid great emphasis on

---

145–85. Laurel Thatcher Ulrich discusses Bushnell's contribution to the creation of the New England regional identity in *The Age of Homespun: Objects and Stories in the Creation of an American Myth* (New York: Vintage Books, 2001) 12–17.

[35] William R. Adamson, *Bushnell Rediscovered* (Philadelphia/Boston: United Church Press, 1966) 122.

[36] Barnes, *Virtuous Republic*, 47–48.

[37] Howard A. Barnes, "The Idea that Caused a War: Horace Bushnell Versus Thomas Jefferson," *Journal of Church and State* 16/1 (Winter 1974): 73–83. See also Bushnell, *Christian Nurture*, 96; and Bushnell, "Reverses Needed," in *The Spirit in Man: Sermons and Selections* (New York: Charles Scribner's Sons, 1910) 164–69.

[38] Fredrickson calls Bushnell "ultraconservative" (*Inner Civil War*, 133). Mullin says that Bushnell's "innovations were all motivated by a profoundly conservative desire to preserve the values and confidences of the world of his youth" (*Puritan as Yankee*, 4). See also Gary Dorrien, *The Making of American Liberal Theology: Imagining Progressive Religion, 1805–1900* (Lousiville KY: Westminster John Knox Press) 111–78, 398–402, acknowledges Bushnell's socially conservative

the duties of motherhood, and he disapproved of the notion of women forsaking those duties in order to assume traditionally male responsibilities such as voting or running civil governments.[39]

However, though Bushnell believed institutions set limits on individual choices, he did not believe that institutions totally overwhelmed the individuality and freedom of their members. In fact, one of the things Bushnell valued about the specific institutions he touted was that they encouraged personal freedom. He understood institutions to be evolving, fluid entities. Though he sometimes struggled to explain this belief philosophically, Bushnell affirmed that we have a degree of freedom to shape the institutions that shape us.[40]

As we shall see, Bushnell's institutional loyalties shaped his vision for an ideal society—a "virtuous republic"[41] that was in many ways similar to the free and orderly Christian society Charles Hodge envisioned. As was the case with Hodge, Bushnell's vision of society influenced his views on slavery and race; but Bushnell's distinct theological orientation influenced his social vision and his statements about slavery and race in distinct ways.

---

tendencies but still describes Bushnell as a formative figure in American liberal theology.

[39] Horace Bushnell, *Women's Suffrage; the Reform Against Nature* (New York: Charles Scribner, 1869) 51–53. In so doing, Bushnell may have been affirming a relatively new "cult of domesticity" and the separate "woman's sphere" that emerged in the U.S. in the nineteenth century with the rise of urbanization and industrialization, but he did not understand himself to be affirming something new. He believed he was affirming the traditional woman's role. See Nancy Cott, *The Bonds of Womanhood: "Woman's Sphere" in New England, 1780–1835* (New Haven: Yale University Press, 1977) 1–18.

[40] Barnes, *Virtuous Republic*, 17. Examples of Bushnell's flexible, evolutionary interpretation of institutions are in the discourses "The Growth of the Law," "The Founders Great in their Unconsciousness," and "The Doctrine of Loyalty," in *Work and Play*, 78–123, 124–66, 343–74.

[41] Barnes, *Virtuous Republic*, 160. See also below, pp. 157–161.

Bushnell on Slavery and Race

As was the case with Charles Hodge, Bushnell's general attitude towards slavery and race arose from a constellation of theological method, normative principles, anthropological assumptions, predominant loyalties, and interpretations of changing circumstances. In each area, Bushnell demonstrated that his and Hodge's different theological commitments were at the root of their differences on slavery and race.

Theological Method

Hodge and Bushnell differed chiefly in their theological methods, their different ways of assessing and interpreting sources of religious knowledge. In other words, the two had profoundly different ways of understanding how God speaks to people, and this had a profound effect on their different views on racial slavery.

Hodge, as we have seen, used a criteria for truth that was at least partly borrowed from the Common Sense philosophy of the Didactic Enlightenment. According to Hodge, God speaks to people in plain, rationally consistent language. More specifically, God speaks authoritatively in the inerrant facts and propositions of the Bible.

Bushnell, on the other hand, was at least partly influenced by the Romantic critique of the Didactic Enlightenment and believed that God speaks to the human emotions and the imagination as much as to the intellect. God speaks in metaphorical language that is much more opaque, multivalent, and paradoxical than Hodge would have it. Bushnell, like Hodge, understood God to speak in a unique and even authoritative way in the Bible, but Bushnell's interpretation of the Bible was more open-ended than Hodge's. Furthermore, Bushnell's method required him to be empathetic to all points of view and open to the spirit of truth in extrabiblical sources of knowledge.

From "Revelation" to God in Christ. Bushnell developed his theological method over time, beginning perhaps when as a student he first struggled through Coleridge's *Aids to Reflection.* His ideas found significant though only partial expression in "Revelation," a commencement address he delivered at Andover Seminary in 1839.[42] In 1843 Bushnell, profoundly affected by the death of his only son, Horace Apthorp Bushnell, began a quest for a more vital faith. One February morning in 1848 he found sudden inspiration, telling his waking wife that he had "seen...the Gospel."[43] That year he published an important article, "Christian Comprehensiveness," which dealt with methodological issues. He also delivered lectures at Harvard, Yale, and Andover Seminary that he would later develop into a book. The resulting 1849 work, *God in Christ*, would serve as the most thorough and controversial explication of his theological method.

With his radical and novel theological method, Bushnell believed he was liberating a living Christian faith from what he understood to be its deadly and divisive shell: the definitions of contemporary theologians, who attempted to reduce religious truth to consistent and static terms.[44] Bushnell construed religious truth as a dynamic force, a force that eludes the precise definitions of scientific theology but avails itself to human experience through the evocative power of poetry. In so doing, Bushnell eschewed the rationalistic Common Sense epistemology in which he and practically all other Anglo-American Protestant clergy of his day had been trained.[45] While Common Sense epistemology construed legitimate knowledge—including knowledge of God—to be rational, immediate, and perspicuous, Bushnell characterized legitimate

---

[42] Horace Bushnell, "Revelation," in David L. Smith, ed., *Horace Bushnell: Selected Writings on Language, Religion, and American Culture* (Chico CA: Scholars Press, 1984) 30–31.

[43] Bushnell, quoted in Cheney, *Life and Letters*, 191–93. Scholars give different accounts of Bushnell's biography and its influence on his theological method (see Mullin, *Puritan as Yankee*, 128–29).

[44] Edwards, *Singular Genius*, 97–109.

[45] Sydney Ahlstrom, "The Scottish Philosophy and American Theology," *Church History* 24/3 (September 1955): 257–72.

knowledge—especially knowledge of God—as affective, nebulous, and essentially undefinable.[46]

Language. An essential part of Bushnell's method was his theory of language. Language, according to Bushnell, can only partially describe and express truth, especially truth about God. While Common Sense philosophy placed great trust in the ability of language to convey even the most profound truths in clear, scientific terms,[47] Bushnell believed that the numinous world of the spirit could never be reduced to precise definitions.

Words—all words—are born out of the sensible world, according to Bushnell. All words, etymologically, refer to something one can touch or smell or see. The "second department of language," those "words of thought" that refer to abstract concepts, all refer metaphorically to sensible objects. In order to speak of ineffable truths, we have to assign them names from the physical world. The word "spirit," for example, literally means breath or wind. Such words have meaning because they evoke an experience in the people who use and hear them. When we speak of the "spirit" of the human being, we have a memory or a sense of the presence of the mysterious force that gives us life.[48]

Bushnell's theory of language made him skeptical of the value of hair-splitting logic and tolerant of contradictions. He argued that theologians who attempt to construct airtight, logical structures forget that their building materials are flawed from the outset. Religious language, because it is metaphorical, is indefinite and partly false. "Words of thought," wrote Bushnell, "…impute form to that

---

[46] Walter H. Conser, *God and the Natural World: Religion and Science in Antebellum America* (Columbia: University of South Carolina Press, 1993) 99–104.

[47] John W. Stewart, *Mediating the Center: Charles Hodge on American Science, Language, Literature, and Politics*, Studies in Reformed Theology and History 3/1 (Princeton: Princeton Theological Seminary, 1995) 52–53.

[48] Horace Bushnell, *God in Christ: Three Discourses, Delivered at New Haven, Cambridge, and Andover, with a Preliminary Dissertation on Language* (New York: Scribner, Armstrong & Company, 1903) 38–53.

which really is out of form."[49] Such language does not lend itself to scientific precision.

Because any set of words can only partially grasp the truth, Bushnell saw the need for many different terms to describe different aspects of the same profound mystery. When such terms logically contradict each other, they do not necessarily rule each other out. Contradictions only reveal the limited capacity of language to describe transcendent truth. In fact, one ought to seek out contradictions because they set in motion a dialectical process that results in a more comprehensive picture of truth. In order to grasp the truth, one must:

> multiply words or figures, and thus to present the subject on opposite sides or many sides. Thus, as form battles form, and one form neutralizes another, all the insufficiencies of words are filled out, the contrarieties liquidated, and the mind settles into a full and just apprehension of the pure spiritual truth. Accordingly we never come so near to a truly well-rounded view of any truth as when it is offered paradoxically; that is, under contradictions; that is, under two or more dictions, which, taken as dictions, are contrary to one another.[50]

Bushnell did embrace contradictions, and this led to his more controversial statements. For example, Bushnell wrote that, unlike other liberal Christians, he never took offense at the idea of proving his orthodoxy by ascribing to a statement of faith or "creed." To the contrary, he was ready "to accept as great a number as fell in [his] way." When he understood them according to his theory of language, even the most apparently incompatible creeds became "so elastic,"

---

[49] Ibid., 48.

[50] Ibid., 55. In "Christian Comprehensiveness," Bushnell also argued that the clash of "repugnant" ideas would result in a broader apprehension of truth. He held out the hope that the most antagonistic of Christian sects would one day embrace each others' contradictory doctrines (459).

and ran "so freely into each other," that he seldom had "any difficulty in accepting as many as are offered" him.[51]

The Bible. Bushnell's theological method affected his interpretation of Scripture. He did not reject the authority of Scripture. In fact, one of his purposes in a later volume, *Nature and the Supernatural, as together Constituting the One System of God*, was to argue that the Bible delivered a unique, supernatural, and authentic revelation. The Bible alone tells the story of the divine "character" of Jesus Christ, who is God's greatest and most effective form of self-expression.[52]

Nevertheless, Bushnell's theory of language implied a very fluid interpretation of the Bible and an open-ended understanding of its authority. Bushnell rejected the Common Sense, literalist method Charles Hodge and many other American Protestants upheld. Bushnell, unlike Hodge, did not construe the Bible chiefly as a catalogue of "facts" or perspicuous, objective doctrines. The Bible was not "a magazine of propositions." Rather, the Bible contained expressive language, "inspirations and poetic forms of life."[53]

For Bushnell, the truth the Bible conveys is not simply information, but rather a kind of aesthetic experience of the divine. The images of the Bible evoke "divine inbreathings and exhalations in us, that we may ascend into their meaning." This transcendent "meaning" cannot be reduced to precise, scientific definitions. In fact, according to Bushnell, the demands of truth do not require the Bible to be free from logical contradictions. Accordingly, a faithful interpretation of the Bible should aim not primarily for logical consistency but for evocative power. If we interpret the Bible according to Bushnell's method, "Our opinions will be less catechetical and definite, using the word as our definers do, but they will be as much broader as they are more divine; as much truer, as

---

[51] Bushnell, *God in Christ*, 82.

[52] Horace Bushnell, *Nature and the Supernatural: as Together Constituting the One System of God* (New York: Charles Scribner's Sons, 1903) 263–318.

[53] Bushnell, *God in Christ*, 93.

they are more vital and closer to the plastic, undefinable mystery of the spiritual life."[54]

In effect, Bushnell's method permitted him to make a broad distinction between the spirit of the Bible and its letter, and even at times to advocate a course of moral action that appeared to contradict the letter of some passages of Scripture. Furthermore, Bushnell found that the Spirit that "lived" within the language of Scripture continues to dwell within nature and in human history. In order to discern the Spirit, one has to be open to the truth that is available outside of the Bible.[55]

Reactions. Bushnell's *God in Christ* caused a fury among Congregational and other Protestant clergy, including Charles Hodge, who meticulously accused Bushnell of at least six heresies. Hodge attacked Bushnell's skepticism about language, saying Bushnell pushed a valid general theory (that language "is an imperfect vehicle of thought") to an absurd extreme: making language so unreliable that he ruined not only the possibility of scientific theology but all "confidence in the ordinary transactions of life."[56] Hodge claimed that Bushnell's poetic interpretation of the Bible was an attempt to turn it into "a cunningly devised fable" rather than a clear message about who God is and what God does. Hodge freely acknowledged that much of the language of the Bible is poetic and affective. But, Hodge insisted, whether the Bible uses propositional, or legal, or poetic language, it delivers the same, rationally coherent message: "The whole healthful power of the things of God over the feelings depends upon their being true to the intellect."[57] Hodge and

---

[54] Ibid.

[55] Bushnell spoke of this general, extrabiblical revelation when he said that "There is a logos in the form of things..." and that God "stands expressed everywhere, so that, turn whichsoever way we please, we behold the outlook of his intelligence" (*God in Christ*, 30).

[56] Munger, *Preacher and Theologian*, 144; Charles Hodge, "Bushnell's Discourses," *BRPR* 21/2 (April 1849): 265–69, 291.

[57] Hodge, "Bushnell's Discourses," 269.

Bushnell had significantly different methods of discerning the truth, and this affected their different views on slavery and race.

Method: Slavery and Race. Bushnell was still developing his theological method during part of the long period he spoke out on slavery and race. Even so, the influence of Bushnell's methodological assumptions on all his statements on slavery and race is evident, as are the ways those assumptions distinguished his policy from that of Charles Hodge.

First of all, Bushnell's method validated emotion as a source of knowledge. For Bushnell emotion was at least equal, if not superior, to reason as an organ of truth. While Hodge coolly censured abolitionists for supplanting rational, principled discussion with emotion-laden stories of the abuse of slaves, Bushnell respected emotion—sympathy and horror—as an important moral indicator. In order to truly understand slavery, according to Bushnell, one must "[d]raw out...the portrait of the domestic slave trade. Describe the disgusting scene of a slave purchase market. Portray the miserable slave-gang marching off to the far south-west, silent, weary, and sick at heart, for the wives and children left behind and never to be seen or heard again on earth."[58]

But Bushnell's method did more than just elevate the significance of affective experience. It allowed him to move beyond the impasse over slavery that the Common Sense, literalist method of biblical interpretation had created for American Evangelicals. In the Bible, Charles Hodge, like many of his Evangelical peers, discovered a set of consistent, inviolable rules written in plain language. Hodge sought to articulate a policy on slavery that was consistent with these rules.[59] Bushnell, on the other hand, rejected this kind of biblical legalism, blaming it for the fruitless debate between proslavery exegetes who "go to [the Bible] to get slavery authorized" and

---

[58] Horace Bushnell, *Discourse on the Slavery Question: Delivered in the North Church, Hartford, Thursday Evening, Jan. 10, 1839* (Hartford: Case, Tiffany, and Company, 1839) 8–9.

[59] See above, pp. 75-77.

abolitionists who, if they do not reject the authority of Scripture entirely, engage in "an obstinate, foredoomed exegesis" to show that "real slavery never was, and never was permitted, either in the Old Testament or the New."[60]

Over and against both these approaches, Bushnell held up an alternative method for discerning the will of God. His method permitted him to make a broad distinction between the spirit of the Bible and its letter and to discern the will of God in contemporary human experience as well as in the Bible. It reshaped the basic principles that undergirded his statements on slavery, enabling him—even compelling him—to take stronger stands than Charles Hodge did, not only against slavery but also in favor of suffrage for former slaves.

However, Bushnell's theological method did little to change and even encouraged his belief in African inferiority. For one thing, it cohered with an organic anthropology that, as we shall see, dovetailed easily with racial theories. For another, Bushnell's method forced him to be open to truth from all quarters and to engage every idea sympathetically[61]—even contemporary pseudoscientific ideas about African inferiority.

Principles

Different theological methods distinguished the basic principles, that guided Hodge and Bushnell's stances on slavery. This difference is evident in the language they used to define their rules as well as the ways they applied these rules. Hodge based his policy on what he understood to be a set of consistent "laws," which were stated in plain

---

[60] Horace Bushnell, *The Census and Slavery, Thanksgiving Discourse, Delivered in the Chapel at Clifton Springs, New York, November 29, 1860* (Hartford: L.E. Hunt, 1860) 18.

[61] Bushnell demonstrated the extent of his open-mindedness when he once instructed his congregation, "You must even be a Mahometan, a Jew, a Pagan,—anything to have a clear conscience." See "The Dissolving of Doubts," in Conrad Cherry, ed. *Horace Bushnell: Sources of American Spirituality* (New York: Paulist Press, 1985) 173.

propositional language in the Bible. Bushnell, on the other hand, articulated his principles in a way that cohered with his open-ended, idealist theological method. Bushnell's policy on slavery was guided not by a set of static "laws" but by something much more nebulous and dynamic: a divine "principle of virtue."

Bushnell imposed his own romantic and idealistic meaning on the "principle of virtue," a philosophical term that had fallen in to common parlance. For Bushnell, the "principle of virtue" could not be exhausted by any set of concrete laws. Rather, it finds partial expression in various legal systems at different times in history. This principle, which finds its highest personal expression in the character of Jesus Christ, is implicit in the moral codes, as well as the narratives and poetry of the Bible. It is also implicit in human experience in general, and especially in the moral progress that human civilizations have made under the influence of the gospel.[62]

The principle of virtue is one the human conscience intuitively apprehends and confirms, though human language consistently fails to give it adequate expression. Language can only describe aspects of this principle. It receives different expressions in different places and times. Even the Bible does not state this principle in explicit terms. Explicit laws, even those written in Scripture, only partially reflect the numinous principle of virtue. Such explicit "moralities of particular action" are mutable and fallible. They are couched in the language of, and accommodate the limitations of, particular cultures in particular times and places. For this reason particular legal codes,

---

[62] Bushnell first applied this "principle" to the problem of slavery in "Growth of the Law," an address he first delivered in 1843 (in *Work and Play*, 78). He expressed his most thorough application of this principle in *The Census and Slavery* in 1860. The idea of an ineffable "principle of virtue" cohered with Bushnell's general understanding of the tension between language and truth, an idea he first expressed in 1839 in "Revelation" and later in *God in Christ*. See Mullin, *Puritan as Yankee*, 63–68. For an early use of the term "principle of virtue," which is quite different from Bushnell's use of the term, see John Gay, "Dissertation Concerning the Fundamental Principle of Virtue or Morality (1731)," in the anthology *The English Philosophers from Bacon to Mill*, ed. Edwin A Burtt (New York: The Modern Library, 1939) 767-85.

even if they are biblical, should not be considered "eternal rules of society." Rather, they are the outward evidence of an invisible pattern of "growth," of moral evolution, that occurs within biblical history and in the history of civilization.[63]

Particular expressions of divine truth need not always be logically consistent in order to be authentic. Even a "positive statute of revelation," a biblical rule, "may lose its applicability" and be replaced by a "new rule contradictory to it in words" and yet remain faithful to the principle that inspired the old rule.[64] In fact, the limitations of human language and human understanding virtually require that such particular expressions of moral truth be inconsistent. Moral rules are meant to change—to evolve in the light of historical circumstances and under the guidance of the Holy Spirit.[65]

Bushnell was not a moral nihilist. He did believe that there were such things as absolute right and absolute wrong. He was skeptical of the capacity of human language, or human action, to grasp those principles in their purest form. He did believe, however, that human language and society could, over time and under the benign influence of the Holy Spirit, become progressively more capable of articulating and embodying these principles. Gradually, the explicit norms that guide the behavior of Christians and regulate Christian society would more closely approximate the divine principle of virtue: "there is a work of progressive legislation continually going forward, by which the moral code is perfecting itself."[66]

Bushnell's "principle of virtue" was at the same time more flexible and more demanding than were Hodge's biblical "laws." It allowed Bushnell to define the evils of slavery in harsher terms than Hodge used. It compelled him, once he had condemned slavery, to be

---

[63] Bushnell, *Census*, 19–20.
[64] Bushnell, "Growth of the Law," 100.
[65] Bushnell, *Census*, 19.
[66] Bushnell, "Growth of the Law," 92.

more forceful in his opposition and in his support of suffrage for former slaves.

Slavery as an Evil. Because Bushnell distinguished between the spirit of the Bible and its letter, and because he distinguished between the numinous divine "principle of virtue" and the concrete laws of the Bible, he was free to condemn slavery in more sweeping terms than Hodge used while avoiding the conundrum of whether or not the Bible, in explicit language, defined slavery as a *malum in se*, a sin under all circumstances.

Charles Hodge believed that biblical laws directly revealed the perfect will of God. As such, they could not authorize a practice that was necessarily evil. If the Bible did not condemn slavery *per se*—if, on the contrary, the God of the Bible permitted and regulated the institution—then slavery was *adiaphora*, of things indifferent—either good or evil depending on circumstances. Slavery, according to Hodge, was a restrictive institution that was, sadly, sometimes necessary in a fallen world (though society might avoid, ameliorate, or abolish it under the proper conditions). Slavery was, at worst, inappropriate under some circumstances. It was, at best, a salutary institution—one that educated slaves and prepared them for freedom.[67]

Bushnell, on the other hand, understood biblical laws to be an indirect reflection of divine perfection. In his view only the numinous principle of virtue was essentially pure. Particular laws, the "moralities of particular action," even biblical laws, could permit actions that were not necessarily free from the taint of evil. Bushnell believed that the God of the Bible could indeed, in accommodating the limitations of a particular time and place, give "'statutes that are not good [Ezekiel 20:25]'" when "they were the best the people were capable of." God makes "patient yieldings, here and there, to barbarism; doing always the best thing possible with men as they were, and then, as better things were possible, raising his standards

---

[67] See above, pp. 77–80, 88–89.

still higher to carry them on still farther."[68] Bushnell, like Hodge, acknowledged that certain passages of Scripture permitted the practice of slavery. Yet unlike Hodge he did not therefore feel compelled to define slavery as a potentially benign institution in order to defend God's goodness or the authority of the Bible.

Bushnell defined slavery as a practice that was basically harmful but not quite as detrimental as other practices. Slavery was a moral evil God had permitted as an accommodation to a barbaric age. This was a more profound definition of the evil of slavery than Hodge allowed for. Slavery, according to Bushnell, was not just a restrictive institution that was unfortunately sometimes necessary. He did not describe slavery as a morally acceptable means of controlling a group of people who were, as of yet, incapable of exercising personal freedom for the sake of the common good. Bushnell did not argue, as did Hodge, that slavery could under some circumstances legitimately restrain barbaric *slaves*.[69] Rather, slavery restrained barbaric *slaveholders*. For Bushnell, enslaving one's enemies was at best a relatively humane alternative to torturing or killing them. He contended that in biblical times God permitted slavery primarily as a means of ameliorating the evil inclinations of the powerful class.[70]

Bushnell's principles permitted him to define the *institution* of slavery as an evil, not just a particular practice of it. It was the "ferocity of *slavery*" as an institution, and not just the abuse of that institution, that hurt and demoralized both slaves and masters. Slavery, with its necessary imbalance of power, was in itself "a frightful system of legalized selfishness" that destroyed families,

---

[68] Bushnell, *Census*, 20.

[69] Charles Hodge, "Slavery," *BRPR* 8/2 (April 1836): 292.

[70] These were not Bushnell's exact words, but they convey his argument. Bushnell compared the Bible's permission of slavery to the Torah's permission of divorce: "Christ himself allows that the law gave husbands a right of divorce by their own act, doing it, 'because of hardness of hearts;' for the barbarity of the times was such that, if husbands were not permitted to put away their wives, they would only do what was worse and more shocking to get rid of them." Bushnell implied that slavery also was an institution God permitted in order to subvert other "worse and more shocking" crimes (*Census*, 19).

encouraged atrocities, and robbed human beings of themselves.[71] Bushnell, as we shall see, considered slavery a systemic evil that involved varying degrees of personal guilt. But whether or not Bushnell considered slaveholding to be a *personal* sin "in all cases, in every moment of its continuance," he did understand it to be an evil *social* practice.[72] Even the most humane slaveholders, who held slaves under the most difficult circumstances, could not rest assured of the moral purity of their acts or intentions.[73]

Abolition of Slavery and Suffrage for Former Slaves. Bushnell's principles not only permitted him to condemn slavery in more sweeping terms than Hodge, they also permitted—even compelled— him to be more direct than Hodge in calling for the practice's abolition and for suffrage for former slaves.

In the 1830s Charles Hodge supported African colonization and fretted about the dangers of immediate emancipation.[74] Horace

---

[71] Bushnell, *Discourse on the Slavery Question*, 7–8, emphasis original.

[72] Ibid., 5.

[73] Bushnell's moral definition of slavery developed over time. At first he seemed to imitate Charles Hodge. Apparently anxious to defend the integrity of the Bible, Bushnell made a distinction between the dehumanizing, abusive system of slavery that existed in the United States and "that institution endured or licensed under the law of Moses" (*Discourse on the Slavery Question*, 8). Similarly, in 1843 Bushnell wrote that the Torah's "permission [for the Israelites] to buy slaves of the nations round about" had "no permanent significance, except in showing that slavery is not in all cases and ages a necessary wrong" ("Growth of the Law," 94). However, even in his 1839 essay, Bushnell insisted that the target of his criticism was the "ferocity of *slavery*" itself, not just particular abuses of that institution (*Discourse on the Slavery Question*, 7–8, emphasis original). Eventually (by 1851) Bushnell moved toward a more consistent condemnation of the practice of slavery *per se*. Bushnell discovered that his theological method did not oblige him to make a distinction between bonded labor in the Bible and slavery in the South in order to defend the authority of Scripture (*Census*, 19–20). Even when reading the earlier statements, however, we can understand Bushnell to be maintaining a tension between the moral imperfection God permits in a particular barbarous era and the perfection of the "principle of virtue." In this case, it is not necessary to read even Bushnell's earlier statements as taking Charles Hodge's tack. Even in these early statements Bushnell was not necessarily defining slavery, even the kind of slavery the Bible permitted, as *adiaphora*, of things indifferent, or potentially benign.

[74] Hodge, "Slavery," 301.

Bushnell, meanwhile, had given up on the colonization scheme and called for the abolition of slavery. Though he criticized the tactics of Garrison and the abolitionists, and though his own political strategy was vague (as was Garrison's),[75] Bushnell still stated that there was no good moral reason for delaying abolition.[76]

After the Civil War, Bushnell called for suffrage for adult male former slaves. Unlike Hodge, Bushnell *was* a proponent of radical reconstruction. Hodge said he was in favor of the political enfran-

---

[75] Garrison, whose attitude toward secular government bordered on anarchy, discouraged his followers from engaging in conventional political action. Many strict Garrisonians refused to vote; see John McKivigan, *The War against Proslavery Religion: Abolitionism and the Northern Churches, 1830–1865* (Ithaca NY: Cornell University Press, 1984) 57).

[76] Bushnell, *Discourse on the Slavery Question*, 6–7, 24. Bushnell's 1839 *Discourse*, like all his writings, is sometimes vague and open to interpretation. Robert Bruce Mullin's reading of *Discourse* raises valid points, though my reading differs in places. Mullin emphasizes how Bushnell's early statements on slavery were typical of "Northern conservative rhetoric" (*Puritan as Yankee*, 212–213). He stresses Bushnell's criticism of abolitionists and his mildness toward Southern slaveholders. I argue that though Bushnell was critical of abolitionists, though he described slavery more as a social sin than a personal sin, and though he believed the North did not have the constitutional power to abolish slavery in the South, he was still stronger in his opposition to slavery than Northern conservatives like Charles Hodge. Bushnell himself said he wanted to prove "not…merely…the ferocity of *some men*, but…the ferocity of *slavery*" (*Discourse on the Slavery Question*, 8 [emphasis original]).

When Bushnell pointed out the most "odious" and inhuman aspects of slavery, he was not calling on Southerners simply to reform the institution but explaining that the institution is irreformable. Inhumanity is "necessary…as a part of the institution" of slavery, and it cannot be made more humane without "sweeping away the whole system down to its very roots" (Ibid., 6).

Bushnell does indeed suggest that Southerners might replace chattel slavery with other milder forms of bonded labor before the final total emancipation (Mullin, *Puritan as Yankee*, 212). However, I believe this suggestion originates from Bushnell's perceived legal inability of Northerners to impose their own plan for abolition on the South rather than from a positive affirmation of this policy.

Finally, Bushnell does say that Northerners may be legally obligated to help Southerners put down a slave revolt. He mentions this, however, not to "assure Southerners" of Northern support (ibid.) but to explain why Northerners have a right and a duty to say something about the immorality of Southern slavery. Because Northerners are legally entangled in the institution, Southerners have no right to say "we have nothing to do with it" (*Discourse on the Slavery Question*, 15).

chisement of former slaves, but he set no deadline for when this should happen. Bushnell, on the other hand, expressed that it should happen immediately, by military force if necessary.[77]

In both these instances, Bushnell's understanding of the "principle of virtue" proved to be at once more flexible and more demanding than the laws that guided Hodge's policies. On the one hand, Bushnell was free to articulate his moral principles without forcing them to agree with a rigid, legalistic interpretation of Scripture. On the other hand, he could hardly set limits on what his fluid and dynamic principles might demand of him in any given context.

For Bushnell, the principle of virtue was an evolving principle that was reaching progressively higher levels of expression as human society developed under the benign influence of the Spirit. It made sense to him that the principle should be more rigorous in one age than in another. In the past, biblical laws permitted slavery as an accommodation to a barbarism. In the present and in the future, the principle of virtue might demand the abolition of slavery and even the full political enfranchisement of former slaves.[78]

Bushnell likewise found clues for discerning the demands of the principle of virtue in current events. When he argued in 1839 that the time for the abolition of slavery had come, he was especially encouraged by the rise of democracies in Europe. He believed the tide of the times was rushing toward freedom.[79] After the Civil War, Bushnell, who saw racially based political discrimination as a residual of the national disease of slavery, portrayed the political enfranchisement of former slaves as the divinely-authorized sequel to abolition. He believed the United States owed it to those soldiers—particularly those African-American soldiers—who had died fighting against Southern slave power to take the next step in the

---

[77] Charles Hodge, "The General Assembly," *BRPR* 36/3 (July 1864): 542. Horace Bushnell, "Our Obligations to the Dead," in *Building Eras in Religion*, 352.

[78] Bushnell, *Census*, 18–21; Horace Bushnell, "Of Distinctions of Color," in *Moral Uses of Dark Things* (New York: Charles Scribner and Sons, 1867) 300–13.

[79] Bushnell, *Discourse on the Slavery Question*, 10.

"extirpation" of slavery from national life.[80] He even interpreted the suffering of the war dead in general, and of African-American veterans in particular, as vicarious suffering—suffering for the sake of others and for a just and loving purpose, analogous to the suffering of Jesus Christ. Bushnell's method did not force such an interpretation of events, but it made this interpretation possible. And once he committed to a particular interpretation of history, he was solemnly obligated to act on it. "Blasted and accursed," he wrote, "be the soul that will forget these dead."[81]

Bushnell's method allowed him, and even compelled him at times, to regard the moral lessons he derived from postbiblical history, or from his own experience, as seriously as Charles Hodge regarded biblical revelation. Part of the reason Hodge did not support abolition sooner or make black suffrage a higher priority was that the Bible did not with any specific mandate force him to do so. For him it was usually enough to do what the law requires, refrain from doing what it forbids, and refrain from forbidding what it permits. Hodge's legalistic biblicism had the effect of sparing him from surprising new religious obligations. For Bushnell, conversely, God's spontaneous action in history could potentially expand the limits of human moral obligation in unexpected ways.

Thus, unrestrained by biblical legalism, Bushnell was free to make a more direct condemnation of slavery and embrace a more active policy against the practice than Hodge. But even as Bushnell's theological method shaped his antislavery principles, it also brought with it certain assumptions that exacerbated his derogation of the African people.

Anthropological Assumptions: Organic Human Nature

Bushnell's theological method implied certain views of human nature—certain anthropological assumptions that significantly influenced his views on slavery and race. On the one hand, Bushnell

---

[80] Bushnell, "Obligations to the Dead," 352–55.
[81] Ibid., 354.

made some of the same conventional, traditional anthropological assumptions as Hodge. Like Hodge, Bushnell accepted the orthodox belief that all human beings share the same essential nature, and this belief played a role in his opposition to slavery.[82] However, Bushnell's anthropology had another unique emphasis: organicism. His organic anthropology, which was integral to his theological method, actually contributed to his opposition to slavery. At the same time it encouraged his racial assumptions, his theories of Anglo-Saxon superiority, and his predictions of African-American extinction.

Revivals and Christian Nurture. Bushnell's organic anthropology was a pervasive theme of his theology, but it found its most developed expression in his work *Christian Nurture*, which was published in several forms over a number of years from the 1830s to its final redaction in 1861.[83] This book, which helped create the modern American understanding of childhood, became a classic of religious and secular education as well as the only book by Bushnell to remain consistently in print to this day.[84]

Christian Nurture began as a critique of revivals. Congregational ministers of Bushnell's day generally saw a "revival" as a sign of divine blessing, an indication of successful ministry, and the normal means of bringing people into the church. A revival consists of a season of intense religious excitement in which large numbers of people confess their sins and commit their lives to Christ. When Bushnell tried and failed to produce a revival at North Church, he began to reflect critically on revival-oriented piety. The Christian life, Bushnell argued, should be more like a gradual ascent, but

---

[82] Bushnell opposed slavery because it did violence to the essential humanity of slaves. It did not recognize the slave as "a creature of conscience, a creature of immortal wants, a creature in God's image" (*Discourse on the Slavery Question*, 7).

[83] Bushnell's critique of revivals began with his article "Spiritual Economy of Revivals of Religion" in the *Christian Spectator* of 1838. This article was also included in *Building Eras in Religion*, 150–81. The Massachusetts Sabbath School Society published his book *Discourses on Christian Nurture* in 1847 but ceased distributing it when it became controversial. Bushnell self-published a revised and amended version the same year. The last revision was published in 1861.

[84] Edwards, *Singular Genius*, 294–95.

revivalism made it a constant succession of peaks and valleys. Furthermore, revivalists tended to make the adult conversion experience (a conscious, voluntary commitment to Christ) the sole means of entry into the Christian faith. In so doing they excluded a whole class of people who were as of yet incapable of such a confession: infants and young children.[85]

Instead of conversion, Bushnell proposed "nurture" as the ordinary initiation into Christian faith. In his view, "entry into the faith was less a momentous event than an elongated process, a life-long turning to God that was appropriately begun in earliest childhood under the influence of Christian parents."[86] Rather than suddenly becoming a Christian as an adult, with proper Christian nurture "the child is to grow up a Christian, and never know himself as being otherwise."[87]

Christian Nurture was, in part, a defense of the practice of infant baptism (as opposed to the exclusive practice of adult or "believer's" baptism) as a legitimate initiation into the Christian faith.[88] However, Bushnell's defense of this old Puritan doctrine contained a novel twist, an idea that happened to be a theme of the Romantic movement[89]: an overriding emphasis on the organic nature of human societies, especially the family.

---

[85] Ibid., 375–78.

[86] Elizabeth Nordbeck, "Christian Nurture Revisited," *PRISM: A Theological Journal for the United Church of Christ* 14/2 (Fall, 1999): 26.

[87] Bushnell, *Christian Nurture*, 10.

[88] H. Shelton Smith, *Changing Conceptions of Original Sin: A Study in American Theology Since 1750* (New York: Charles Scribner's Sons, 1955) 142–43.

[89] The organic nature of human society was an important theme for Friedreich Schleiermacher, especially in his understanding of original sin and of the communication of the Holy Spirit. See *The Christian Faith*, English trans. of the 2d German ed., ed. H.R. Mackintosh and J. S. Stewart (Edinburgh: T&T Clark, 1989) 279, 425, 560–65 (originally published in German in 1830). Bushnell, who did not read German, would have been familiar with some of Schleiermacher's ideas through the interpretation of John Daniel Morell, though Bushnell developed many of his ideas independently (Mullin, *Puritan as Yankee*, 97–98).

The Meaning of "Organism." Bushnell's use of the term "organism" as a metaphor for human society had a number of implications. First, Bushnell implied that human beings are not strictly individuals. We are each bound together in a web of solidarity. At times Bushnell spoke of the whole human race as an organism. He also spoke of smaller human societies as organisms. Various social organizations constitute distinct clusters of cells, each sustaining interdependent relationships with the others within the larger whole. The most basic and influential organic unit, according to Bushnell, is the family. Other social clusters—churches, governments, and even races—also constitute relatively distinct organic entities. These organic communities extend across time and space, connecting generations as well as contemporaries. Human history consists of the growth, life, and interaction of organic communities.[90]

Each organic entity—each family, church, nation, or race—is a whole greater than the sum of its parts. By calling these entities "organisms," Bushnell implied that they each are living creatures. Each whole has a distinct "spirit" that is encoded in its parts. Each individual member bears the distinct traits—virtues and vices—of the organic communities of which he or she is a part. The whole has a kind of personality. It has a kind of will and can take actions, which have consequences.[91]

By referring to human societies as organisms, Bushnell was also surrounding them with an aura of mystery. As is the case with all living creatures, one cannot entirely explain how organic communities come into being or what holds them together. An organic society is certainly not a voluntary association. People do not willfully create them. People are born into organic communities and formed by them. Organic communities are, in a sense, orders of

---

[90] Bushnell, *Christian Nurture*, 31, 90–122.
[91] Ibid., 104.

creation. Language with only faltering adequacy captures the ineffable spirit of an organic community.[92]

While organic communities are deeply rooted and enduring, they are not entirely rigid. Because they are living entities, they possess a degree of spontaneity. They can change and grow. Growth is generally a gradual process, however. If one attempts to force change suddenly on an organic community or its members, the results are often ineffective or dangerous to the health of the whole and of all its parts.[93]

Finally, our organic communities make us who we are. The family in particular shapes the personalities of its members. Bushnell believed the strongest influence on the individual personality was parental nurture. Parents transmit their values to their children from infancy. These values are transmitted in many subtle ways: not only consciously through language but unconsciously through attitudes and actions. Parents mold the "plastic" nature of children like wax.[94] The influence of family and other institutions continues beyond childhood: "We are never at any age so completely individual as to be clear of organic connections that affect our character."[95]

Bushnell believed that the moral influence of parents on children begins even before birth. The moral character of the mother affects

---

[92] For example, Bushnell said that the foundational documents of the United States, the Declaration of Independence and the Constitution, did not create or even adequately explain the spirit of the nation. These documents expressed, with only limited adequacy, the spirit of an organic entity, a unified people, which had been developing for many decades and continues to develop in North America. See "Popular Government by Divine Right," in *Building Eras in Religion, Literary Varieties, III* (New York: Charles Scribner's Sons, 1881) 286–318. See also Conrad Cherry, "Structure of Organic Thinking: Horace Bushnell's Approach to Language, Nature, and Nation," *Journal of the American Academy of Religion* 40/1 (March 1972): 13–18, and Mullin, *Puritan as Yankee*, 96.

[93] Revivals are often, though not always, contrived efforts to force growth, according to Bushnell (*Christian Nurture*, 59–63). One of the reasons Bushnell was critical of Garrison's style of advocating abolition was that Bushnell believed he attempted to force institutional change in an unnatural way (*Census*, 16).

[94] Bushnell, *Christian Nurture*, 239–41.

[95] Ibid., 95.

the child in the womb. The effects of one's moral character may extend to two or even three generations of his or her progeny.[96] Furthermore, the moral influence of the family goes even beyond nurture; it affects nature. Like other nineteenth-century thinkers, Bushnell believed that the acquired physical and spiritual characteristics of one generation can be inherited by the second.

Organicism and Individuality. Bushnell pushed the idea of the organic nature of human society to the extent that it raised a philosophical problem for him: to what extent are we free, self-determining individuals and to what extent are our actions determined by the organic communities to which we belong? If a person is thoroughly formed by his community, particularly his family, can he be held morally accountable for his actions?[97] Bushnell raised this question in a later essay. He answered with the assertion "that no human being is so far dominated" by the influence of his community "as to be wholly unconscious of wrong." There is an "everlasting, ideal principle of right" that extends across all human communities.[98] Bushnell maintained the idea of individual freedom and accountability alongside his emphasis on the organic unity of human society, but he did not completely resolve the tension between these two poles of his understanding of human nature.

Organicism and Nurture. Bushnell's organic anthropology was important for his argument in favor of nurture-centered, as opposed to conversion-centered, piety. His emphasis on the image of "growth" and development helped him make the case that the acquisition of Christian faith was a gradual process rather than a sudden transformation. His emphasis on the influential power of the

---

[96] Ibid., 227–33.

[97] Daniel Walker Howe, "The Social Science of Horace Bushnell," *Journal of American History* 70/2 (September 1983): 311, says, "In its way, Bushnell's scheme was almost as deterministic as the old Calvinist one: in place of God's bestowal of supernatural grace on his elect, he set the power of parents over their helpless, suggestible offspring."

[98] Horace Bushnell, "Of the Conditions of Solidarity," in *Moral Uses of Dark Things*, 147–48.

organic community helped him describe Christian faith as something that is transmitted (primarily and ordinarily) through family nurture rather than revival-oriented preaching. It was on the basis of the organic unity of the family that Bushnell made the case for infant baptism. He claimed that members of a family share a corporate identity, so much so that children share in the faith of their parents long before they are able to make any conscious confession of faith. Infant baptism is legitimate, according to Bushnell, because it is an outward affirmation of the faith that an infant already has by virtue of her organic unity with her parents. Bushnell argued that the organic connections between parents and children were the conduits not only of personality but even of sin and grace.[99]

Organicism and Method. Bushnell's organic anthropology and his theological method were implicitly connected. His organic model of human society was the natural means for communicating his particular conception of religious truth. According to Bushnell's thinking, truth is "organic." It is a vital whole that is greater than the sum of its parts. Truth is not an objective set of ideas that can be communicated through detached, rational explanation. It is a dynamic mystery that can only be known through subjective, interpersonal experience. It is a living system of ideas and habits that can not be separated from the historical communities in which it grows, lives, and bears fruit. Christian faith is not assent to an objective set of doctrines but a "life," an emerging "character," a subtle set of attitudes one learns by experience and through close contact with other Christians. The proper channel for this kind of truth is an organically connected community: a group whose members communicate, not primarily through words but through

---

[99] Bushnell, *Christian Nurture*, 110–19, 123–61. See also Daniel J. Earhart-Brown, "Baptism in the Theologies of Horace Bushnell, Charles Hodge, and John W. Nevin" (Ph.D. diss., Union Theological Seminary-Presbyterian School of Christian Education, 2001) 98–105.

mutual participation in a common life. Bushnell described the family (as well as other institutions) as such an organism.[100]

Organicism against Slavery. Bushnell's organic anthropology had important moral consequences. In a number of ways it contributed to his opposition to slavery. Viewed from a broad perspective, Bushnell's anthropology united the whole human race in a web of solidarity and mutual obligation. This enabled Bushnell to appeal to "common feelings of humanity" when he pleaded for the welfare of slaves.[101]

Bushnell's organic language also helped him define slavery as a systemic, institutional evil: a germ-like infection that got into a society's blood, defiling the character of each individual member and of that society's various institutions.[102] This helped Bushnell define slavery as a *social* sin while avoiding the conundrum of whether slavery was "always and everywhere" a *personal* sin. In his view the slaveholding society was a whole greater than the sum of its parts, an organic entity with its own vitality—even, in a sense, its own will. Slavery was a real sin committed by a real agent, but the agent was society as a whole, not necessarily each individual member. Some members of a slaveholding society, presumably those with more political power and greater consciousness of the wrongs of slavery, doubtlessly "incur great personal guilt." Others simply are "born into the institution, and it is one of the amiable and dutiful tendencies of human nature to approve or rest in the established habits and

---

[100] Cherry, "Structure of Organic Thinking," 3–20. The connection between Bushnell's theological method and his organic anthropology are especially evident in his "Unconscious Influence," in *Sermons for the New Life* (New York: Charles Scribner's Sons, 1871) 186–205. This sermon was originally delivered in 1846 (Mullin, *Puritan as Yankee*, 95–96).

[101] Bushnell, *Discourse on the Slavery Question*, 6.

[102] Horace Bushnell, *Crisis of the Church* (Hartford: Daniel Burgess and Company, 1835) 18–20, and "Barbarism the First Danger," in *Work and Play*, 249–51.

customs of ancestors."[103] In this way, Bushnell was able to account for the moral complexity of slavery as an institutional evil.

Organicism and Race. However, Bushnell's organicism also had a troubling aspect. It led to his essentialized understanding of race, his theory of Anglo-Saxon superiority, and his repeated predictions of African-American extinction.

Bushnell described the family as the most influential human community. He spoke of children as organically connected to their parents and of family connections as the conduits of human character (and even of sin and grace). He even argued that the family's influence on the individual worked antenatally across generations. All this resulted in his assuming that, to a large degree, the personality of each individual is determined by pedigree. From here it was a short step to speaking of humankind in terms of races and stocks. When one takes a closer look at Bushnell's organic model of the human race, one finds the larger web of human solidarity made up of many smaller networks. Among these subgroups were rigidly defined races.

Bushnell believed the Anglo-Saxon race to be the superior race. It was the one race to have the benefit of centuries of the right kind of nurture. It was the one race that was genetically equipped for cultural dominance in the United States. "Out of all the inhabitants of the world,...a select stock, the Saxon, and out of this the British family, the noblest of the stock, was chosen to people our country; that our eagle, like that of the prophet, might have the cedars of Lebanon, and the topmost branches of the cedars, to plant his great waters."[104]

Not only did Bushnell believe in Anglo-Saxon superiority, he also predicted African-American extinction. Though individuals might survive and thrive, the African race as a whole would be

---

[103] Bushnell, *Discourse on the Slavery Question*, 5. See also his *Census*, 20–21. Bushnell's understanding of slavery as a social sin is also implicit in his argument that slaveholders should not be excluded from the international Evangelical Alliance. See Horace Bushnell, "The Evangelical Alliance," *New Englander and Yale Review* 5/1 (January 1847): 105–106, 120; Mullin, *Puritan as Yankee*, 94–95.

[104] Bushnell, "The True Wealth or Weal of Nations," in *Work and Play*, 45.

gradually phased out of existence in America in the same manner as the American Indians and other "barbarous" peoples. Blacks were not capable of surviving in the United States as a free people. Slavery itself was keeping them alive, but after emancipation they would die out, just "as the herd will dwindle when the herdsman withdraws his care."[105]

Bushnell's odd combination of moral rigor and racial fatalism put him in an ironic position. He understood African Americans to be rational, moral creatures endowed with the same right to liberty and political participation as other people. At the same time, he depicted African Americans as tragically predestined for extinction due to their racial characteristics. He was at once obligated to defend their rights yet unable to avert their inevitable demise, which he believed would result from their attaining their rights: "Though it opens no very bright and hopeful prospect to the African race, [emancipation] will at least bring them to an acknowledgment of their manhood," Bushnell stated with resignation.[106]

Bushnell repeated this prediction many times up to, during, and (as we shall see) after the Civil War. In *Nature and the Supernatural* (1858), Bushnell argued that "No savage race of the world has ever been raised to civilization...by mere natural development." To the contrary, the "savage races" of Bushnell's day were "beings or races physiologically run down, or become effete, under sin; fallen at last below progress, below society, become a herd no longer capable of public organization, and a true, social life. It signifies nothing for such races to ask for more time; time can do nothing for them better than extinction."[107] In his *Census and Slavery* (1860), he stated, "I know of no example in human history, where an inferior and far less cultivated stock has been able, freely intermixed with a superior, to hold its ground. On the other hand, it will always be seen that the superior lives the other down, and finally quite lives it away. And

---

[105] Bushnell, *Discourse on the Slavery Question*, 14.
[106] Ibid.
[107] Bushnell, *Nature and the Supernatural*, 211.

indeed, since we must all die, why should it grieve us that a stock a thousand years behind, in the scale of culture, should die with fewer and still fewer children to succeed, till finally the whole succession remains in the more cultivated race?"[108]

In the 1861 edition of *Christian Nurture*, Bushnell wrote that it was the duty of Christians to spread the gospel, not primarily through evangelism but through the "out-populating power" of the "Christian stock," and that barring some miraculous intervention of providence, the white "Christian nations" would displace the "feebler" races even in the latter's own lands.[109] Bushnell stated his racial theories with important caveats, some of which we will explore later, but his basic message was one of Anglo-Saxon superiority and African-American extinction.

Organicism and Charles Hodge. Bushnell certainly was not the only white man in his day to divide the human race into rigid racial categories, or to believe in Anglo-Saxon superiority, or even to predict the extinction of the African race. He was, however, at least unusual in placing so much theological value on the "natural" conduits of race. His was a view of race that was part and parcel of his particular organic anthropology.[110]

---

[108] Bushnell, *Census*, 12.

[109] Bushnell, *Christian Nurture*, 195, 207.

[110] In 1813 American children read in their textbooks, "The religion of nature, the light of revelation, and the pages of history, are combined in the proof, that God has ordered that nations shall become extinct, and that others shall take their places," quoted in Martin E. Marty, *Righteous Empire: The Protestant Experience in America* (New York: Dial Press, 1970) 14. Even so, Bushnell's predictions of African-American extinction were unusual in that they were situated in the midst of protests *against* slavery. "Proslavery writers, of course, had often argued that Negro extermination was the inevitable consequence of emancipation and had used this prediction to make a case for slavery on psuedohumanitarian grounds"; see George M. Fredrickson, *The Black Image in the White Mind: The Debate on Afro-American Character and Destiny, 1817–1914* (New York: Harper and Row, Publishers, 1971) 155. Bushnell was also unusual in that he specifically denied the possibility of humanitarian action averting African-American extinction. He described extinction as the tragic but inevitable consequence of the progress of civilization. Finally, his predictions were also unusual in that used language that sounded social Darwinism

Charles Hodge differed from Bushnell in his general anthropological assumptions and his views on race. Hodge, in a review of the 1847 edition of *Christian Nurture*, accepted to a point Bushnell's organic model of human society and the family. However, Hodge criticized what he termed Bushnell's "naturalism." Hodge feared that Bushnell had virtually bound the grace of God to the organic conduits of the family. Bushnell seemed to claim that the grace of God not only *may* but *must* travel through these conduits. In this way, Bushnell appeared to reduce "the mighty power of God" to "some organic law."[111] Hodge stopped short of lending family and, by extension, race the same theological importance that Bushnell did.

This is not to say that Bushnell was more racist than Hodge. Such a statement would be nearly impossible to prove. Racism is a complex set of attitudes that are difficult to quantify. A person's racism might be gauged, not only by evaluating the opinions he holds or even the strange racial theories he expresses, but by his actions and particularly by his use of political and personal power. In many ways the African American had a better friend in Bushnell than in Hodge, not only because of his political stances but because of his respectful, egalitarian relationships with individual African Americans.[112]

Furthermore, Hodge used some of the same racial rhetoric that Bushnell did, even referring to the possibility that Africans might become extinct in America. But Hodge also set limits on his

---

twenty years before Darwin published his *Origin of the Species*. All these factors, however, still did not make Bushnell's racial extinction theory absolutely unique (ibid., 154–59).

[111] Charles Hodge, "Bushnell on Christian Nurture," *BRPR* 19/4 (October 1847): 522–24, 532. Hodge could also use organic language when speaking of the nation, but his use of the term was not tied to Bushnell's extended biological metaphor and his particular understanding of the organic influence of human society and the family on individual destiny; see J. Carwardine, "The Politics of Charles Hodge," in *Charles Hodge Revisited: A Critical Appraisal of His Life and Work*, ed. John W. Stewart and James Moorhead (Grand Rapids: Eerdmans Publishing Company, 2002) 252–53.

[112] Cheney, *Life and Letters*, 465–67; Bushnell, *Nature and the Supernatural*, 486–90; Edwards, *Singular Genius*, 55.

understanding of the significance of racial differences. Despite his acceptance of racial categories, he understood the grace of God to be a force that could level racial inequalities.[113] Despite his occasional musings about the bonds of "blood,"[114] Hodge admitted that questions about the destinies of races were ones that he "need not discuss"—beyond his jurisdiction as a theologian. If Hodge, on one occasion, raised the specter of the extinction of the African race on the American continent in an *ad hominem* argument for colonization, he did so because he believed extinction should be averted through humanitarian action.[115]

Hodge did not share Bushnell's commitment to a racial extinction theory. Hodge did not repeatedly present the extinction of a whole race of people as the tragic but necessary consequence of the progress of the gospel. Whether or not it can be proven that Hodge was "more" or "less" racist than Bushnell, it is the case that Bushnell indulged in certain religious theories about race that did not preoccupy Hodge, at least not to the same extent. Hodge was not driven to them by a commitment to an organic anthropology.

Predominant Loyalty: A Virtuous Republic

As was the case with Hodge, Bushnell's policy on slavery was shaped by his "predominant loyalty" to a social vision, one that grew out of his theological convictions and his abiding loyalty to the institutions that nurtured him. Bushnell's vision for an ideal Christian society was

---

[113] "Nothing is plainer from the teachings of Scripture than that all believers are one body in Christ, that all are the partakers of the Holy Spirit, and by virtue of their union with Him are joint and equal partakers of the benefits of his redemption; that if there be any difference between them, it is not in virtue of national or social distinctions, but solely of individual character and devotion"; this text is in a passage in which Hodge argues against the idea that "the Jews…are to be restored to their own land" before the second advent of Christ. See Charles Hodge, *Systematic Theology*, 3 vols. (New York: Scribner, Armstrong and Company, 1872; reprint, Grand Rapids: Eerdmans Publishing Company, 1997) 3:810 (page number corresponds to the reprint ed.). This

[114] Charles Hodge, "The State of the Country," *BRPR* 33/1 (January 1861): 3.

[115] Charles Hodge, "Emancipation," *BRPR* 21/4 (October 1849): 588, 595.

a "virtuous republic," that is, "a stable society of ladies and gentlemen in which each individual would be free to achieve his highest potential."[116]

The social visions Hodge and Bushnell pursued were actually quite similar. Both men tempered a love of freedom with a love of order. Both valued equality, but both tempered their egalitarian ideals with a relatively flexible elitism (and a relatively inflexible sexism). Both valued strong social institutions—governments, churches, and schools as well as families—which they believed would nurture the moral values in their members that would make them more capable of the responsible exercise of personal freedom. Both ascribed to a doctrine of social progress. Hodge and Bushnell both believed that a Christian society should allow for a progressively wider enjoyment of wealth, knowledge, virtue, social equality, and freedom. Finally, both saw slavery as ultimately incompatible with the social visions they espoused.[117]

Teleology against Slavery. Unlike Hodge, Bushnell's flexible theological method gave him greater freedom to define his social vision over and against slavery and to oppose slavery and "slave power" more directly. Hodge dealt with slavery and other moral problems with a "deontological" (rule-centered) moral orientation. He based his policy toward slavery on inviolable moral rules, which he derived from his commonsense interpretation of the Bible. Bushnell, on the other hand, had a "teleological" (goal-centered) moral orientation. He had both the freedom and the responsibility to articulate moral policy on the basis of practical consequences and to adapt moral rules in order to pursue a worthy goal. Hodge tended to evaluate the various aspects of Southern slavery on the basis of whether or not they cohered with biblical laws in *theory*. But Bushnell

---

[116] Barnes, *Virtuous Republic*, 160.

[117] For Charles Hodge's social vision, see above pp. 62–69, 86–91. For Horace Bushnell's vision see his "True Wealth or Weal of Nations," 43–77; *Crisis of the Church*, passim.; *Politics under the Law of God, A Discourse Delivered in the North Congregational Church, Hartford* (Hartford: Edwin Hunt, 1844) passim; and "Barbarism the First Danger," 226–67. See also Barnes, *Virtuous Republic*, 160.

evaluated the various aspects of Southern slavery on the basis of their consequences in *practice* and whether these consequences cohered with his goal of a "virtuous republic."

For example, Hodge pointed out that even those "atrocious" Southern slave laws, which mete out harsh punishments to slaves who commit crimes, acknowledge the humanity of slaves in theory: "by holding a slave responsible for his acts, suppose him to be a human being." Bushnell, on the other hand, argued that the more "humane" Southern slave laws, those that supposedly *protected* the life and limb of slaves against abusive masters, did not actually acknowledge the humanity of slaves because they did not guarantee that slaves could testify against their masters in court and therefore did not protect slaves in practice.[118]

Partly because of his teleological orientation, Bushnell was more forceful than Hodge in his opposition to Southern politicians and the influence they had on the national government. Slavery, for Bushnell, was not simply as involuntary servitude in the abstract. It was a concrete social practice with real social consequences. It was a hostile power, an institution with its own dynamic spirit—a spirit that opposed the values of the virtuous society he pursued. The political actions of slaveholding states were the effects of this demonic force as it sought to encroach on American (and New England) institutions. Bushnell evaluated these political actions less on the basis of the principles on which they were purportedly based and more on the kind of experience they generated and the consequences they entailed.

For example, Hodge prescribed obedience to the Fugitive Slave Law of 1850, saying that it theoretically cohered with biblical and constitutional principles.[119] Yet Bushnell attacked the law on the basis

---

[118] Charles Hodge, "Abolitionism," *BRPR* 16/4 (October 1844): 555; Bushnell, *Discourse on the Slavery Question*, 7.

[119] Charles Hodge, "Civil Government," *BRPR* 23/1 (January 1851): 125–31; Laura L. Mitchell, "Matters of Justice between Man and Man: Northern Divines, the Bible, and the Fugitive Slave Act of 1850," in *Religion and the Antebellum Debate*

of its practical consequences. Publicly Bushnell called the law unfit to be passed and unenforceable. Privately he promised to "violate and spurn" it.[120] Bushnell indeed objected to the law on the basis of the US Constitution, which he said protected only the right of slaveholders to reclaim their own slaves, not to force Northerners to catch fugitives for them. However, Bushnell understood the Fugitive Slave Law to be more than just the South's claim for protection of constitutionally recognized property. The intended consequences of the legislation extended beyond the principles on which it was purportedly based. The legislation sought to manipulate the experience and the interests of Northerners in order to destroy the Northern antislavery spirit: "It was meant to insult us, and crack the lash in our faces." The legislation sought to demoralize not only Northern law enforcement but ordinary Northern citizens, "conscientiously principled against slavery as a wrong," by enlisting them in "the Marshall's *posse*" to catch fugitive slaves. The legislation rewarded slave-catchers 10 dollars for each prisoner sent into slavery and only 5 dollars for each prisoner set free, creating a bias against protecting the innocent and in favor of propping up the institution of slavery.[121] Thus Bushnell, with his teleological orientation, exposed a host of potential evil consequences of the Fugitive Slave Law that Hodge passed over.[122]

Similarly, while Hodge stewed silently over the Kansas-Nebraska Act of 1854,[123] which repealed the Missouri Compromise, Bushnell publicly attacked it on the basis of its intended consequences. He called it an attempt by Southern politicians to weaken "the Northern iron." He saw it as one of a series of actions intended to impose "plantation attitudes"—slaveholding values—on the

---

over Slavery, ed. John McKivigan and Mitchell Snay (Athens: University of Georgia Press, 1998) 134–68.

[120] Bushnell, *Census*, 22; Horace Bushnell to Cyrus A. Bartol, 8 September 1851, quoted in Cheney, *Life and Letters*, 248–49.

[121] Bushnell, *Census*, 21–22.

[122] Hodge, "Civil Government," passim.

[123] See ibid., 115.

nation. He called on his listeners to resist such impositions and to punish Northern compromisers at the ballot box.[124]

Teleology and Race. In this way, Bushnell's teleological orientation freed him to oppose slavery and "slave power" in the name of social progress. At the same time, his organic anthropology affected his understanding of how social progress would happen, particularly the role race would play in bringing about his vision of a "virtuous republic." While Bushnell's ideal vision for society precluded racial slavery, it did not seem to have a place for the newly freed African-American people.

Part of the problem was that Bushnell's descriptions of this ideal society were culturally conditioned and parochial. He visualized it as a grand projection of a New England village. The more serious problem was that he depicted this society being created in and through the organic conduits of race. One could not enter this society without appropriating its values: an organic set of attitudes and habits that one was to absorb, virtually unconsciously, over a lifetime—primarily through family nurture. The Anglo-Saxon race had the benefit of generations of the right kind of nurture. The African race, sadly, had not. As a people they did not have the necessary strength of character to help create the virtuous society to which Bushnell aspired, or to thrive, or even to survive in such a society.

The creation of the virtuous society depended on the perseverance and purity of the properly nurtured "stock" of people. For this reason, Bushnell charged the US government with the responsibility of protecting the well-being of the nation by passing legislation to protect the biological purity of the Anglo-Saxon race. "Who shall respect a people," he said, "who do not respect their own blood?"[125]

---

[124] Bushnell, *The Northern Iron* (Hartford.: Edwin Hunt and Son, 1854) 28.

[125] Bushnell, "True Wealth or Weal of Nations," 63. This statement, made in a speech before the Society of Phi Beta Kappa at Yale in 1837, was probably not a direct affirmation of miscegenation laws that prevented marriage between blacks and whites. More likely, Bushnell was arguing in favor of legally restricting European

Historical Circumstances

Bushnell's theological method, his dynamic understanding of the principle of virtue, and his teleological orientation led him to conceive history as an evolutionary process that, though explosive and uneven, was gradually moving toward a higher degree of civilization and a wider dispersion of freedom. Like other Romantics, Bushnell conceived of history as the gradual actualization of an ideal.[126] Unlike Hodge, Bushnell was free to pursue this ideal without being confined to rigid legalistic obedience to the laws of the past, particularly those laws that permitted slavery. For Bushnell, the Spirit of history militated against slavery.

True, Bushnell criticized Garrisonian abolitionists, accusing them of poor tactics, bad exegesis, and "rudeness."[127] He also predicted that the gradual systemic influence of America's successful free institutions (like free labor) would do infinitely more than the agitation of the American Antislavery Society to vanquish slavery.[128] Nevertheless, as we have seen, in almost every circumstance Bushnell was more forceful and direct than Hodge in his opposition to slavery and his support of suffrage for former slaves.

History against Slavery. In his 1839 *Discourse on the Slavery Question*, Bushnell not only objected to the tactics of the Garrisonians, but also he, like Hodge, assumed that the Northern states lacked the constitutional power to coerce the Southern states to abolish slavery. Even so, he attacked slavery as directly as he could given the legal and tactical limitations he set for himself. As we have seen, Bushnell was brave enough to tell Southerners they had no moral excuse for perpetuating slavery any longer, he opposed remunerating slaveholders for emancipated slaves, and he criticized the colonization scheme.

---

immigration. Nevertheless, it illustrates the importance racial connections played in the realization of Bushnell's vision of a virtuous republic.

[126] See below, pp. 37–39.

[127] Bushnell, *Discourse on the Slavery Question*, 17.

[128] Bushnell, *Census*, 16.

In 1839 Bushnell, like Hodge, generally advocated abolition through moral persuasion rather than through political action. Even at this early date, however, Bushnell supported the legal abolition of slavery in the District of Columbia, which he believed was not Southern territory—a political measure Hodge never considered.[129] Also at this time, though he was unable to garner support from his colleagues, Bushnell attempted to call a special convention of Connecticut congregational clergy to meet in Hartford and prepare an antislavery address to the churches.[130]

In the 1850s, as we have seen, Bushnell unlike Hodge forcefully and publicly opposed both the Fugitive Slave Law and the Kansas-Nebraska Act. Also during this time, Bushnell added his name to those of forty-three Connecticut leaders in a letter to President James Buchanan protesting the use of Federal troops to restrain Free Soilers of Lawrence, Kansas, who had undertaken to establish their own (antislavery) local government.[131]

Bushnell's militant attacks on "the essentially immoral, or unmoral, habit of slavery" and slave power carried on throughout the Civil War. Bushnell construed the Southern rebellion as particularly wicked and the Union victory as particularly important. He cheerfully greeted a young member of North Church, home on leave from the Union Army, by saying, "Glad to see you, Metcalf. Killed anybody yet?" and added, "Time you had. That's what you went for." Bushnell, like Hodge, saw emancipation as a providential blessing of the war, even if the North's initial goal in the war was the restoration of the Union, not the abolition of slavery. However, as we have seen, Bushnell was more forceful than Hodge in calling for immediate suffrage for adult male former slaves.[132]

---

[129] Bushnell, *Discourse on the Slavery Question*, 15, 17–18.

[130] Edwards, *Singular Genius*, 53.

[131] Ibid., 200.

[132] Bushnell, "Reverses Needed," in *The Spirit in Man*, 175; William A. Clebsch, "Christian Interpretations of the Civil War," *Church History* 30/2 (June 1961): 212–22; Edwards, *Singular Genius*, 231; Bushnell, "Obligations to the Dead," 352.

History and Race. One might assume that the Civil War and its aftermath would transform Bushnell's notions of race. His crusading antislavery attitude during the war, along with his passionate advocacy of suffrage for former slaves after the war, seemed to contrast starkly with his previous statements. After the war, Bushnell expressed gratitude to the former slaves and other African Americans who had fought for the Union. He claimed that the newly reunited nation owed it to them to "see that every vestige of slavery is swept clean" by ensuring the political enfranchisement of former slaves. "We are bound, if possible, to make emancipation work well," he wrote.[133]

But did Bushnell really believe this was possible? Would the effort white Americans were to expend in order to put "the despised race...upon the footing of men"[134] effectively give the African-American people as a whole a place in American society? Or was the effort, though morally obligatory, also doomed to failure? Would the African-American people, despite all the efforts made on their behalf, still dwindle towards extinction? Did Bushnell's negative attitude toward the African race, and particularly his bleak predictions of African-American extinction, change over time?

The answer is yes and no, with an emphasis on no. Bushnell's understanding of history did little to ameliorate, and in some ways exacerbated, his rigid notions of racial differences and his bleak prognostications for the African race. Bushnell's understanding of the nation's moral obligation to former slaves caused him to press his imagination and his racial assumptions as far as he could in order to hold out the best hope for the future of the African people, either on the American continent or elsewhere. However, he could only push so far without rendering himself incoherent. This he was not willing to do. After the war, Bushnell essentially said what he had said before. He claimed that white Americans were morally obligated to do all they could to include the African people in American society, but he

---

[133] Bushnell, "Obligations to the Dead," 352.
[134] Ibid., 353.

doubted that these efforts would be successful. Evidence of the ambivalent progress (or lack of progress) in his racial attitudes can be found in his often misunderstood 1867 essay "Of Distinctions of Color," to which we alluded in the beginning of this chapter.

"Of Distinctions of Color": An Ambivalent Essay

In 1867 Bushnell published *Moral Uses of Dark Things*, a volume of essays that dealt with the age-old problem of evil: "Why does a supposedly good God permit such 'dark things' as disease, pain, bad government, the venom of the snake, or acute hunger?"[135] One essay, "Of Distinctions of Color," dealt with the hardships that resulted from racial differences, particularly the differences between the "white" European peoples and the "black" African race.[136]

This could well be the most bizarre and convoluted essay Bushnell ever wrote. In it he seemed to hold several opinions at once. At times he referred to Africans as an inferior, even hopeless people; but he also speculated that they might some day be superior to all other peoples. He repeated his condemnation of racial slavery and his support of African-American suffrage but he also made ambiguous references to the polygenetic theory of human origins, unintentionally lending credence to the idea that blacks were a separately created, inferior species of animal—less human than white people. Not only did Bushnell express ambiguous ideas in this essay, but he did so with a particularly erratic and eclectic style: picking up ideas, dropping them, later retrieving them in different contexts as well as moving from logical argument to poetic flourish to hypothetical fiction—even science fiction. Not surprisingly, different scholars have interpreted this essay to mean different things.

---

[135] Edwards, *Singular Genius*, 83. This volume began as a series of sermons in 1846, which Bushnell later collected and revised for publication. "Of Distinctions of Color" was a new essay in 1867.

[136] Bushnell, "Distinctions of Color," 296. For a longer analysis of this same essay see David Torbett, "Horace Bushnell and 'Distinctions of Color': Interpreting an Ambivalent Essay on Race," *PRISM: A Theological Journal for the United Church of Christ* 14/2 (Fall 1999): 3–24.

African Inferiority, Racial Extinction. Contrary to the claims made by some of Bushnell's modern supporters,[137] a careful reading shows he did not renounce his belief in African inferiority or his racial extinction theory in "Of Distinctions of Color." In this essay, Bushnell described black Americans as inferior. They labored under a vague "condition of immense disadvantage." Former slaves, "emancipated by the fortunes of war," would likely never be self-sufficient as a people in the United States. It was not just systemic racism that blocked African-American progress. Bushnell also referred to some interior flaw that will make African Americans "a prey to themselves."[138] Bushnell described this inferiority vaguely as physical,[139] moral, and intellectual.[140] At times he seemed to be describing only those individuals who were once slaves in the United States as inferior. At times he seemed to describe the whole African race in this way.[141] While he did not restate his racial extinction theory explicitly, in one particularly pathetic passage he dwelt on the apparently hopeless future for black people in America. One "cannot pass a little colored child on the street," he wrote: "...without sighing inwardly and sometimes with a moistening eye—'poor hapless one, what place or good possibility is there in the world for you? Growing up, you grow into what; for what can you be? Scarcely have you a right to be, or become, anything?'"[142]

Qualifications of African Inferiority. Yet while Bushnell did not drop his belief in African inferiority or renounce his racial extinction theory after the Civil War, he did articulate these theories with the same caveats he offered before. As he had in the past,[143] Bushnell affirmed and celebrated the universal essential human nature, "the

---

[137] Edwards, *Singular Genius,* 257–58.

[138] Bushnell, "Distinctions of Color," 296.

[139] Ibid., 306, 315.

[140] Ibid., 297, 298.

[141] Ibid., 296–97, 306.

[142] Ibid., 297.

[143] Bushnell had attacked slavery on the basis that slaves were human beings, created on the divine image. See Bushnell, *Discourse on the Slavery Question,* 7.

undersoul, the man, the everlasting, divinely moral personality" that undergirded the superficial but significant inequalities between races.[144] As he had in the past, he blamed African inferiority on environmental factors, particularly the demoralizing effect of slavery and other forms of white oppression: "the stigma we have ourselves put upon them by our wrong."[145]

Bushnell laid greater emphasis on these caveats in 1867 than he had in 1839, exerting all the effort he could to open up better prospects for the future of the African people. He showed himself open to the possibility that he might be wrong, even implying that his own racial prejudice might have skewed his judgements. He allowed that Africans, at least, lack the "dry revenge and prowling wolfishness" of American Indians. Africans may be like the Jews, Bushnell speculated, who, though "a generally disrespected race" were also "among the most talented, if not the very most, of all races of mankind."[146]

As he had in the past,[147] Bushnell allowed that a surprising intervention of divine providence might reverse the scenario of racial extinction. What he once spoke of briefly as a remote possibility he now spoke of at length as a hopeful scenario. The sovereign God might yet do surprising things with the African people. Bushnell argued that it "belongs to the genius of Christianity to prove itself by remarkable inversions of order, which it may well do here." The African race might be the locus of the "grand final chapter of inversion." Bushnell imagined that Africans would advance to the point that the world would look to them as prophets. Former slaves might yet establish a superior culture, but not in the United States where they suffer great disadvantages. "Perhaps they were allowed to be brought hither," Bushnell wrote, "that they might obtain conceptions of society and government for Africa, perhaps to open a

---

[144] Bushnell, "Distinctions of Color," 300.

[145] Ibid., 296. See also Bushnell, *Discourse on the Slavery Question*, 8–9.

[146] Bushnell, "Distinctions of Color", 297–99.

[147] Bushnell, *Christian Nurture*, 195, 207, and *Nature and the Supernatural*, 211.

way into the English tongue and its books, and so into the possibility of creating an Anglicized Africa."[148] Clearly even Bushnell's most hopeful prediction for Africans was tinged by Anglo-Saxon ethnocentrism.

Rigidity of Race. The problem for Bushnell was that race was an essential category. It is true that he did not bind the sovereign will of God to the fortunes of a particular race. While he assumed that God had and would continue to favor the Anglo-Saxon race, he was willing to concede that God could possibly work redemptively through another race, even the African race. But this very caveat draws attention to the general problem of Bushnell's rigid and insuperable notion of race. Yes, God can work redemptively through one race as well as another, but even God must work through the organic conduits of race and not outside of them. While Bushnell affirmed that all human beings of all races share the "unreducible diamond of the moral nature,"[149] he still subdivided the human family into rigid racial categories. Bushnell did not suggest that membership in the Christian community dissolved the boundaries of race. Much less did he approach the twentieth-century critique that the notion of distinct races is an ideological construct and not an essential truth.

According to Bushnell, history flowed through the organic, biological conduits of family, and therefore through the organic conduits of race. The spirit of history could not destroy the channels through which it flowed. Race was an aspect of the natural system, which God chose to create and work through. Racial differences were a set of barriers that even God could not remove, though God could work surprising results within them. Bushnell's emphasis on race, so intimately bound to his particular theology, is not totally excused by

---

[148] Bushnell, "Distinctions of Color," 314–17.

[149] Ibid., 301. One might say Bushnell believes that certain solidarities are greater and more important than the solidarities of race, but these greater solidarities never dissolve racial differences. In "Of Distinctions of Color," Bushnell argues that one's membership in the human race is of greater moral significance than one's membership in a particular race, but he never lets go of the idea that particular races are distinct subgroups within the greater network of human solidarity.

his being a man of his time. Charles Hodge, as we have seen, stopped short of lending family and race the same theological importance that Bushnell did.

"Open-mindedness" and the Polygenetic Theory. Bushnell's flexible understanding of revelation and his openness to new forms of truth, rather than helping him modify his rigid views of race, led him down a path of confusion and ambiguity regarding the "polygenetic theory" of human origins.

Bushnell's "comprehensive" method affected how he dealt with any novel or challenging idea his contemporary culture produced. He had to be open to new ideas, especially the new ideas of science. Even when he did choose to attack an opponent, he did not rely on objective authorities, or dogmatic assertions, or even strict logic. Rather, he used a rhetorical style that appealed to the imagination and the emotions of his auditors. Such a style required Bushnell to empathize even with his opponents. It often resulted in a fluid interplay of ideas that leant a degree of validity to his opponents' views, even when his opponents were promoters of pseudoscientific theories of African inferiority. Bushnell disagreed with the "American school" of ethnologists, who claimed that the different races were separately created species. But in "Of Distinctions of Color," Bushnell engaged these opponents so sympathetically that his misled many readers into thinking that this opponents' views were his own.

For example, delving briefly into science fiction, Bushnell encouraged his readers to imagine a hypothetical species of apes, "hairy and wild creatures to look at," with human-like morals, culture, and intelligence. Though "not physiologically descended from the stock of Adam," these creatures would be not "a whit less human." Furthermore, Bushnell argued, if these hypothetical "mere animal creatures of the forest" could demonstrate their humanity, how much more has the African race already done so? Thus he attempted to demonstrate that moral and intellectual qualities, rather than blood kinship, define human nature.[150]

---

[150] Bushnell, "Distinctions of Color," 302–304.

At another point Bushnell conceded that he was less troubled by the existence of the polygenetic theory than the "morally bad uses that are made of it." He went on to suggest that Africans might benefit more in terms of self-esteem from the polygenetic origins theory than from his own monogenetic origins theory. Bushnell said that if he were black, he would prefer to think of himself as a member not of a deteriorated form of the white race but of "an original race, not yet raised by culture to their true pitch of power and possible eminence." Bushnell speculated on the possibility that it might be "God's plan to finish the race last, and set them upon the summit, when their day shall come, as the topstone of all righteous peace, and most inspired religion."[151]

It is important to note that never once in these fanciful diversions did Bushnell infer that Africans were animals or that they were created separately from other peoples, but his convoluted argument has led many critics, including some friendly ones, to assume that this is exactly what he did.[152] Like the liberal educator he was, Bushnell tried to make his point with imagination and empathy for his opponents' views. However, he demonstrated that such a method can be confusing and tainted by potentially insulting racial stereotypes.

However ambivalent Charles Hodge was on the subject of slavery, he was clear in his rejection of the polygenetic theory. With his dogmatic, direct, and rational style, he did not confuse his readers

---

[151] Ibid., 307–308. With this singular turn of argument, Bushnell anticipated twentieth-century black nationalists, like Wallace Fard and the Nation of Islam, who also sought to empower African Americans by construing blacks and whites as the products of separate creations, though of course Fard claimed that Africans were created first. See Mattias Gardell, *In the Name of Elijah Muhammad: Louis Farrakan and the Nation of Islam* (Durham NC: Duke University Press, 1996) 59. That Bushnell could approach this anachronism while at the same time holding to his nineteenth-century Anglo-Saxon prejudices is a testimony to the territories his free-ranging imagination could take him in a single essay.

[152] Cross, *Minister to a Changing America*, 41–49; Fredrickson, *Inner Civil War*, 44–45; Cole, "Bushnell on the Slavery Question," 20; Edwards, *Singular Genius*, 257–58. Luker corrects these mistaken interpretations (408–16).

to the point of making them believe he agreed with the American school and its exclusion of Africans from the human species.

In sum, Bushnell's attitude toward race, just like his moral stance on slavery, cohered with his general theological commitments. To restate our thesis, Horace Bushnell's particular constellation of theological method, normative principles, anthropological assumptions, predominant loyalties, and circumstantial considerations enabled and inspired his opposition to slavery and his post-Civil War support of African-American suffrage. This same constellation also enabled and inspired him to embrace theories of Anglo-Saxon superiority and African inferiority.

It is tempting for Bushnell's supporters to consider his racial attitudes to be accidental to his general thought—to suggest that one may remove a prophetic kernel from its profane husk. One scholar argues that Bushnell was ahead of his time in many ways; if only he had thoroughly pursued all the "prophetic" implications of all his ideas, "his theology of the organic growth of humanity, of God's use of family, and of language," he would have overcome the bigoted racial assumptions of his contemporaries, just as he challenged their theological assumptions.[153] As we have seen, however, every one of Bushnell's "prophetic" ideas—his organic model for human society, his emphasis on the family, and even his open-ended theological method with its particular theory of language—all contributed to his essentialized construal of race and his persistent theory of the extinction of the African people on the American continent. Ironically, the same theological ideas that enabled and even compelled him to attack slavery also enabled and encouraged his Anglo-Saxon racism.

With Hodge, we have a reverse irony. The same rigid biblical legalism that encouraged him to defend slavery *per se* as morally permissible also put him in a position of defending the essential unity and equality of all races. His opposition to slavery, such as it was, was based on the inescapable biblical "fact" of human unity and equality.

---

[153] Weeks, "Bushnell on Black America," 41.

In fact, Hodge's biblicism may have set limits on his own personal racism. The next chapter will further explore these mirroring ironies and their legacies.

4

Hodge, Bushnell, and Their Legacies

Charles Hodge and Horace Bushnell were neither Garrisonian abolitionists nor proslavery fire-eaters. They were both moderate opponents of racial slavery, even though they also harbored some racial prejudices. They both understood the Civil War to be primarily a war to preserve the Union, yet they both welcomed the abolition of slavery as a providential blessing of the war. When viewed from this broad perspective, they had much in common with each other and with many other Northern Protestant clergy of their day.

Yet if we narrow our focus and look at the particular stances they took over time, we see a difference in their attitudes toward slavery and race. We see on the one hand Charles Hodge, whose opposition to slavery took an indirect route. For much of his career he was primarily concerned with countering the abolitionist argument that all slaveholding was a sin *per se*. Southern slaveholders regarded him as an ally. His articles were reprinted and redistributed throughout the South.[1]

The other side of his attitude toward slavery, that it was not an essentially good institution—that it should in a civilized Christian society eventually be discarded—passed virtually unnoticed until the polarizing sectional conflict over slavery drew out its implications.

---

[1] Hodge, with typical naivete, understood the popularity of his essay "Slavery" in the South to be a sign that most Southerners agreed with his opinion that slavery was not "itself a good." See Charles Hodge, "West India Emancipation," *BRPR* 10/4 (October 1838): 609n.

Hodge showed himself to be a moderate opponent of slavery, if only by contrast to those increasingly vocal supporters of the institution. After the Civil War, despite his former support of African colonization and despite his misgivings about radical reconstruction, Hodge showed himself to be, at least in theory, a proponent of political equality for former slaves in the United States.

Horace Bushnell, on the other hand, saw the institution of slavery itself as essentially evil. Bushnell came out, sooner and more forcefully than Hodge, against slavery, against colonization, and in favor of full citizenship for former slaves. But even as he opposed slavery and supported radical reconstruction, Bushnell predicted the extinction of the African people on the American continent. He later modified but never really renounced this racial extinction theory, a theory Hodge did not share.

Many factors were at the root of Hodge and Bushnell's different policies toward slavery and their differing attitudes toward race, but an essential factor was theology. Each man had a distinct set of religious beliefs. These beliefs formed two coherent systems of thought. They shaped the ways in which Hodge and Bushnell negotiated the options their culture presented for responding to the problems of slavery and race.

Central to Hodge's policy was his theological method, his understanding of authoritative sources of knowledge. It was Hodge's high regard for the Bible that kept him from denouncing slavery as a sin *per se*. It is true that, all beliefs about the Bible aside, Hodge, the former slaveholder, had other reasons for finding such a denunciation unattractive. Nevertheless, he made a strong case that, while adhering to his Common Sense, legalist interpretation of the Bible, one could not successfully make the abolitionist argument that the employment of slave labor was always wrong.

Hodge's moderate opposition to slavery was also grounded in his theological orientation—his belief in the essential unity of humankind and the universal human right to "the means of improvement." These beliefs were confirmed by and implicit in his theological method. Hodge made excuses for racial slavery as a *temporary* institution, but he could not excuse a system that *permanently* denied a whole group of people access to the means of improvement on the basis of race. Despite Hodge's many racial prejudices, he opposed slavery in the United States on the ground that it was *racial* slavery; it singled out a particular race for permanent social inequality.

Bushnell's position on slavery and race was also grounded in his theological method. It is true that his opposition to slavery may have also been based partly on his "New England chauvinism"—his loyalty to a society that had long ago rejected slavery, partly for moral and partly for economic reasons.[2] But whatever mixed motivations Bushnell had, he also had a solid theological foundation from which to oppose slavery. His method freed him from the literalistic, legalistic interpretation of Scripture that Hodge and so many other of Bushnell's contemporaries espoused. It permitted—even compelled—him to take his own moral sentiments and his own reading of history as a kind of divine revelation, similar to the revelation in the Bible. While such a method does not necessitate an antislavery stance, it did enable Bushnell to build up an argument against slavery while avoiding a number of unacceptable alternatives: engaging in a "foredoomed exegesis" in order to prove that the Bible literally forbade slavery, rejecting the authority of the Bible entirely, or defending slavery *per se* in order to defend the integrity of Scripture, a trap that ensnared not only Charles Hodge but a number of other Northern evangelicals.[3]

---

[2] George M. Fredrickson, *The Inner Civil War: Northern Intellectuals and the Crisis of the Union*, 2d ed. (Chicago: University of Illinois Press, 1993) 46. In his antislavery message, Bushnell reminded his congregants, "you are the sons of New England"; see Horace Bushnell, *Discourse on the Slavery Question: Delivered in the North Church, Hartford, Thursday Evening, Jan. 10, 1839* (Hartford: Case, Tiffany, and Company, 1839) 31.

[3] Mark Noll, "The Bible and Slavery," in *Religion and the American Civil War*, ed. Randall M. Miller, Harry S. Stout, and Charles Reagan Wilson (New York/Oxford: Oxford University Press, 1998) 43–44.

However, while Bushnell's method enabled him to take a stronger stance against slavery, it also entailed an anthropology that leant a theological importance to race. Bushnell's organicism—his idea that human beings are enmeshed in and formed by particular organic communities, by their biological families and (by extension) races—was integral to his theological method. This anthropology enabled him to speak of human beings as locked into particular, inexorable racial destinies. Even many of Bushnell's friendly critics cannot deny the fact of his racism and the connection between Bushnell's use of racial categories and his organic anthropology.[4] Furthermore, Bushnell's openness to truth from all sources implied an openness to nativist, racist attitudes of the nineteenth-century United States.

Thus, theology truly had a formative effect on Hodge and Bushnell's views on slavery and race. The proof of the integrity of their theological presuppositions lay in the difficulties they caused. Hodge and Bushnell's views on racial slavery were each distinctly awkward. In each of their stances, one can see their theological commitments locked in conflict with other presuppositions. One can see how their theological assumptions led them to draw different conclusions than they would have otherwise drawn, had they different beliefs.

Hodge appeared to believe in racial equality almost in spite of himself. In his first major article on slavery, he found himself in the position of defending the possible establishment of an integrated, biracial, egalitarian society in the United States, even though he personally found such a social arrangement unlikely and even unattractive. Hodge was forced, at times, to allow his belief in the

---

[4] Howard A. Barnes, *Horace Bushnell and the Virtuous Republic*, American Theological Library Monograph 27 (Metuchen NJ: Scarecrow Press, 1991) 34; David L. Smith, *Symbolism and Growth: The Religious Thought of Horace Bushnell* (Ann Arbor MI: Edwards Brothers, Inc., Distributed by Scholar's Press, 1981) 74; Glenn Alden Hewitt, *Regeneration and Morality: a Study of Charles Finney, Charles Hodge, John W. Nevin, and Horace Bushnell* (Brooklyn: Carlson, 1991) 134.

biblical doctrine of the unity of humankind to set limits on his "commonsense" racial assumptions.

With contradistinct irony, Bushnell adhered to rigid racial categories in spite of himself. These unyielding categories became a burden to him, yet he could not let them go. Once Bushnell had built up a structure of assumptions, theories, and predictions about certain races, he could not easily disassemble it. He was compelled by his sense of right to resist slavery and fight for the political rights for former slaves. Yet at the same time Bushnell appeared hopeless, or at least very doubtful, that these efforts to help the African-American people would bear fruit. He was too committed to the idea that God's grace works slowly through the natural, organic channels of family and race. This process had taken centuries to elevate the Anglo-Saxon race to its state of excellence. The African people could not hope to catch up. The most likely scenario was that they would be phased out of existence on the American continent, replaced by the superior race. Even when, as in his post-war "Of Distinctions of Color," Bushnell tried to imagine an extraordinary act of providence—a "remarkable...inversion" that would result in Africans establishing a superior culture—he could only do so within the confines of rigid racial categories.

Both Hodge and Bushnell left significant intellectual legacies, which we can only glance at briefly. Yet even this limited purview allows us to see that the different aspects of their ambivalent views on slavery and race were part of their particular legacies.

Two decades after the end of the Civil War and African-American slavery, Charles Hodge's nephew, Presbyterian minister J. Aspinwall Hodge, tenaciously defended the African colonization scheme using frankly racial language: "For reasons not clearly understood by us, God has divided men into races, and through all time he has kept these great families distinct...Amalgamation of the three great races is not God's will and has never received the mark of His approbation. Loyalty to race, which holds them apart, is a divinely implanted instinct...the African race must and ought to remain...a distinct people."[5]

J. A. Hodge represented one aspect, but not the only aspect, of his uncle's legacy. He signified Charles Hodge the colonizationist, who assumed that Africans were generally incompetent for freedom, who assumed that whites had the right and responsibility for deciding what was to be done with former slaves, who assumed that the United States was an Anglo-Saxon nation, who cringed at racial "amalgamation," and who supported African colonization as a solution to America's racial problem for most of his career.

But just as there were two aspects of Hodge's attitudes toward race, there are at least two aspects of the legacies of these views. There was an important part of Hodge's views on race that his nephew did not emphasize: Hodge's belief in the unity of humankind, which set limits on the validity of any speculations about the importance of "loyalty to race." This orthodox doctrine formed the basis of Hodge's moderate opposition to slavery. For his students, who spelled out the idea in more radical terms than their teacher did, the doctrine of the unity of humankind served as a weapon in the struggle against racism and racial oppression.[6] For the frontier editor Elijah Lovejoy, human unity and equality necessitated the immediate abolition of slavery.[7] For the Presbyterian pastor and activist Francis Grimké, it necessitated the end of racial discrimination in the United States.

Grimké, a former slave, was born in 1850 in Charleston, South Carolina, the son of a black slave and her white master. After the Civil War brought him freedom, Francis went North, eventually to

---

[5] J. Aspinwall Hodge, *America and Africa* (Washington DC: American Colonization Society, 1888) 7, quoted in Andrew E. Murray, *Presbyterians and the Negro—a History* (Philadelphia: Presbyterian Historical Society, 1966) 82.

[6] In addition to Elijah Lovejoy and Francis Grimké, see Benjamin Breckinridge Warfield, "On the Antiquity and Unity of the Human Race," *Princeton Theological Review* 9/1 (January 1911): 1–25.

[7] John Gill, *Tide without Turning: Elijah Lovejoy and Freedom of the Press* (Boston: Starr King Press, 1958) 30–33 et passim.

attend Lincoln and Howard Universities and, in 1875, Princeton Theological Seminary (thanks in part to the generosity of his aunts, the famous abolitionists Sarah and Angelina Grimké, formerly of South Carolina). The aging Charles Hodge remembered Grimké as "equal to the ablest of his students"[8] and Grimké remembered encountering little if any racial prejudice at the seminary.[9] After graduating, Grimké served Fifteenth Street Presbyterian Church in Washington, DC, except for a two-year hiatus, until his death in 1937.

Grimké was nicknamed "the Black Puritan" because so much of his preaching focused on personal morality and the Protestant work ethic. In a manner reminiscent of Hodge, Grimké encouraged his African-American congregation to improve themselves—morally, intellectually, and materially—in order to rise in American society and effect racial equality. But Grimké was also a realist who knew that no amount of black self-improvement could achieve justice without structural change. He was one of the founders of the National Association for the Advancement of Colored People and was a supporter of the uncompromising civil rights advocate W. E. B. Dubois. He was a critic of the former slave Booker T. Washington, whose program for "elevating" the African-American people focused almost exclusively on self-improvement and who accommodated a degree of racial discrimination.[10] From his pulpit in Washington, Grimké spoke out fearlessly against any form of racism he could uncover—disparaging his local presbytery for tolerating racial segregation, exposing and denouncing the practice of lynching in the South, and protesting the segregation of the armed forces in World War I.[11]

---

[8] James McCosh, quoted in Francis Grimké, *The Works of Francis Grimké*, 4. vols., ed. Carter G. Woodson (Washington DC: Associated Publishers, 1942) 1:x.

[9] Grimké, *Works of Francis Grimké*, 1:526.

[10] Grimké, *Works of Francis Grimké*, 3:8.

[11] For Francis Grimké's struggles against racism, see Darryl M. Trimiew, *Voices of the Silenced: The Responsible Self in a Marginalized Community* (Cleveland: Pilgrim Press, 1993) 49–62; Louis Weeks, "Racism, World War I and the

At the absolute center of all Grimké's antiracist arguments was his belief in the unity of humankind—the idea that all human beings are essentially similar and essentially equal in God's eyes: "With God a white skin carries no more weight than a black skin, or skin of any other hue."[12] Hodge, the colonizationist, might not have agreed with Grimké's radical social application of the principle of human equality. Even so, Grimké's stance was in line with Princeton's affirmation of the essential unity of the human species. Grimké articulated the principle in classic Princetonian language—on the basis of an infallible Bible, viewed through the lens of the moderate Enlightenment.[13] Grimké even used Princetonian language against Princeton Theological Seminary when he denounced his beloved alma mater ("not only the oldest, but the greatest of our theological schools") for adopting a policy of racially segregating dormitories. "Things have...changed" since he attended and lived with white students in the dormitories, he wrote.[14]

The basic difference between Hodge and Grimké was one of perspective. Grimké understood American racism from the victim's point of view. This resulted in a more thorough criticism of the distortions of white prejudice, a more truthful assessment of the competence of the African-American people, and a more realistic understanding of the evils of any form of legal or popular racial discrimination. Grimké, the strict biblicist, might have had difficulty

---

Christian Life: Francis Grimké in the Nation's Capital," in *Black Apostles: Afro-American Clergy Confront the Twentieth Century*, ed. Randall K. Burkett and Richard Newman, 57–75 (Boston: G. K. Hall, 1978); Henry Justin Ferry, "Francis James Grimké: Portrait of a Black Puritan" (Ph.D. diss., Yale University, 1970) passim; and Clifton E. Olmstead, "Francis James Grimké (1850–1937): Christian Moralist and Civil Rights," in *Sons of the Prophets: Leaders of Protestantism from Princeton Seminary*, ed. Hugh T. Kerr (Princeton: Princeton University Press, 1963) 161–75.

[12] Grimké, *Works of Francis Grimké* 1:480.

[13] Ibid., 319–23. This is not to say that Princeton was the only influence on Grimké. He also drew inspiration from abolitionists like Frederick Douglass (ibid., 34–80) and Sojourner Truth (ibid., 513).

[14] Ibid., 526.

answering Hodge's argument that the employment of involuntary servitude was not a sin *per se*. However, Grimké would no doubt find fault with Hodge's presumption that African Americans were temporarily "incompetent" for freedom or that slavery could ever serve as a tool for "improving" and educating slaves for freedom and political equality with whites. However, despite their different perspectives, the continuity between Hodge's anthropological assumptions and Grimké's is clear. Grimké represents an aspect of the Princeton legacy.

Horace Bushnell's most prominent legacy was the Social Gospel movement of the late nineteenth and early twentieth centuries. Among the leaders of this movement were liberal Christian theologians and pastors like the Congregationalists Washington Gladden (whose installation sermon Bushnell preached) and Josiah Strong. Probably the most famous and eloquent spokesman for the movement was Walter Rauschenbusch, whose theology bore the imprint of his eleven-year pastorate at Second German Baptist Church in the Hell's Kitchen district of New York City.[15]

The goal of the Social Gospel movement was to realize the Kingdom of God on earth: to bring an end to social injustice through the redemption of individuals and social institutions, to heal the systemic evils, especially the evils of unbridled industrial capitalism, that corrupted individuals and society as a whole. In pursuit of this goal, Rauschenbusch and other proponents of the Social Gospel established a pattern of church-based social activism that was to endure for generations.[16]

Bushnell, who told his parishioners they had a moral obligation to become rich,[17] may not have joined in Rauschenbusch's

---

[15] For Walter Rauschenbusch, see Doris Robinson Sharpe, *Walter Rauschenbusch* (New York: MacMillan, 1942) passim, and Paul M. Minus, *Walter Rauschenbusch: American Reformer* (New York: MacMillan, 1988) passim.

[16] Robert T. Handy, ed., *The Social Gospel in America* (New York: Oxford University Press, 1966) 3–16.

[17] Bushnell, "Prosperity our Duty," in *The Spirit in Man: Sermons and Selections* (New York: Charles Scribner's Sons, 1910) 135–58. Bushnell believed,

condemnation of capitalism. But the connection between his ideas and the Social Gospel are clear. The image of human society and human history as a set of organically connected institutions, the idea that human actions have far-reaching consequences within the vast web of human solidarity, the notion that sin and evil—as well as grace and redemption—are transmitted through organically connected human communities, the image of human history as an evolutionary process in which God is immanently present—all these themes of Bushnell's thought are also themes of the Social Gospel.[18]

The ambivalent aspects of Bushnell's views on race and slavery are also present in the Social Gospel. On the one hand, the Social Gospel movement affirmed Bushnell's emphasis on political equality, along with his understanding of the social nature of sin and salvation. These elements of the Social Gospel had a direct influence on the struggle for racial justice in America. Martin Luther King, Jr. wrote that Rauschenbusch's *Christianity and the Social Crisis* left "an indelible imprint on my thinking by giving me a theological basis for...social concern."[19]

However, the other side of Bushnell's attitude toward race also left an imprint on his intellectual legacy. Proponents of the Social Gospel inherited Bushnell's organic anthropology. They also inherited his propensity to be open to the insights of contemporary science. These tendencies are evident when Rauschenbusch and other Social Gospel advocates adopt Bushnell's habit of categorizing humankind into races or "stocks."

"Contemporary science" in the late nineteenth and early twentieth centuries was virtually synonymous with Darwinian evolution and social Darwinism. While the success of Darwin's theory ended serious discussion of the polygenetic theory of human

---

however, that personal wealth should be used for the common good. See also Barnes, *Virtuous Republic*, 44–46.

[18] Walter Rauschenbusch, *A Theology for the Social Gospel* (New York/Nashville: Abingdon Press, 1945) 131–45 et passim.

[19] Martin Luther King, Jr., *Stride toward Freedom: The Montgomery Story* (New York: Harper and Brothers, Publishers, 1958) 91.

origins, it did not do away with pseudoscientific racism. In fact, as the history of the twentieth century would show, the influence of pseudoscientific racism was just beginning. As did the polygenecists of the earlier nineteenth century, social Darwinists used contemporary science to prop up theories of Anglo-Saxon superiority. Most notably, the philosopher Herbert Spencer applied the idea of survival of the fittest to human races and asserted the essential superiority of the "Aryan" race.[20]

Ironically, Bushnell himself criticized Darwin's theory of evolution, seeing it as an entirely materialistic system that left no room for God.[21] Nevertheless, Bushnell's organic understanding of human nature, his emphasis on the influential power of the biological family, and his understanding of history as an evolutionary process meshed comfortably with social Darwinism. Bushnell's racial extinction theory, which he presented years before Darwin published his *Origin of Species*, certainly seemed like a social application of the notion of "survival of the fittest."

Bushnell's successors in the Social Gospel movement inherited his organic anthropology and his general openness to modern science but not his qualms about Darwinism. Rather, they embraced Darwinian evolution, applying a particularly optimistic idea of evolution to all areas of life.[22] Despite their sympathy with the weak and vulnerable, Social Gospel theologians were not immune to some of the more ruthless aspects of social Darwinism, including its racial applications. Sticking out like a sore thumb in Rauschenbusch's long

---

[20] J. C. [Josiah] Nott, a Southern member of the "American school" ethnologists, quickly adopted and adapted the Darwinian theory to serve a racist agenda. See Nott, "The Problem of the Black Races," *DeBow's Review* ns 1/3 (March 1866): 266–70, and "Instincts of Races," *New Orleans Medical and Surgical Journal* 19 (1866): 1–16, 145–56, quoted in William Stanton, *The Leopard's Spots: Scientific Attitudes Toward Race in America, 1815–59* (Chicago: University of Chicago Press, 1960) 187. See also Thomas F. Gossett, *Race: The History of an Idea in America* (Dallas: Southern Methodist University Press, 1963) 145–52.

[21] Robert L. Edwards, *Of Singular Genius, of Singular Grace: A Biography of Horace Bushnell* (Cleveland: Pilgrim Press, 1992) 206–207.

[22] Sharpe, *Walter Rauschenbusch*, 5.

list of the evils of unbridled capitalism is the accusation that American corporations had imported "cheap and docile labor" from the south and east of Europe: "They have burdened our cities with an undigested mass of alien people; they have lowered the standard of living for millions of native Americans; they have checked the propagation of the Teutonic stock; they have radically altered the racial future of our nation; and they have set a new destiny for our national religion."[23]

While Rauschenbusch's awkward references to race are rare, other Social Gospel thinkers were more forthright with their racial theories, especially Josiah Strong. A Congregational minister and missionary from Ohio, Strong was an outspoken critic of "the blight of the cities and the vast ranges of social injustice which industrialism and exploitation were creating."[24] However, Strong also "advocated the rapid territorial expansion of the United States based on Darwinism, Protestantism, and the supposed superiority of the Anglo-Saxon 'race.'"[25] In his *Our Country*, which virtually laid the ideological groundwork for American colonialism, Strong predicted a time when the world would

---

[23] Rauschenbusch, *Christianizing the Social Order* (New York: MacMillan Company, 1912) 278. Racial assumptions may also have been one of the causes of the typically optimistic Rauschenbusch's despair at racial conflict in the American South, which "for years has seemed to me so tragic, so insoluble, that I have never yet ventured to discuss it in public." Though at last Rauschenbusch did affirm that "no solution will satisfy the Christian spirit of our united nation which does not provide for the progressive awakening of hope and pride for the individual Negro and the awakening of race pride and race ambition in all Negro communities"; see *The Belated Race and the Social Problem* (N.p.: American Missionary Association, n.d.), quoted in Sharpe, *Walter Rauschenbusch*, 166.

[24] Sydney Ahlstrom, "New Introduction to the Reprint Edition," in Josiah Strong, *The New Era, or The Coming Kingdom* (New York: Baker and Taylor Company, 1893; reprint, Hicksville, NY: Regina Press, 1975) 3i–5i (page numbers correspond to the reprint edition).

[25] Michael LaRosa and Frank O. Mora, eds., *Neighborly Adversaries: Readings in U.S.-Latin American Relations* (Lanham MD: University Press of America, 1999) 21.

...enter on a new stage of its history—the final competition of races, for which the Anglo-Saxon is being schooled. ...Then this race of unequaled energy, with all its majesty of numbers and the might of wealth behind it—the representative, let us hope, of the largest liberty, the purest Christianity, the highest civilization—having developed peculiarly aggressive traits calculated to impress its institutions upon mankind, will spread itself all over the earth. And can anyone doubt that the result of this competition will be the survival of the fittest?[26]

Thus we see a tendency toward racial thinking among Social Gospel proponents that was, if nothing else, an awkward blemish on the broad and inclusive picture of justice they upheld. While Strong (and certainly Rauschenbusch) would never deny that people of African descent were human beings and merited equal and just treatment, Strong (and to a lesser degree Rauschenbusch) had difficulty finding a place for the African-American (or any other dark-skinned) people as a whole in the redeemed society he imagined. Bushnell was not the only influence who contributed to this ambivalence, but it was an ambivalence he shared. It was an ambivalence that his theological ideas did not resolve but rather encouraged. There is at least a continuity of thought in the racial attitudes of Bushnell and those of later proponents of the Social Gospel.

---

[26] Josiah Strong, *Our Country*, rev. ed. (New York: Baker and Taylor Company, 1893; reprint ed., Cambridge: Belknap Press of Harvard University Press, 1963) 213–14 (page numbers correspond to the reprint edition). Strong differed from other racial thinkers in that he did not disapprove of racial "amalgamation." He believed the Anglo-Saxon race had and would continue to strengthen itself by biologically absorbing other races.

Conclusion

Lessons for the Future

So what lessons might twenty-first-century Christian theologians learn from this case study of Hodge and Bushnell, of liberal and conservative Protestantism, and of slavery?

One is simply the extent to which racist assumptions influenced both of these Northern opponents of slavery. They both assumed the inferiority of African-American slaves. They both speculated in a condescending tone on "what to do for them."[1] Apparently neither ever thought slaves themselves might have something to say about their situation, their needs, and their future. To read Hodge and Bushnell and the writings of many of their peers is to have a new and sympathetic understanding of the argument of James Cone in his *Black Theology of Liberation*: "American white theology…has been basically a theology of the white oppressor."[2] In fact, one might write a whole book just on the ways in which Hodge and Bushnell's judgements about slavery and race were influenced by their racial prejudices.

But this is not the only lesson to be learned from these men. Every theologian has labored, to a certain extent, under the limitations and prejudices of his or her age. Hodge and Bushnell raise the question, to what extent can one's theological method transcend those limitations? Their examples show us the possibilities and

---

[1] Horace Bushnell, "Of Distinctions of Color," in *Moral Uses of Dark Things* (New York: Charles Scribner and Sons, 1867) 296.

[2] James Cone, *A Black Theology of Liberation* (Marynoll NY: Orbis, 1996) 4.

dangers implicit in two distinct, enduring methodological orientations.

Hodge, the "conservative," prescribed strict obedience to the Bible, which he understood to be a transparent objective standard. His literalistic, legalistic interpretation of the Bible led him to conclude that slaveholding cannot be a sin "per se." It made his discussion of slavery one of abstract principles rather than of real human experience. It led him, at least for many years, to tolerate an institution that created an extreme imbalance of power, with many evil consequences even he acknowledged, on the grounds that it was biblically sanctioned. It diminished the moral significance of human experience, particularly the suffering of African-American slaves.

Bushnell's "liberal" open-ended theological method freed him from an inerrantist interpretation of the Bible and its authority. It freed him to make judgements based on his belief in a dynamic and immanent religious truth. Bushnell was free to take human experience (including the suffering of slaves) seriously, and to adapt rules (even apparent biblical sanctions) for the sake of relieving human suffering. This enabled him to condemn slavery as essentially evil despite the Bible's apparent permission of slavery.

However, Bushnell's method also entailed an organic anthropology that dovetailed with a kind of racial fatalism. He believed that we human beings are all enmeshed in and formed by our particular organic communities, by our biological families and (by extension) our racial pedigrees. Logically speaking, organicism does not necessarily and inevitably lead to racism, but this is a direction in which it might lead. In Bushnell's case it did. This in itself is a lesson to twenty-first-century Christian theologians, who in fact employ the organic metaphor for human society a great deal. Feminists, liberation theologians, ecologists, and others commonly affirm the "connectedness" of the human family.[3] While the use of this metaphor is certainly valid, Bushnell's example admonishes us to use

---

[3] Marjorie Suchocki, "Weaving the World," *Process Studies* 14/2 (Summer 1985): 76-86.

it carefully—to be aware of what the "connections" are, to consider what kind of cultural assumptions go into the construction of any particular model of human solidarity.

Perhaps the more disturbing problem with Bushnell's theological method is that it put him in the position of always being "open to new ideas," especially the new ideas of science. But in Bushnell's day, the "new idea" that had gained the respect of the scientific community was the polygenetic theory of human origins, a theory that divided the human family into rigid racial categories. "In times past," wrote one polygenecist, "historians...treated mankind as a unit," but "this delusion is now passing away, and a change is coming 'over the spirit of our dream.'" Now, enlightened people "talk of races—their physical and psychical peculiarities—their fitness for certain forms of government—their capacities for moral and intellectual culture—their true positions in the social scale."[4] Racial prejudices were old, but scientific racism was a new thing in the nineteenth century. And it would survive, in different forms, until its culmination in a "final solution" in twentieth-century Europe.[5]

Bushnell, with his open-ended understanding of the source of truth, lacked an objective standard with which to challenge these racial theories. Even when making the most basic point, that Africans really are human beings, he appealed mainly to the subjective, affective experience of his readers. In effect, he asked the rhetorical questions, even if blacks and whites are separately created species, can we not tell in our hearts that they are both equally human? Does our experience not affirm that blacks and whites share the same moral nature?[6] This approach was dangerous in two ways. For one, it was so roundabout that many readers never understood what he was saying.

---

[4] J. C. [Josiah] Nott, "Diversity of the Human Race," *DeBow's Review* 10/2 (February 1851): 113–14.

[5] George M. Fredrickson, *The Black Image in the White Mind: The Debate on Afro-American Character and Destiny, 1817–1914* (New York: Harper and Row, Publishers, 1971) xvii, 320–32; Yehuda Bauer, *A History of the Holocaust* (Danbury CT: Franklin Watts, 1982) 40–47.

[6] See above, pp. 169–172.

More disturbingly, Bushnell put the African people in the position of proving their humanity by appealing to the subjective emotions of whoever was observing them.

In 1902 Tom Dixon, Jr., a Baptist minister from Shelby, North Carolina, published *The Leopard's Spots*, an extraordinarily popular "romance of the white man's burden." In the wake of his success, he vowed to devote the rest of his life to preaching against "the black ape." His other white supremacist novels, *The Clansmen* (1905), *The Traitor* (1907) and *The Flaming Sword* (1939) followed. How would Dixon answer Bushnell's rhetorical question? Would Dixon say that, based on his experience, he knew that blacks and whites were equally human? Would not some observers, guided by their racial prejudices, look at the African people and see something more bestial than even Bushnell saw? Is this not exactly what happened, both during Bushnell's day and afterwards?[7]

This weakness of Bushnell's approach leads one to appreciate Hodge's appeal to a dogmatic standard. One sees the need for a theological method that draws a line in the sand, saying "hitherto shalt thou come, but no further." At least Hodge did not confuse his readers about where he stood on the polygenetic theory of human origins. At least he did not mislead his readers into thinking he believed Africans were not human beings. Hodge's dogmatism set limits on the kind of propositions he could ever seriously consider accepting. It may even have set limits on his own racism.

A comparison of Hodge and Bushnell confirms the need for Christian theology to rely on some objective standard, some kind of special revelation that stands over and against any human subjective judgement. Of course, many difficult questions arise. What would that standard be? On what would its authority be based? How do we

---

[7] H. Shelton Smith, *In His Image, but...Racism in Southern Religion, 1790–1810* (Durham NC: Duke University Press, 1972) 274–77. Dixon's novels were the basis for D. W. Griffith's film *Birth of a Nation*, which has been described as a major stride for cinema and for the cause of racism. See Thomas Cripps, *Slow Fade to Black: The Negro in American Film, 1900–1942* (New York: Oxford University Press, 1977) 41–69.

articulate it and the limits it sets? Can it set limits and also allow a degree of freedom to value knowledge culled from human experience—especially the experience of human suffering? Can any standard allow for this kind of freedom without becoming totally compliant, thereby losing its force? The answer to these questions is beyond the ken of this essay, but they are the questions a comparison of Hodge and Bushnell raise, and they are questions that will continue to preoccupy Christian theologians well into the present century.

Works Cited

Primary Sources: Horace Bushnell

Books and Pamphlets

Bushnell, Horace. *Building Eras in Religion*. Volume 3 of *Literary Varieties*. New York: Charles Scribner's Sons, 1881.

———. *The Census and Slavery, Thanksgiving Discourse, Delivered in the Chapel at Clifton Springs, New York, November 29, 1860*. Hartford: L. E. Hunt, 1860.

———. *Christ and His Salvation: In Sermons Variously Related Thereto*. New York: Charles Scribner, 1864.

———. *Christian Nurture*. New York: Charles Scribner, 1861. Reprint, Grand Rapids: Baker Book House, 1979.

———. *Crisis of the Church*. Hartford: Daniel Burgess and Company, 1835.

———. *Discourse on the Slavery Question: Delivered in the North Church, Hartford, Thursday Evening, Jan. 10, 1839*. Hartford: Case, Tiffany, and Company, 1839.

———. *Forgiveness and Law, Grounded in Principles Interpreted by Human Analogies*. New York: Scribner, Armstrong, 1874. Republished, with supplementary notes, as *Vicarious Sacrifice*, volume 2. New York: Charles Scribner, 1877.

———. *God in Christ: Three Discourses, Delivered at New Haven, Cambridge, and Andover, with a Preliminary Dissertation on Language*. New York: Charles Scribner's Sons, 1903.

———. *Moral Uses of Dark Things*. Volume 2 of *Literary Varieties*. New York: Charles Scribner, 1905.

———. *Nature and the Supernatural: as Together Constituting the One System of God*. New York: Charles Scribner's Sons, 1903.

———. *The Northern Iron, a Discourse Delivered in the North Church of Hartford, on the Annual State Fast, April 14, 1854*. Hartford: Edwin Hunt, 1854.

———. *Politics under the Law of God, A Discourse Delivered in the North Congregational Church, Hartford*. Hartford: Edwin Hunt, 1844.

———. *Sermons for the New Life*. New York: Charles Scribner's Sons, 1871.

———. *Sermons on Christ and His Salvation*. New York: Charles Scribner's Sons, 1876.

———. *Sermons on Living Subjects*. New York: Scribner, Armstrong, 1872.

———. *The Spirit in Man: Sermons and Selections by Horace Bushnell*. New York: Charles Scribner's Sons, 1903.

———. *The Vicarious Sacrifice, Grounded in Principles of Universal Obligation*. New York: Charles Scribner, 1866.

———. *Women's Suffrage; the Reform Against Nature*. New York: Charles Scribner, 1869.

———. *Work and Play; or Literary Varieties*. New York: Charles Scribner, 1864.

Discourses and Essays in Books

Bushnell, Horace. "The Age of Homespun." In *Work and Play; or Literary Varieties*, 374–408. New York: Charles Scribner, 1864.

———. "Barbarism the First Danger." In *Work and Play*, 227–67. New York: Charles Scribner's Sons: 1881.

———. "Christian Comprehensiveness." In *Building Eras in Religion*, 386–459. New York: Charles Scribner's Sons: 1881.

———. "The Dissolving of Doubts." In *Horace Bushnell: Sources of American Spirituality*, edited by Conrad Cherry, 162–73. New York: Paulist Press: 1985.

———. "The Doctrine of Loyalty." In *Work and Play*, 343–74. New York: Charles Scribner's Sons: 1881.

———. "The Founders Great in their Unconsciousness." In *Work and Play*, 124–66. New York: Charles Scribner's Sons: 1881.

———. "The Growth of the Law." In *Work and Play*, 78–123. New York: Charles Scribner's Sons: 1881.

———. "Of Distinctions of Color." In *Moral Uses of Dark Things*, 297–318. New York: Charles Scribner and Sons, 1867.

———. "Of the Conditions of Solidarity." In *Moral Uses of Dark Things*, 142–64. New York: Charles Scribner's Sons: 1905.

———. "Our Obligations to the Dead." In *Building Eras in Religion*, 319–55. New York: Charles Scribner's Sons: 1881.

———. "Popular Government by Divine Right." In *Building Eras in Religion*, 286–318. New York: Charles Scribner's Sons, 1881.

———. "Prosperity Our Duty." In *The Spirit in Man: Sermons and Selections*, 135–58. New York: Charles Scribner's Sons, 1910.

———. "Revelation." In *Horace Bushnell: Selected Writings on Language, Religion, and American Culture*, edited by David L. Smith, 30–31. Chico CA: Scholars Press, 1984.

———. "Reverses Needed." In *The Spirit in Man: Sermons and Selections*, 159–84. New York: Charles Scribner's Sons, 1910.

———. "The True Wealth or Weal of Nations." In *Work and Play*, 43–77. New York: Charles Scribner's Sons: 1881.

———. "Unconscious Influence." In *Sermons for the New Life*, 186–205. New York: Charles Scribner's Sons, 1871.

Letter

Bushnell, Horace, to Cyrus A. Bartol. 8 September 1851. Quoted in Mary Bushnell Cheney, *Life and Letters of Horace Bushnell*, 248–49. New York: Harper and Brothers, Publishers, 1880.

Primary Sources: Charles Hodge

Books

Hodge, Charles. *A Commentary on the Epistle to the Ephesians*. New York: Robert Carter and Brothers, 1875.

———. *A Commentary on the Epistle to the Romans*. Philadelphia: Grigg and Eliot, 1835.

————. *A Commentary on the Epistle to the Romans: New Edition, Revised and in a Great Measure Rewritten*. Philadelphia: W. S. and A. Martin, 1864.

————. *Conference Papers, or Analyses of Discourses, Doctrinal and Practical, Delivered on Sabbath Afternoons to the Students of the Theological Seminary, Princeton, New Jersey*. New York: Charles Scribner's Sons, 1879.

————. *The Constitutional History of the Presbyterian Church in the United States of America*. 2 volumes. Philadelphia: William S. Martien, 1839–1840.

————. *An Exposition on the First Epistle to the Corinthians*. New York: Robert Cart and Brothers, 1878.

————. *An Exposition of the Second Epistle to the Corinthians*. New York: George H. Doran Company, 1859.

————. *Systematic Theology*. 3 volumes. New York: Charles Scribner, 1871 (volumes 1–2); Scribner, Armstrong and Company, 1872 (volume 3). Reprint, Grand Rapids: Eerdmans Publishing Company, 1999.

————. *The Way of Life*. Edited by Mark Noll. New York/Mahwah NJ: Paulist Press, 1987.

————. *What Is Darwinism?: and other Writings on Science and Religion*. Edited and with an introduction by Mark Noll and David N. Livingston. Grand Rapids: Baker Book House, 1994.

Essays in Books

Hodge, Charles. "The Bible Argument on Slavery." In *Cotton Is King, and Pro-slavery Arguments*, third edition, edited by E. N. Elliot, 841–77. Augusta GA: Pritchard, Abbot and Loomis, 1860. Reprint, New York: Johnson Reprint Corp, 1968. Excised version of "Slavery," *Biblical Repertory and Princeton Review* 8/2 (April 1836).

————. "The Fugitive Slave Law." In *Cotton Is King, and Pro-slavery Arguments*, third edition, edited by E. N. Elliot, 811–40. Augusta GA: Pritchard, Abbot and Loomis, 1860. Reprint, New York: Johnson Reprint Corp, 1968. Formerly published as "Civil

Government," *Biblical Repertory and Princeton Review* 23 (January 1851).

Articles in the Biblical Repertory and Princeton Review (BRPR)
The articles of the *BRPR* are not signed. The *Biblical Repertory and Princeton Review: Index Volume from 1825 to 1828* (Philadelphia: Peter Walker, 1871) lists the authors of the major articles. I have assumed that Charles Hodge was the author of the "Short Notices" that were published while he was editor.

Hodge, Charles. "Abolitionism." *BRPR* 16/4 (October 1844): 545–81.
———. "American Board." *BRPR* 21/1 (January 1849): 1–42.
———. "Bushnell on Christian Nurture." *BRPR* 19/4 (October 1847): 502–39.
———. "Bushnell on Vicarious Sacrifice." *BRPR* 38/2 (April 1866): 161–94.
———. "Bushnell's Discourses." *BRPR* 21/2 (April 1849): 259–98.
———. "The Church and the Country." *BRPR* 23/2 (April 1861): 322–76.
———. "Civil Government." *BRPR* 23/1 (January 1851): 125–59.
———. "Diversity of Species in the Human Race." *BRPR* 34/3 (July 1862): 435–64.
———. "Emancipation." *BRPR* 21/4 (October 1849): 583–607.
———. "England and America." *BRPR* 34/1 (January 1862): 147–77.
———. "The General Assembly of 1835." *BRPR* 7/3 (July 1835): 440–82.
———. "The General Assembly of 1836." *BRPR* 8/3 (July 1836): 415–76.
———. "The General Assembly." *BRPR* 18/3 (July 1846): 418–56.
———. "General Assembly." *BRPR* 25/3 (July 1853): 450–527.
———. "The General Assembly." *BRPR* 31/3 (July 1859): 538–618.
———. "The General Assembly." *BRPR* 33/3 (July 1861): 511–68.
———. "The General Assembly." *BRPR* 34/3 (July 1862): 464–524.
———. "The General Assembly." *BRPR* 36/3 (July 1864): 506–74.

———. "The General Assembly." *BRPR* 37/3 (July 1865): 458–515.

———. "Latest Forms of Infidelity." *BRPR* 12/1 (January 1840): 31–71.

———. "Preaching the Gospel to the Poor." *BRPR* 43/1 (January 1871): 80–95.

———. "President Lincoln." *BRPR* 37/3 (July 1865): 435–58.

———. "The Princeton Review on the State of the Country and of the Church." *BRPR* 37/4 (October 1865): 627–57.

———. "The Relation of Church and State." *BRPR* 35/4 (October 1863): 679–93.

———. "Retrospect of the Princeton Review." *BRPR* index volume (1871): 1–39.

———. "Short Notices." *BRPR* 25/1 (January 1853): 138–50

———. "Short Notices." *BRPR* 25/3 (July 1853): 528–38.

———. "Short Notices." *BRPR* 29/4 (October 1857): 719–32.

———. "Short Notices." *BRPR* 34/2 (April 1862): 358–68.

———. "Short Notices." *BRPR* 34/3 (July 1862): 549–58.

———. "Slavery." *BRPR* 8/2 (April 1836): 268–305.

———. "State of the Church." *BRPR* 9/2 (April 1838): 243–70.

———. "The State of the Country." *BRPR* 33/1 (January 1861): 1–36.

———. "The Sunday Laws." *BRPR* 31/4 (October 1859): 733–67.

———. "Sunday Mails." *BRPR* 3/1 (January 1831): 86–134.

———. "The Unity of Mankind." *BRPR* 31/1 (January 1859): 103–49.

———. "The War." *BRPR* 35/1 (January 1863): 140–69.

———. "West India Emancipation." *BRPR* 10/4 (October 1838): 602–44.

Letters

Hodge, Charles, to Hugh Hodge. 12 December 1828. Papers of Charles Hodge, box 9, folder 3. Firestone Library, Princeton University, Princeton NJ.

———, to Hugh Hodge. 18 March 1829. Papers of Charles Hodge, box 9, folder 3. Firestone Library, Princeton University, Princeton NJ.

————, to Hugh Hodge. 1 October 1831. Quoted in *The Life of Charles Hodge, by His Son, Alexander A. Hodge*, 217. London: T. Nelson, 1880.

————, to Hugh Hodge. 9 January 1834. Papers of Charles Hodge, box 9, folder 5. Firestone Library, Princeton University, Princeton NJ.

Other Primary Sources

Books, Pamphlets, Essays, Articles, Public Documents, and Newspapers

Adger, John B. "Northern and Southern Views of the Province of the Church." *Southern Presbyterian Review* 16 (1866): 409. Quoted in Peter J. Wallace, "The Defense of the Forgotten Center: Charles Hodge and the Enigma of Emancipationism in Antebellum America," *Journal of Presbyterian History* 75/3 (Fall 1997): 174.

An Act for the Gradual Abolition of Slavery [New Jersey]. Facsimile in Graham Russell Hodges, *Slavery and Freedom in the Rural North: African Americans in Monmouth County, New Jersey, 1665–1865*, 129. Madison NJ: Madison House, 1997.

Anonymous. "The Assembly of 1863 on Slavery." *Presbyter* (23 September 1863). Quoted in Lewis G. Vander Velde, *The Presbyterian Churches and the Federal Union, 1861–65*, 165. Cambridge: Harvard University Press, 1932.

————. "The Biblical Repertory." *Presbyter* (3 August 1864). Quoted in Lewis G. Vander Velde, *The Presbyterian Churches and the Federal Union, 1861–65*, 136. Cambridge: Harvard University Press, 1932.

————. "Position Defined." *Presbyter* (13 July 1864). Quoted in Lewis G. Vander Velde, *The Presbyterian Churches and the Federal Union, 1861–65*, 128. Cambridge: Harvard University Press, 1932.

————. *Southern Baptist* (23 October 1850). Quoted in Mitchell Snay, *Gospel of Disunion: Religion and Separatism in the Antebellum South*, 62–63. Cambridge: Cambridge University Press, 1993.

Alexander, Archibald. "History of the American Colony in Liberia." *BRPR* 12/2 (April 1840): 205–25.

————. *A History of Colonization on the Western Coast of Africa.*
    Philadelphia: W. S. Martien, 1846.

Beecher, Lyman. *A Plea for the West* (1835). In *God's New Israel: Religious
    Interpretations of American Destiny*, revised edition, edited by Conrad
    Cherry, 122–30. Chapel Hill: University of North Carolina Press,
    1998.

Blanchard, J., and N. L. Rice. *A Debate on Slavery Held in the City of
    Cincinnati, on the First, Second, Third, and Sixth Days of October, 1845,
    upon the Question: Is Slave-Holding in Itself Sinful, and the Relation
    between Master and Slave, a Sinful Relation?* Cincinnati: Wm. H.
    Moore, 1846. Quoted in J. Albert Harrill, "The Use of the New
    Testament in the American Slave Controversy: A Case History in
    the Hermeneutical Tension between Biblical Criticism and
    Christian Moral Debate," 151. *Religion and American Culture: A
    Journal of Interpretation* 10/2 (Summer 2000).

Breckinridge, Robert J. "Colonization and Abolition." *BRPR* 5/3 (July
    1833): 281–305.

Calhoun, John. *The Works of John C. Calhoun.* Volume 2. Edited by
    Richard Cralle. New York: n.p., 1853. Quoted in William Sumner
    Jenkins, *Pro-Slavery Thought in the Old South*, 80. Chapel Hill:
    University of North Carolina Press, 1935.

Dabney, Robert L. *A Defense of Virginia (and through Her of the South) in
    Recent and Pending Contests against the Sectional Party.* New York: E. J.
    Hale and Son, 1867.

Davies, Samuel. *The Duty of Christians to Propagate Their Religion Among
    Heathens, Earnestly Recommended to the Masters of Negroe Slaves in
    Virginia. A Sermon Preached in Hanover, January 8, 1757.* London: J.
    Oliver, 1757. Quoted in Andrew E. Murray, *Presbyterians and the
    Negro: A History*, 11. Philadelphia: Presbyterian Historical Society,
    1966.

Dew, Thomas Roderick. *Review of the Debate in the Virginia Legislature of
    1831 and 1832.* Richmond VA: T. W. White, 1832.

Douglass, Frederick. "An Evaluation of Racial Anthropology." In *Racial
    Thought in America*, volume 1 of *From the Puritans to Abraham*

Lincoln, edited by Louis Ruchames, 478–92. Amherst: University of Massachusetts Press, 1969.

———. *Narrative of the Life of Frederick Douglass*. Boston: Anti-Slavery Office, 1845. Reprint, New York: Dover Publications, Inc., 1995.

Eastman, Mary. *Aunt Phillis's Cabin; or, Southern Life as It Is*. Philadelphia: Lippincott, Grumbo, 1852. Reprint, New York: Negro Universities Press, 1968.

Garrison, William Lloyd. *Liberator* (3 September 1831). Excerpted in *William Lloyd Garrison*, edited by George M. Fredrickson, 25. Englewood Cliffs NJ: Prentice Hall, 1968.

———. *Liberator* (29 December 1832). Excerpted in *Against Slavery: An Abolitionist Reader*, edited by Mason Lowance, 112–17. New York: Penguin Books, 2000.

———. *Liberator* (15 December 1837). Excerpted in *William Lloyd Garrison*, edited by George M. Fredrickson, 47–51. Englewood Cliffs NJ: Prentice Hall, 1968.

———. *Liberator* (31 May 1844). Excerpted in *William Lloyd Garrison*, edited by George M. Fredrickson, 52–55. Englewood Cliffs NJ: Prentice Hall, 1968.

———. *Thoughts on African Colonization: or an Impartial Exhibition of the Doctrines, Principles, and Purposes of the American Colonization Society*. Boston: Garrison and Knapp. Excerpted in *Racial Thought in America*, volume 1: *From the Puritans to Abraham Lincoln*, edited by Louis Ruchames, 311–21. Amherst: University of Massachusetts Press, 1969.

Gay, John. "Dissertation Concerning the Fundamental Principle of Virtue or Morality (1731)." In *The English Philosophers from Bacon to Mill*, edited by Edwin A. Burtt, 767–85. New York: The Modern Library, 1939.

Grimké, Francis. *The Works of Francis Grimké*. 4 volumes. Edited by Carter G. Woodson. Washington DC: Associated Publishers, 1942.

Hammond, John Henry. "Laws of Nature—Natural Rights—Slavery." Manuscript in a private collection. Quoted in William Sumner

Jenkins, *Pro-Slavery Thought in the Old South*, 129. Chapel Hill: University of North Carolina Press, 1935.

Hodge, J. Aspinwall. *America and Africa*. Washington DC: American Colonization Society, no date. Quoted in Andrew E. Murray, *Presbyterians and the Negro: A History*, 82. Philadelphia: Presbyterian Historical Society, 1966.

Hopkins, Erastus. "African Colonization." *BRPR* 12/1 (January 1833): 257–80.

Jefferson, Thomas. *Notes on the State of Virginia*. Edited by William Peden. Chapel Hill: University of North Carolina Press, 1955.

McLeod, Alexander. *Negro Slavery Unjustifiable*. In *Against Slavery: An Abolitionist Reader*, edited by Mason Lowance, 70–84. New York: Penguin Books, 2000.

McNiell, George. *North Carolina Presbyterian* (19 January 1861). Quoted in Richard Carwardine, *Evangelicals and Politics in Antebellum America*, 317. New Haven and London: Yale University Press: 1993.

Nott, J. C. [Josiah]. "Diversity of the Human Race." *DeBow's Review* 10/2 (February 1851): 113–32.

———. "Instincts of Races." *New Orleans Medical and Surgical Journal* 19 (1866): 1–16, 145–56. Quoted in William Stanton, *The Leopard's Spots: Scientific Attitudes Toward Race in America, 1815–59*, 187. Chicago: University of Chicago Press, 1960.

———. "Nature and Destiny of the Negro." *DeBow's Review* 10/3 (March 1851): 329–32.

———. "The Problem of the Black Races." *DeBow's Review* new series 1/3 (1866): 266–83. Quoted in William Stanton, *The Leopard's Spots: Scientific Attitudes Toward Race in America, 1815–59*, 187. Chicago: University of Chicago Press, 1960.

Paley, William. *Moral and Political Philosophy*. 8th edition. Boston: West and Richardson, 1815.

Parker, Theodore. "The Function and Place of Conscience in Relation to the Laws of Men." In *Against Slavery: An Abolitionist Reader*, edited by Mason Lowance, 275–85. New York: Penguin Books, 2000.

Presbyterian Church in the USA. *General Assembly, Minutes.*
    Philadelphia: no publisher, 1818. 692ff. Quoted in Andrew E.
    Murray, *Presbyterians and the Negro: A History*, 27. Philadelphia:
    Presbyterian Historical Society, 1966.
Presbyterian Church in the USA. [Old School]. *Minutes of the General
    Assembly.* Volume 16. Philadelphia: no publisher, 1861. 329–30.
    Quoted in Lewis G. Vander Velde, *The Presbyterian Churches and the
    Federal Union, 1861–65*, 58. Cambridge: Harvard University Press,
    1932.
Rauschenbusch, Walter. *The Belated Race and the Social Problem.* No
    place: American Missionary Association, no date. Quoted in Doris
    Robinson Sharpe, *Walter Rauschenbusch*, 166. New York: MacMillan
    Company, 1942.
———. *Christianizing the Social Order.* New York: MacMillan Company:
    1912.
———. *A Theology for the Social Gospel.* New York and Nashville:
    Abingdon Press, 1945.
Reid, Thomas. *An Inquiry into the Human Mind on the Principles of
    Common Sense.* Edited by Timothy Duggan. Chicago: University of
    Chicago Press, 1970. Quoted in Keith Lehrer, *Thomas Reid*, 31.
    London and New York: Routledge, 1989.
Ruffin, Thomas. *The Papers of Thomas Ruffin.* Volume 4. Edited by J. G.
    deRoulhac Hamilton. Raleigh NC: no publisher, 1918–1920.
    Quoted in Eugene Genovese, *Roll Jordan Roll: The World the Slaves
    Made*, 35. New York: Vintage, 1976.
The Saybrook Platform. In Williston Walker, *The Creeds and Platforms of
    Congregationalism*, 502–506. New York: Charles Scribner's Sons,
    1893.
Scheiermacher, Friedreich. *The Christian Faith.* English translation of the
    second German edition. Edited by H. R. Mackintosh and J. S.
    Stewart. Edinburgh: T&T Clark, 1989.
Smith, Samuel Stanhope. *Essay on the Causes of the Variety of Complexion
    and Figure in the Human Species.* Second edition. New Brunswick NJ:
    J. Simpson and Company, 1810.

Stowe, Harriet Beecher. *The Annotated Uncle Tom's Cabin*. Edited by Philip Van Doren Stern. New York: Bramhall House, 1964.

Strong, Josiah. *Our Country*. Revised edition. New York: Baker and Taylor Company, 1893. Reprint, Cambridge: Belknap Press of Harvard University Press, 1963.

Taylor, Nathaniel William. "*Concio ad Clerum*: A Sermon." In *Theology in America: The Major Protestant Voices from Puritanism to Neo-Orthodoxy*, 211–49. Edited by Sydney Ahlstrom. Indianapolis: Bobbs-Merril Company, 1967.

Thornwell, James Henley. *The Rights and Duties of Masters. A Sermon Preached at the Dedication of a Church Erected in Charleston, South Carolina, for the Benefit and the Dedication of the Coloured Population*. Charleston: Walker and James, 1850.

Walker, David. *David Walker's Appeal*. New York: Hill and Wang, 1965.

Warfield, Benjamin Breckinridge. "On the Antiquity and Unity of the Human Race." *Princeton Theological Review* 9/1 (January 1911): 1–25.

Wayland, Francis. *Elements of Moral Science*. Boston: Gould, Kendall, and Lincoln, 1835. Reprint, edited by Joseph F. Blau, Cambridge: Belknapp University Press, 1963.

Worcester, Samuel et al. "On the Racial Theory of Slavery." In *Racial Thought in America*. Volume 1 of *From the Puritans to Abraham Lincoln*, 300–10. Edited by Louis Ruchames. Amherst: University of Massachusetts Press, 1969.

Wright, Henry C. *Liberator* (11 May 1848). Quoted in Wayne A. Meeks, "The 'Haustalfen' and American Slavery: A Hermeneutical Challenge," in *Theology and Ethics in Paul and His Interpreters: Essays in Honor of Victor Paul Furnish*, edited by Eugene H. Lovering, Jr., and Jerry L. Sumney, 251. Nashville: Abingdon Press, 1996.

Letters

Bacon, Leonard, to Amos A. Phelps. 29 August 1845. Quoted in Hugh Davis, "Leonard Bacon, the Congregational Church and Slavery, 1845–1861," in *Religion and the Antebellum Debate over Slavery*, edited by John McKivigan and Mitchell Snay, 226. Athens and London: University of Georgia Press, 1998.

Cunningham, Rev. W. M., to C. C. Jones. 18 February 1861. In Robert Manson Myers, *The Children of Pride: A True Story of Georgia and the Civil War*, 645. New Haven: Yale University Press, 1972.

Dabney, Robert L., to G. Woodhouse Payne. 20 January 1840. Quoted in James Oscar Farmer, Jr., *The Metaphysical Confederacy: James Henry Thornwell and the Synthesis of Southern Values*, 206. Macon GA: Mercer University Press, 1986.

McEwen, Robert, to Mary Apthorp Bushnell. No date. Quoted in Mary Bushnell Cheney, *Life and Letters of Horace Bushnell*, 55–56. New York: Harper and Brothers, Publishers, 1880.

Talcott, Russell G., to John Seymour. 15 January 1839. Quoted in Robert L. Edwards, *Of Singular Genius, of Singular Grace: A Biography of Horace Bushnell*, 51. Cleveland: Pilgrim Press, 1992.

Tappan, Lewis, to Charles Hodge. 25 November 1849. Papers of Charles Hodge. Firestone Library, Princeton University, Princeton NJ. Box 19, folder 1.

Secondary Sources

Books

Adamson, William R. *Bushnell Rediscovered*. Philadelphia: United Church Press, 1966.

Ahlstrom, Sydney. *A Religious History of the American People*. New Haven: Yale University Press, 1972.

———, editor. *Theology in America: The Major Protestant Voices from Puritanism to Neo-Orthodoxy*. Indianapolis: Bobbs-Merril Company, Inc.: 1967.

Andrews, William L., editor. *Sisters of the Spirit: Three Black Women's Autobiographies of the Nineteenth Century*. Bloomington: Indiana University Press, 1986.

Barnes, Howard A. *Horace Bushnell and the Virtuous Republic*. American Theological Library Monograph 27. Metuchen NJ: Scarecrow Press, 1991.

Bauer, Yehuda. *A History of the Holocaust*. Danbury CT: Franklin Watts, 1982.

Bozeman, Theodore Dwight. *Protestantism in an Age of Science: the Baconian Ideal and Antebellum American Religious Thought*. Chapel Hill: University of North Carolina Press, 1977.

Carwardine, Richard. *Evangelicals and Politics in Antebellum America*. New Haven: Yale University Press: 1993.

Cheney, Mary Bushnell. *Life and Letters of Horace Bushnell*. New York: Harper and Brothers, Publishers, 1880.

Cherry, Conrad, editor. *Horace Bushnell: Sources of American Spirituality*. New York: Paulist Press, 1985.

Commager, Henry Steele. *Theodore Parker*. Boston: Little, Brown, and Company, 1936.

Cone, James. *A Black Theology of Liberation*. Marynoll NY: Orbis, 1996.

Conforti, Joseph A. *Jonathan Edwards, Religious Tradition and American Culture*. Chapel Hill: University of North Carolina Press, 1995.

————. *Samuel Hopkins and the New Divinity Movement: Calvinism, the Congregational Ministry, and Reform in New England between the Great Awakenings*. Grand Rapids: Christian University Press, 1981.

Conklin, Paul K. *The Uneasy Center: Reformed Christianity in Antebellum America*. Chapel Hill: University of North Carolina Press, 1995.

Cott, Nancy. *The Bonds of Womanhood: "Woman's Sphere" in New England, 1780–1835*. New Haven: Yale University Press, 1977.

Conser, Walter H. *God and the Natural World: Religion and Science in Antebellum America*. Columbia: University of South Carolina Press, 1993.

Cripps, Thomas. *Slow Fade to Black: The Negro in American Film, 1900–1942*. New York: Oxford University Press, 1977.

Cross, Barbara M. *Horace Bushnell: Minister to a Changing America*. Chicago: University of Chicago Press, 1958.

Davis, David Brion. *The Problem of Slavery in Western Culture*. Ithaca NY: Cornell University Press, 1966.

Davis, Hugh. *Leonard Bacon: New England Reformer and Antislavery Moderate*. Baton Rouge: Louisiana State University Press, 1998.

Diamond, Peter J. *Common Sense and Improvement: Thomas Reid as a Social Theorist*. Frankfurt am Main: Peter Lang, 1998.

Dorrien, Gary. *The Making of American Liberal Theology: Imagining Progressive Religion, 1805–1900*. Louisville KY: Westminster John Knox, 2001.

Duke, James O. *Horace Bushnell, on the Vitality of Biblical Language*. Chico CA: Scholars Press, 1984.

Dyck, Arthur J. *On Human Care: An Introduction to Ethics*. Nashville: Abingdon Press, 1977.

Edwards, Robert L. *Of Singular Genius, of Singular Grace: A Biography of Horace Bushnell*. Cleveland: Pilgrim Press, 1992.

Farmer, James Oscar, Jr. *The Metaphysical Confederacy: James Henry Thornwell and the Synthesis of Southern Values*. Macon GA: Mercer University Press, 1986.

Faust, Drew Gilpin. *The Ideology of Slavery: Proslavery Thought in the Antebellum South, 1830–1860*. Baton Rouge: Louisiana State University Press, 1981.

Filler, Louis. *The Crusade against Slavery, 1830–1860*. New York: Harper and Row, Publishers, 1960.

Finkleman, Paul. *Slavery and the Founders: Race and Liberty in the Age of Jefferson*. Armonk NY: M. E. Sharpe, 1996.

Foner, Eric. *Free Soil, Free Labor, and Free Men: The Ideology of the Republican Party before the Civil War*. Oxford/New York: Oxford University Press, 1970.

Fredrickson, George M. *The Black Image in the White Mind: The Debate on Afro-American Character and Destiny, 1817–1914*. New York: Harper and Row, Publishers, 1971.

———. *The Inner Civil War: Northern Intellectuals and the Crisis of the Union*. New York: Harper and Row, Publishers, 1965.

————, editor. *William Lloyd Garrison*. Englewood Cliffs NJ: Prentice-Hall, Inc., 1968.

Gardell, Mattias. *In the Name of Elijah Muhammad: Louis Farrakan and the Naton of Islam*. Durhman NC: Duke University Press, 1996.

Garrison, Wendell Phillips, and Francis Jackson Garrison. *William Lloyd Garrison, 1805-1879: The Story of His Life Told by His Children*, volume 3 of 4. New York: The Century Company, 1889.

Genovese, Eugene. *Roll Jordan Roll: The World the Slaves Made*. New York: Vintage, 1976.

————. *The Slaveholder's Dilemma: Freedom and Progress in Southern Conservative Thought, 1820–1860*. Columbia: University of South Carolina Press, 1992.

Gill, John. *Tide without Turning: Elijah Lovejoy and Freedom of the Press*. Boston: Starr King Press, 1958.

Goen, C. C. *Broken Churches, Broken Nation: Denominational Schisms and the Coming of the American Civil War*. Macon GA: Mercer University Press, 1985.

Gosset, Thomas F. *Race: The History of an Idea in America*. Dallas: Southern Methodist University Press, 1963.

Gustafson, James M. *Christian Ethics and the Community*. Philadelphia: United Church Press, a Pilgrim Press Book, 1971.

Haddorff, David W. *Dependence and Freedom: The Moral Thought of Horace Bushnell*. Lanham MD: University Press of America, Inc., 1994.

Handy, Robert T., editor. *The Social Gospel in America*. New York: Oxford University Press, 1966.

Harding, Vincent. *A Certain Magnificence: Lyman Beecher and the Transformation of American Protestantism, 1775–1863*. Brooklyn NY: Carlson Publishing, 1991.

Hatch, Nathan O. *The Democratization of American Christianity*. New Haven and London: Yale University Press, 1989.

Hewitt, Glenn Alden. *Regeneration and Morality: a Study of Charles Finney, Charles Hodge, John W. Nevin, and Horace Bushnell*. Brooklyn NY: Carlson, 1991.

Hodge, Archibald Alexander. *The Life of Charles Hodge, by His Son, Alexander A. Hodge*. London: T. Nelson, 1880.

Hoffecker, W. Andrew. *Piety and the Princeton Theologians: Archibald Alexander, Charles Hodge, and Benjamin Warfield*. Grand Rapids: Baker Book House, 1981.

Holifield, E. Brooks. *The Gentlemen Theologians: American Theology in Southern Culture, 1795–1860*. Durham NC: Duke University Press, 1978.

————. *Theology in America: Christian Thought from the Age of the Puritans to the Civil War*. New Haven: Yale University Press, 2003.

Howe, Daniel Walker. *The Political Culture of the American Whigs*. Chicago: University of Chicago Press, 1979.

Hudson, Winthrop. *Religion in America*. Third revised edition. New York: Charles Scribner's Son's, 1981.

Jacobs, Harriet. *Incidents in the Life of a Slave Girl: Written by Herself*. Edited by Jean Fagan Yellin. Cambridge: Harvard University Press, 1987.

Jamison, A. Leland, and James Ward Smith, editors. *The Shaping of American Religion*. Volume 1 of Religion in American Life. Princeton: Princeton University Press, 1961.

Jenkins, William Sumner. *Pro-Slavery Thought in the Old South*. Chapel Hill: University of North Carolina Press, 1935.

Jordan, Winthrop D. *White over Black: American Attitudes toward the Negro, 1550–1812*. Chapel Hill: University of North Carolina Press.

Kerber, Linda K. *Federalists in Dissent: Imagery and Ideology in Jeffersonian America*. Ithaca NY: Cornell University Press, 1970.

Kerr, Hugh T., editor. *Sons of the Prophets: Leaders of Protestantism from Princeton Seminary*. Princeton: Princeton University Press, 1963.

King, Martin Luther, Jr. *Stride toward Freedom: The Montgomery Story*. New Yorker: Harper and Brothers, Publishers, 1958.

LaRosa, Michael, and Frank O. Mora, editors. *Neighborly Adversaries: Readings in U.S.-Latin American Relations*. Lanham MD: University Press of America, 1999.

Lehrer, Keith. *Thomas Reid*. London and New York: Routledge, 1989.

Lerner, Gerda. *The Grimké Sisters of South Carolina: Pioneers for Women's Rights and Abolition*. New edition. New York/Oxford: Oxford University Press, 1998.

Loetscher, Lefferts, A. *The Broadening Church: A Study of Theological Issues in the Presbyterian Church since 1869*. Philadelphia: University of Pennsylvania Press, 1957.

————. *Facing the Enlightenment and Pietism: Archibald Alexander and the Founding of Princeton Theological Seminary*. Westport CT: Greenwood, 1983.

Loveland, Anne C. *Southern Evangelicals and the Social Order, 1800–1860*. Baton Rouge: Louisiana State University Press, 1980.

Lowance, Mason, editor. *Against Slavery: An Abolitionist Reader*. New York: Penguine Books, 2000.

Marsden, George M. *The Evangelical Mind and the New School Presbyterian Experience*. New Haven: Yale University Press, 1970.

Marty, Martin E. *Righteous Empire: The Protestant Experience in America*. New York: Dial Press, 1976.

Mathews, Donald G. *Religion in the Old South*. Chicago: University of Chicago Press, 1977.

May, Henry. *The Enlightenment in America*. New York: Oxford University Press, 1976.

McKivigan, John, R. *The War against Proslavery Religion: Abolitionism and the Northern Churches, 1830–1865*. Ithaca NY: Cornell University Press, 1984.

———— and Mitchell Snay, editors. *Religion and the Antebellum Debate over Slavery*. Athens: University of Georgia Press, 1998.

McLoughlin, William G., Jr. *Revivals, Awakenings, and Reform*. Chicago History of American Religion. Edited by Martin Marty. Chicago: University of Chicago Press, 1978.

Mead, Sidney. *Nathaniel William Taylor, 1786–1858: A Connecticut Liberal*. Chicago: University of Chicago, 1942.

Miller, Perry. *The Life of the Mind in America from the Revolution to the Civil War*. New York: Harcourt, Brace and World, 1965.

Miller, Samuel Jr. *Life of Samuel Miller*. Volume 1 of 2. Philadelphia: Claxton, Remsen, and Haffelfinger, 1869.

Minus, Paul M. *Walter Rauschenbusch: American Reformer*. New York: MacMillan, 1988.

Mitchell, Laura L. "Matters of Justice between Man and Man: Northern Divines, the Bible, and the Fugitive Slave Act of 1850." In *Religion and the Antebellum Debate over Slavery*, edited by John McKivigan and Mitchell Snay, 134–68. Athens: University of Georgia Press, 1998.

Morgan, Edmund S. *American Slavery, American Freedom: The Ordeal of Colonial Virginia*. New York: W. W. Norton, 1975.

Mullin, Robert Bruce. *The Puritan as Yankee: A Life of Horace Bushnell*. Foreword by Allen C. Guelzo. Grand Rapids: Eerdmans Publishing Company, 2002.

Munger, Theodore T. *Horace Bushnell: Preacher and Theologian*. Boston: Houghton, Mifflin and Company, 1900.

Murray, Andrew, E. *Presbyterians and the Negro: A History*. Philadelphia: Presbyterian Historical Society, 1966.

Nichols, James Hastings. *Romanticism in American Theology: Nevin and Schaff at Mercersburg*. Chicago: University of Chicago Press, 1961.

Niebuhr, H. Richard. *The Kingdom of God in America*. New York: Harper and Row, Publishers, 1937. Reprint, Middletown CT: Wesleyan University Press, 1988.

———. *The Social Sources of Denominationalism*. New York: Henry Holt and Company, 1929.

Noll, Mark A. *America's God: From Jonathan Edwards to Abraham Lincoln*. Oxford: Oxford University Press, 2002.

———. *A History of Christianity in the United States and Canada*. Grand Rapids: Eerdmans Publishing Company, 1992.

————. *Evangelicalism: Comparative Studies of Popular Protestantism in North America, The British Isles, and Beyond, 1700–1990*. Edited by David W. Bebbington and George A. Rawlyz. New York/Oxford: Oxford University Press, 1994.

————. *Princeton and the Republic, 1768–1822*. Princeton: Princeton University Press, 1989.

————, editor. *The Princeton Theology, 1812–1921: Scripture, Science, and Theological Method from Archibald Alexander to Benjamin Breckinridge Warfield*. Phillipsburg NJ: Presbyterian and Reformed Publishing Company, 1981.

Olender, Maurice. *The Languages of Paradise: Race, Religion and Philology in the Nineteenth Century*. Translated by Arthur Goldhammer. Cambridge: Harvard University Press, 1992.

Peterson, Thomas Virgil. *Ham and Japheth: The Mythic World of Whites in the Antebellum South*. Metuchen NJ: Scarecrow Press, 1978.

Potter, Ralph B. *War and Moral Discourse*. Richmond VA: John Knox Press, 1970.

Rogers, Jack B., and Donald K. McKim. *The Authority and Interpretation of the Bible: An Historical Approach*. San Francisco: Harper and Row, Publishers, 1979.

Ruchames, Louis, editor. *Racial Thought in America*. Volume 1. *From the Puritans to Abraham Lincoln*. Amherst: University of Massachusetts Press, 1969.

Scott, William Berryman. *Some Memories of a Palaeontologist*. Princeton: Princeton University Press, 1939.

Sharpe, Doris Robinson. *Walter Rauschenbusch*. New York: MacMillan, 1942.

Sirmans, Mariam E. *Colonial South Carolina: A Political History*. Chapel Hill: University of North Carolina Press.

Smith, David L. *Symbolism and Growth; The Religious Thought of Horace Bushnell*. Ann Arbor MI: Edwards Brothers, Inc., Distributed by Scholars Press, 1981.

————, editor. *Horace Bushnell: Selected Writings on Language, Religion, and American Culture*. New York: Oxford University Press, 1965.

Smith, H. Shelton. *Changing Conceptions of Original Sin: A Study in American Theology Since 1750.* New York: Charles Scribner's Sons, 1955.

———. *In His Image, but...: Racism in Southern Religion, 1780–1910.* Durham NC: Duke University Press, 1972.

———, editor. *Horace Bushnell, Twelve Selections.* A Library of Protestant Thought. New York: Oxford University Press, 1965.

Smith, Timothy L. *Revivalism and Social Reform: American Protestantism on the Eve of the Civil War.* New York and Nashville: Abingdon Press, 1957.

Snay, Mitchell. *Gospel of Disunion: Religion and Separation in the Antebellum South.* Cambridge: Cambridge University Press, 1993.

Stackhouse, Max. *Public Theology and Political Economy: Christian Stewardship in Modern Society.* Lanham MD: University Press of America, 1991.

Stanton, William. *The Leopard's Spots: Scientific Attitudes Toward Race in America, 1815–59.* Chicago: University of Chicago Press, 1960.

Staudenraus, P. J. *The African Colonization Movement 1812–1865.* New York: Columbia University Press, 1961.

Stewart, John W., and James H. Moorhead, editors. *Charles Hodge Revisited: A Critical Appraisal of His Life and Work.* Grand Rapids: Eerdmans Publishing Company, 2002.

Stewart, John W. *Mediating the Center: Charles Hodge on American Science, Language, Literature, and Politics.* Studies in Reformed Theology and History 3/1. Princeton: Princeton Theological Seminary, 1995.

Sweet, Leonard I., editor. *The Evangelical Tradition in America.* Macon GA: Mercer University Press, 1984.

Thompson, Ernest Trice. *Changing Emphases in American Preaching.* Philadelphia: Westminster Press, 1943.

———. *Presbyterians in the South, 1607–1861.* Volume 1 of 3. Richmond VA: John Knox Press, 1961.

Tise, Larry E. *Proslavery: A History of the Defense of Slavery in America, 1701–1840.* Athens: University of Georgia Press, 1987.

Trimiew, Darryl M. *Voices of the Silenced: The Responsible Self in a Marginalized Community* Cleveland: Pilgrim Press, 1993.

Ulrich, Laurel Thatcher. *The Age of Homespun: Objects and Stories in the Creation of an American Myth.* New York: Vintage Books, 2002.

Vander Velde, Lewis G. *The Presbyterian Churches and the Federal Union, 1861–65.* Cambridge: Harvard University Press, 1932.

Von Rohr, John. *The Shaping of American Congregationalism.* Cleveland: Pilgrim Press, 1992.

Walker, Williston. *A History of the Congregational Churches in the United States.* American Church History 3/1. New York: Christian Literature Company, 1894.

Wyatt-Brown, Bertram. *Lewis Tappan and the Evangelical War against Slavery.* Cleveland: Press of Case Western Reserve University, 1969.

Articles and Essays

Ahlstrom, Sydney. "New Introduction to the Reprint Edition." In reprint of Josiah Strong, *The New Era, or The Coming Kingdom,* 1i–6i. New York: Baker and Taylor Company, 1893. Reprint, Hicksville, NY: Regina Press, 1975.

———. "The Scottish Philosophy and American Theology," *Church History* 24/3 (September 1955): 257–72.

———. "Theology in America: A Historical Survey." In *The Shaping of American Religion,* volume 1 of *Religion in American Life,* edited by James Ward Smith and A. Leland Jamison, 279–85. Princeton: Princeton University Press, 1961.

Baker, William S. "The Social Views of Charles Hodge (1797–1878): A Study in 19th-Century Conservatism." *Presbyterion: Covenant Seminary Review* 32/1 (Spring 1975):1–22.

Barnes, Howard A. "Idea that Caused a War: Horace Bushnell versus Thomas Jefferson." *Journal of Church and State* 16/1 (Winter 1974): 73–84.

Beuttler, Fred W. "Making Theology Matter: Power, Polity, and the Theological Debate over Homosexual Ordination in the

Presbyterian Church (U.S.A.)." *Journal of Presbyterian History* 79/1 (Spring 2001): 5–22.

———. "Response to Paul E. Capetz." *Journal of Presbyterian History* 79/1 (Spring 2001): 40–42.

Van Broekhoven, Deborah Bingham. "Suffering with the Slaveholders: The Limits of Francis Wayland's Antislavery Witness." In *Religion and the Antebellum Debate over Slavery*, edited by John McKivigan and Mitchell Snay, 196–220. Athens: University of Georgia Press, 1998.

Braude, Benjamin. "The Sons of Noah and the Construction of Ethnic and Geographical Identities in the Medieval and Early Modern Periods." *The William and Mary Quarterly*, third series, 14/1 (January 1997): 120–42.

Brauer, Jerald C. "Conversion: From Puritanism to Revivalism." *Journal of Religion* 58/3 (July 1978): 227–43.

Capetz, Paul E. "Defending the Reformed Tradition? Problematic Aspects of the Appeal to Biblical and Confessional Authority in the Present Theological Crisis Confronting the Presbyterian Church (U.S.A.)." *Journal of Presbyterian History* 79/1 (Spring 2001): 23–39.

———. Response to Fred W. Beuttler. *Journal of Presbyterian History* 79/1 (Spring 2001): 43–45.

Carwardine, Richard. "The Politics of Charles Hodge." In *Charles Hodge Revisited*, edited by John W. Stewart and James H. Moorhead, 247–97. Grand Rapids: Eerdmans Publishing Company, 2002.

Cashdollar, Charles D. "Pursuit of Piety: Charles Hodge's Diary, 1819–1820." *Journal of Presbyterian History* 55/3 (Fall 1977): 267–84.

Cherry, Conrad. "Structure of Organic Thinking: Horace Bushnell's Approach to Language, Nature, and Nation." *Journal of The American Academy of Religion* 40/1 (March 1972): 3–20.

Childress, James F. "Situation Ethics." In *The Westminster Dictionary of Christian Ethics*, edited by Childress and John Macquarrie, 586–87. Philadelphia: Westminster Press, 1986.

Clark, Elizabeth B. "'The Sacred Rights of the Weak': Pain, Sympathy, and the Culture of Individual Rights in Antebellum America." *Journal of American History* 82/2 (September 1995): 463–91.

Clebsch, William A. "Christian Interpretations of the Civil War." *Church History* 30/2 (June 1961): 212–22.

Cole, Charles C., Jr. "Horace Bushnell and the Slavery Question." *New England Quarterly* 23/1 (March 1950): 19–30.

Corrigan, John. "The Enlightenment." In *Encyclopedia of the American Religious Experience*, volume 2 of *Studies of Traditions and Movements*, edited by Charles Lippy and Peter Williams, 1185–2000. New York: Charles Scribner's Sons, 1988.

Davis, David Brion. "Constructing Race: A Reflection." *The William and Mary Quarterly*, third series, 14/1 (January 1997): 7–18.

Davis, Hugh. "Leonard Bacon, the Congregational Church and Slavery, 1845–1861." In *Religion and the Antebellum Debate over Slavery*, edited by John McKivigan and Mitchell Snay, 221–48. Athens and London: University of Georgia Press, 1998.

Faust, Drew Gilpin. "Evangelicalism and the Meaning of the Proslavery Argument." *Virginia Magazine of History and Biography* 85/1 (January 1977): 3–17.

Flanders, Ralph. "Slavery." In *Dictionary of American History*, volume 5, edited by James Thruslow and R. V. Gleman, 95–96. New York: Charles Scribner's Sons, 1940.

From, Joel L. "The Uniform Operations of Grace: Nature, Mind, and Gospel in Early Nineteenth Century Evangelicalism." *Fides et Historia*, combined issue 37/2 (Summer/Fall 2005); 38/1 (Winter/Spring 2006): 137–50.

Genovese, Eugene, and Elizabeth Fox-Genovese. "The Culture of the Old South." In Eugene Genovese, *The Southern Front: History and Politics in the Culture War*, 51–78. Columbia MO and London: University of Missouri Press, 1995.

Genovese, Eugene. "Larry Tise's *Proslavery*: An Appreciation and a Critique." *Georgia Historical Quarterly* 72/4 (1988): 670–83.

Gladden, Washington. "Horace Bushnell and Progressive Orthodoxy." *Pioneers of Religious Liberty in America*, edited by Samuel A. Eliot, 227–63. Boston: American Unitarian Association, 1903.

Guelzo, Allen C. "Charles Hodge's Antislavery Moment." In *Charles Hodge Revisited*, edited by John W. Stewart and James H. Moorhead, 299–325. Grand Rapids: Eerdmans Publishing Company, 2002.

Hogeland, Ronald W. "Charles Hodge, the Association of Gentlemen and Ornamental Womanhood: 1825–1855." *Journal of Presbyterian History* 53/3 (Fall 1975): 239–55.

Holifield, E. Brooks. "Hodge, the Seminary, and the American Theological Context." In *Charles Hodge Revisited*, edited by John W. Stewart and James H. Moorhead, 102–28. Grand Rapids: Eerdmans Publishing Company, 2002.

Howe, Daniel Walker. "The Social Science of Horace Bushnell." *Journal of American History* 70/2 (September 1983): 305–22.

Ilahi, Au'Ra Muhammad Abdullah. "Racism." In *Historical Encyclopedia of World Slavery*, volume 2, edited by Junius Rodriguez, 537. Santa Barbara CA: ABC-CLIO, Inc., 1997.

Kennedy, Earl W. "From Pessimism to Optimism: Francis Turretin and Charles Hodge on 'the Last Things.'" In *Servant Gladly: Essays in Honor of John W. Beardslee the Third*, edited by Jack D. Klunder, 104–16. Grand Rapids: Eerdmans Publishing Company, 1989.

Leith, John. "Presbyterianism, Reformed." In *Encyclopedia of Religion*, volume 11, edited by Mircea Eliade et al., 523–24. New York: MacMillan Publishing Company, 1987.

Luker, Ralph E. "Bushnell in Black and White: Evidences of the 'Racism' of Horace Bushnell." *New England Quarterly* 45/3 (September 1972): 408–16.

Meeks, Wayne A. "The 'Haustafeln' and American Slavery: A Hermeneutical Challenge." In *Theology and Ethics in Paul and His Interpreters: Essays in Honor of Victor Paul Furnish*, edited by Eugene H. Lovering, Jr., and Jerry L. Sumney, 232–53. Nashville: Abingdon Press, 1996.

Miller, Glenn T. "God's Light and Man's Enlightenment: Evangelical Theology of Colonial Presbyterianism." *Journal of Presbyterian History* 51/2 (Summer 1973): 97–115.

Mullin, Robert B. B. "Biblical Critics and the Battle over Slavery." *Journal of Presbyterian History* 61/2 (Summer 1983): 210–26.

Murchie, David. "From Slaveholder to American Abolitionist: Charles Hodge and the Slavery Issue." In *Christian Freedom: Essays in Honor of Vernon C. Grounds*, edited by Kenneth W. M. Wozniak and Stanley J. Grenz, 127–52. Lanham MD: University Press of America, 1986.

Noll, Mark A. "The Bible and Slavery." In *Religion and the American Civil War*, edited by Randall M. Miller, Harry S. Stout, and Charles Reagan Wilson, 43–73. New York and Oxford: Oxford University Press, 1998.

———. "Charles Hodge as an Expositor of the Spiritual Life." In *Charles Hodge Revisited*, edited by John W. Stewart and James H. Moorhead, 181–216. Grand Rapids: Eerdmans Publishing Company, 2002.

Nordbeck, Elizabeth. "Christian Nurture Revisited." *PRISM: A Theological Journal for the United Church of Christ* 14/2 (Fall 1999): 25–33.

Olmstead, Clifton E. "Francie James Grimké (1850–1937): Christian Moralist and Civil Rights." In *Sons of the Prophets: Leaders of Protestantism from Princeton Seminary*, edited by Hught T. Kerr, 161–75. Princeton: Princeton University Press, 1963.

Padgett, Chris. "Evangelicals Divided: Abolition and the Plan of Union's Demise in Ohio's Western Reserve." In *Religion and the Antebellum Debate over Slavery*, edited by John McKivigan and Mitchell Snay, 249–72. Athens and London: University of Georgia Press, 1998.

Raboteau, Albert J. "The Black Experience in American Evangelicalism: The Meaning of Slavery." In *Evangelical Tradition in America*, edited by Leonard Sweet, 181–97. Macon GA: Mercer University Press, 1984.

Ray, Stephen G. "The Remembrance of Integrity: African-American New England Congregationalists and the Politics of History."

PRISM: A Theological Journal of the United Church of Christ 14/1 (Spring 1999): 30–42.

Schmidt, Jean Miller. "Holiness and Perfection." In *Encyclopedia of the American Religious Experience*, volume 2 of *Studies of Traditions and Movements*, edited by Charles Lippy and Peter Williams, 813–29. New York: Charles Scribner's Sons, 1988.

Scott, John Anthony. "Kemble, Francis Anne (1809–1893)." In *Dictionary of Afro-American Slavery*, edited by Randall M. Miller and John David Stout, 382–83. New York, Westport, and London: Greenwood Press, 1988.

Shriver, George. "Romantic Religion." In *Encyclopedia of the American Religious Experience*, volume 2 of *Studies of Traditions and Movements*, edited by Charles Lippy and Peter Williams, 1103–15. New York: Charles Scribner's Sons, 1988.

Stevenson, Louise L. "Charles Hodge, Women and Womanhood, and Manly Ministers." In *Charles Hodge Revisited*, edited by John W. Stewart and James H. Moorhead, 247–97. Grand Rapids: Eerdmans Publishing Company, 2002.

Suchocki, Marjorie. "Weaving the World." *Process Studies* 14/2 (Summer 1985): 76–86.

Sweet, Leonard. "Nineteenth Century Evangelicalism." In *Encyclopedia of the American Religious Experience*, volume 2 of *Studies of Traditions and Movements*, edited by Charles Lippy and Peter Williams, 875–99. New York: Charles Scribner's Sons, 1988.

Swezey, Charles. "The Role of Religious Participation and Religious Belief in Biomedical Decision Making." In *Society's Choices: Social and Ethical Decision Making in Biomedicine*, edited by Ruth Ellen Bulger, Elizabeth Meyer Bobby, and Harvey V. Fineberg, 358–87. Washington DC: National Academy Press, 1995.

Torbett, David. "Horace Bushnell and 'Distinctions of Color': Interpreting an Ambivalent Essay on Race." *PRISM: A Theological Journal for the United Church of Christ* 14/2 (Fall 1999): 3–24.

Turner, James. "Charles Hodge and the Intellectual Weather of the Nineteenth Century." In *Charles Hodge Revisited*, edited by John W.

Stewart and James H. Moorhead, 247–97. Grand Rapids: Eerdmans Publishing Company, 2002.

Varnon, Elizabeth R. "Evangelical Womanhood and the Politics of the African Colonization Movement in Virginia." In *Religion and the Antebellum Debate over Slavery*, edited by John McKivigan and Mitchell Snay, 169–95. Athens and London: University of Georgia Press, 1998.

Wallace, Peter J. "The Defense of the Forgotten Center: Charles Hodge and the Enigma of Emancipationism in Antebellum America." *Journal of Presbyterian History* 75/3 (Fall 1997): 165–77.

Weeks, Louis. "Horace Bushnell on Black America." *Religious Education* 68/1 (January–February 1973): 28–41.

———. "Racism, World War I and the Christian Life: Francis Grimké in the Nation's Capital." In *Black Apostles: Afro-American Clergy Confront the Twentieth Century*, edited by Randall K. Burkett and Richard Newman, 57–75. Boston: G. K. Hall, 1978.

Unpublished Paper and Letter

Ottati, Douglas F. "Assessing Moral Arguments: A Study Paper" (1987). Typed manuscript (photocopy). From the author at Union Theological Seminary-Presbyterian School of Christian Education, Richmond VA.

Stevenson, Louise L., e-mail message to author, 27 September 2000.

Dissertations

Beardslee, John Walter, III. "Theological Development at Geneva under Francis and Jean Alphonse Turretin (1648–1737)." Ph.D. dissertation, Yale University, 1956.

Earhart-Brown, Daniel J. "Baptism in the Theologies of Horace Bushnell, Charles Hodge, and John W. Nevin." Ph.D. dissertation, Union Theological Seminary-Presbyterian School of Christian Education, 2001.

Ferry, Henry Justin. "Francis James Grimké: Portrait of a Black Puritan." Ph.D. dissertation, Yale University, 1970.

Kennedy, Earl William. "An Historical Analysis of Charles Hodge's Doctrines of Sin and Particular Grace." Ph.D. dissertation, Princeton Theological Seminary, 1968.

Murchie, David Nell. "Morality and Social Ethics in the Thought of Charles Hodge." Ph.D. dissertation, Drew University, 1980.

St. Amant, Penrose. "The Rise and Early Development of the Princeton School of Theology." Ph.D. dissertation, University of Edinburgh, 1952.

Swezey, Charles M. "What is Theological Ethics?: A Study of the Thought of James M. Gustafson." Ph.D. dissertation, Vanderbilt University, 1978.

Index